THE CHRISTOLOGY OF EARLY JEWISH CHRISTIANITY

STUDIES IN BIBLICAL THEOLOGY

A series of monographs designed to provide clergy and laymen with the best
work in biblical scholarship both in this country and abroad

STUDIES IN BIBLICAL THEOLOGY

Second Series · 17

THE CHRISTOLOGY OF EARLY JEWISH CHRISTIANITY

RICHARD N. LONGENECKER

ALEC R. ALLENSON INC.
635 EAST OGDEN AVENUE
NAPERVILLE, ILL.

© *SCM Press Ltd 1970*

ISBN 0–8401–3067–8

Library of Congress Catalog Card No. 78–131588

Published by Alec R. Allenson Inc.

Naperville, Ill.

Printed in Great Britain

CONTENTS

ACKNOWLEDGMENTS

IT IS A pleasure to record publicly my appreciation to the following persons and organizations for assistance in the present project. To Professor C. F. D. Moule, whose writings have given direction at many points in the argument and who graciously offered a number of helpful suggestions towards the improvement of the manuscript. To Dean Kenneth S. Kantzer for his early inspiration, continued confidence and constant encouragement. To the American Association of Theological Schools and to Trinity Evangelical Divinity School for substantial grants enabling me to carry on the research and writing. To my students of past years, whose interaction in a seminar course on The Theology of Early Jewish Christianity has been invaluable. And to *New Testament Studies* (XIV, 1968), *The Evangelical Quarterly* (XLI, 1969), and the *Journal of the Evangelical Theological Society* (XII, 1969) for permission to incorporate in revised form my articles published earlier in those journals. My debt to many others who have written in the areas of Jewish Christianity and early christology is all too feebly indicated in the footnotes of the work. Even when in disagreement, I have often profited immensely; and while attempting to make a distinctive contribution, I have frequently been conscious of building on the work of my predecessors.

ABBREVIATIONS

Multi-volume Reference Works

Ap. & Ps. *The Apocrypha and Pseudepigrapha of the Old Testament*, 2 vols., ed. R. H. Charles, 1913

Beginnings *The Beginnings of Christianity*, 5 vols., ed. F. J. Foakes Jackson and K. Lake, 1920–33

JE *The Jewish Encyclopedia*, 12 vols., ed. I. Singer, 1901–6

NT Apoc. *New Testament Apocrypha*, 2 vols., ed. E. Hennecke and W. Schneemelcher, 1959–64, Eng. trans. ed. R. McL. Wilson, 1963–5

Str.-Bil. *Kommentar zum Neuen Testament aus Talmud und Midrasch*, 5 vols., H. L. Strack and P. Billerbeck, 1922–56

TWNT *Theologisches Wörterbuch zum Neuen Testament*, 7 vols. (to date), ed. G. Kittel and G. Friedrich, 1932ff., Eng. trans., *Theological Dictionary of the New Testament*, ed. G. W. Bromiley, 1964ff.

Journals

BA *The Biblical Archaeologist*

BASOR *Bulletin of the American Schools of Oriental Research*

BJRL *Bulletin of the John Rylands Library*

EvangT *Evangelische Theologie*

ExpT *The Expository Times*

HTR *The Harvard Theological Review*

Interp *Interpretation*

IEJ *Israel Exploration Journal*

JBL *Journal of Biblical Literature*

JJS *The Journal of Jewish Studies*

JQR *The Jewish Quarterly Review*

JTS *The Journal of Theological Studies*

NTS *New Testament Studies*

NovT *Novum Testamentum*

RSR   *Recherches de Science Religieuse*
RB   *Revue Biblique*
RQ   *Revue de Qumran*
SJT   *Scottish Journal of Theology*
TS   *Theological Studies*
TZ   *Theologische Zeitschrift*
VC   *Vigiliae Christianae*
VT   *Vetus Testamentum*
VTS   *Vetus Testamentum Supplement*
ZAW   *Zeitschrift für die alttestamentliche Wissenschaft*
ZNW   *Zeitschrift für die neutestamentliche Wissenschaft*
ZTK   *Zeitschrift für Theologie und Kirche*

Bible Versions

NEB   New English Bible
LXX   The Septuagint
MT   Masoretic Text

Dead Sea Scrolls

1QS   Manual of Discipline (*serek hayohad*)
1QS^a   Appendix, Manual of Discipline
1QS^b   Benedictions, Manual of Discipline
1QH   Psalms of Thanksgiving (*hodayot*)
1QM   War Scroll (*milhamah*)
1QHab   Commentary on Habakkuk 1 and 2
1QIs^a   Isaiah Scroll, exemplar a (complete)
1QMic   Commentary on portions of Micah
1QApoc   Genesis Apocryphon
4QTes   Testimonia Fragment
4QFlor.   Florilegium: Comments on Selected Portions
4QPatr.   Patriarchal Blessings
4QPs. 37   Commentary on Psalm 37 (fragmentary)
4QAng.Lit. Angelic Liturgy (*serek sirot 'olat hassabbat*)
CDC   Cairo Damascus Covenant (6QD and 4QD^b of
            Qumran)
11QMelch.   Melchizedek Scroll

Talmudic materials are abbreviated as in H. Danby, *The Mishnah*,
and the Soncino editions of the Gemaras and Midrashim. The
letters j and b signal the Palestinian Talmud (*Talmud jerusalmi*) and

the Babylonian Talmud (*Talmud babli*) respectively; R signifies Rabbah in the Midrashim, and Tos. indicates the Tosephta.

References to the Qumran materials are given according to column and line. CDC references are also given according to chapter and verse in parentheses, as in *AP. & Ps.*, as a convenient way of indicating the relations between fragments A and B and the complete text. References to Josephus are given according to book, chapter, and section (as Whiston) and according to book and section (as Loeb).

All other abbreviations are customary or self-explanatory.

I

INTRODUCTION: ISSUES AND SCOPE

THE STUDY OF early Christian thought regarding the person and work of Jesus of Nazareth has tended generally to follow one or the other of two paths: (1) an emphasis upon discontinuity in the development of early christology, coupled with a readiness to declare as primitive the residue after most of the Pauline features have been subtracted; or (2) a stress upon continuity, or even identity, in early Christian conviction and expression, coupled with a willingness to incorporate most elements of early christology into the framework of Paulinism. There is, of course, some overlapping between the two approaches, for hardly anyone representing the one position is prepared to deny completely the relevancy of certain observations put forward by those of the other. To date, however, the camps are rather solidly entrenched, and the discussion seems to have reached something of a stalemate.

It is the thesis of the present work that the newer evidence from the Dead Sea Scrolls and the Nag Hammadi texts enables us to put early Jewish Christianity into better focus, both directly and by awakening a fuller appreciation for the significance of other materials for the study of this phenomenon, and that therefore scholarship is in a better position than before to work responsibly in the field of early Jewish Christian christology on such issues as (1) distinctiveness and development, (2) continuity and discontinuity, and (3) underlying convictions and circumstantial expressions. And it is this thesis which the following pages are attempting to explicate.

DEFINITION OF TERMS

The expression Jewish Christianity is employed in a variety of ways today. To the layman the phrase immediately connotes *nationality* and means simply the Christian faith as held and practised by persons of Jewish ancestry. Certainly, of course, this is involved. But as a definition suitable for historical inquiry, it is both much too broad and somewhat too narrow. To treat the first Christian century on this basis, for example, is to make Jewish Christianity synonymous with almost the entirety of the New Testament, with only the Lucan writings as possible exceptions. But such inclusiveness defies further delineation and confuses the historical picture. Likewise, to treat the patristic materials on this basis is to confine oneself too severely to those writings demonstrably authored by Jews, which also blunts our historical sensibilities.

Those who stand in comparative religionist traditions usually define Jewish Christianity along the lines of *christology*, asserting that the term represents Jews who regarded Jesus as a prophet or as the Jewish Messiah, but not as divine.[1] The expression in this context is equivalent to the 'Ebionites' and those lesser known groups who sought to combine allegiance to Jesus with a strict numerical monotheism, and who later gave rise on hellenistic soil to Nestorian views. Those opposed to this radical christological distinction have usually defined the term in relation to the *Mosaic law,* insisting that Jewish Christians should be viewed as Jews whose acceptance of the messiahship of Jesus implied certain affirmations regarding his divinity, but who also felt keenly about the perpetuity and obligatory nature of the Law.[2]

Of late, Jewish Christianity is being understood more along the lines of *conceptual imagery and terminology,* regardless of the individual's connection with the Jewish community or the Jerusalem church.[3] It is also employed in terms of a *specific period of time,*

---

[1] E.g., O. Pfleiderer, *Das Urchristentum,* 2 vols. (1887); E. Hatch, *The Influence of Greek Ideas and Usages upon the Christian Church* (1890); R. Reitzenstein, *Die hellenistischen Mysterienreligionen* (1910); W. Bousset, *Kyrios Christos* (1913, 1921); H. Lietzmann, *Geschichte der alten Kirche,* 3 vols. (1932–8); W. Bauer, *Rechtgläubigkeit und Ketzerei im ältesten Christentum* (1934); R. Bultmann, *Theologie des Neuen Testaments,* 2 vols. (1948, 1951); *idem, Das Urchristentum im Rahmen der antiken Religionen* (1949); H. J. Schoeps, *Theologie und Geschichte des Judenchristentums* (1949); and S. G. F. Brandon, *The Fall of Jerusalem and the Christian Church* (1951), to name only a representative few expressing Tübingen, *religionsgeschichtliche,* and Bultmannian opinions, together with their seminal works.

[2] E.g., F. J. A. Hort, *Judaistic Christianity* (1894); J. Jocz, *The Jewish People and Jesus Christ* (1949); and F. V. Filson, *Three Crucial Decades* (1963).

[3] E.g., L. Goppelt, *Christentum und Judentum im Erstem und Zweiten Jahrhundert* (1955); and J. Daniélou, *The Theology of Jewish Christianity* (ET 1964). G. Dix, *Jew and Greek* (1953), also fits into this category, though not consistently so.

whether confined to Palestinian Christianity as it existed prior to the destruction of Jerusalem in AD 70[4] or having reference to Christianity, whether Jewish or Gentile, as it existed on the site of Jerusalem during the first four centuries of the Christian era;[5] though such chronological demarcations may also be included in any of the three definitions above as a secondary feature.

The need that arises in speaking of Jewish Christianity is for a definition that includes (1) a sufficient degree of particularity and specifity to enable precision of treatment, yet (2) a breadth of designation that will allow for possible variation within the entity studied. While a definition based on a particular doctrine, whether that of christology or that of Law, meets the first requirement, it tends to ignore other facets of the study, to impose an unwarranted uniformity, and to determine conclusions in advance. This is not to discredit entirely the insights gained from these approaches, nor to relieve ourselves from the necessity of following out the research which each has undertaken, for each in its own way is dealing with vital concerns involved in the study of early Christianity. But it is to suggest that one is ill-advised to wed himself too closely to either, for an investigation of early Christian faith in its Jewish expression which defines its subject only in terms of christology or Law restricts itself much too severely at its inception. On the other hand, it is all too true that a definition based primarily on conceptual imagery and terminology tends to become unmanageable and is in constant danger of a vagueness such as would prohibit any adequate checking of data.

Recognizing the dangers of which we have just spoken, I believe, however, that it is this latter approach which offers the most appropriate point of departure and promises to be the most fruitful in the study of the subject at hand. Yet of itself, it is not sufficiently restrictive to be fully serviceable. I therefore propose to speak of Jewish Christianity in a twofold sense:

1. Ideologically, with reference to early Christians whose conceptual frame of reference and whose expressions were rooted in semitic thought generally and Judaism in particular.

2. Geographically, with reference to early Christianity which

---

[4] J. Munck, 'Jewish Christianity in Post-Apostolic Times', *NTS*, VI (1960), pp. 103–16; and S. G. F. Brandon, *Fall of Jerusalem and the Christian Church* (1951).

[5] H. Chadwick, *The Circle and the Ellipse* (1959).

was either centred in Jerusalem or looked to the church in Jerusalem (whether actually or ideally) as its 'Mother Church', and sought to continue its ministry.

In speaking of 'early' Jewish Christianity, I mean to signal my interest in Jewish Christianity of the first Christian century – that is, of the period between the resurrection of Jesus (AD 30) and the outbreak of the disastrous war with Rome which resulted in the end of the Second Jewish Commonwealth and the Jewish expulsion from Jerusalem (AD 132) – and particularly the apostolic period of that century.

Jewish Christianity itself, of course, cannot be contained within the confines of my delineations. It will therefore be necessary to range more widely in order to cast light upon our subject. But in so confining our interest and in so defining our topic, we will be provided with the specifics of locality and time, yet allowed flexibility in the treatment of more crucial concerns where both unity and diversity are factors. The treatment of Jewish Christianity in the patristic period must be left to others.[6]

RECURRENT HYPOTHESES

Underlying every investigation are certain hypotheses which motivate the research and which, if found worthy, become controlling theses in the presentation. Such is true for this work as well. During the course of investigation and composition various alterations, modifications, and clarifications have come about in regard to the original working hypotheses. But amid many important issues herein considered, five major theses have emerged. These find repeated statement in different contexts throughout, being woven into the warp and woof of the presentation. It is impossible here to develop them at any length, to designate contexts, or to indicate implications. That is what the rest of the work is about. But it is well to state them as briefly as possible at the start, with the hope that their presence will be discernible in what follows.

Early Jewish Christianity a distinguishable entity. The study of Jewish Christianity as a distinguishable entity is decidedly modern, coming to the fore only within the last century and a half. And

---

[6] The many volumes from the pen of Jean Daniélou provide us with an excellent treatment of Jewish Christianity in the second and third centuries, especially his synthetic work on *The Theology of Jewish Christianity* (ET 1964).

roughly speaking, it has progressed in three phases. The first dates from the 1830's, and is associated with the Tübingen School's understanding of apostolic history along Hegelian lines. It was Ferdinand Christian Baur[7] who, on a theory of antithetical relations between Petrine and Pauline Christianity, first clearly treated Jewish Christianity as an entity; in this case, a distinct as well as distinguishable entity. But in the general discrediting of Hegelian philosophy, the demolishing of the literary basis for Tübingen's view by J. B. Lightfoot and Theodor Zahn,[8] and the more adequate reconstruction of early Christian history by the Cambridge triumvirate of J. B. Lightfoot, F. J. A. Hort, and B. F. Westcott,[9] the superstructure of Tübingen was considered by most to have fallen; though from the debris, it has been rebuilt of late in a somewhat revised form by H. J. Schoeps and S. G. F. Brandon.[10] The second phase dates from the 1880's, and corresponds to the dominance of *religionsgeschichtliche* concepts in New Testament scholarship. Otto Pfleiderer, Edwin Hatch, Richard Reitzenstein, and Wilhelm Bousset eloquently stated the thesis of genealogical relationships between hellenistic religious philosophy and the theology of the New Testament, arguing that beneath the hellenic encrustation lay the pristine faith of the original Palestinian believers. This approach came to classic expression in the works of Hans Lietzmann and Walter Bauer, and is continued in large measure in the treatments of Rudolf Bultmann[11] and the many who have received inspiration from him. The third phase dates from the 1950's, and is marked by the discoveries, publication and study of the Dead Sea Scrolls and the Nag Hammadi (Chenoboskion) texts. While these newer materials tend to substantiate

[7] F. C. Baur, 'Die Christuspartei in der korinthischen Gemeinde, der Gegensatz des petrinischen und paulinischen Christenthums in der ältesten Kirche', *Tübinger Zeitschrift* (1831), pp. 61–206; *idem, Paulus, der Apostel Jesu Christi* (1845).

[8] J. B. Lightfoot, *The Apostolic Fathers,* 5 vols. (1869–85); T. Zahn, *Ignatius von Antiochien* (1873).

[9] J. B. Lightfoot, *Epistle to the Galatians* (1865); *idem, Essays on 'Supernatural Religion'* (1889); *idem, Dissertations on the Apostolic Age* (1892); F. J. A. Hort, *Judaistic Christianity* (1894); *idem, The Epistle of St. James* (1909); B. F. Westcott, *The Epistle to the Hebrews* (1889); *idem, The Gospel according to St. John,* 2 vols. (1908).

[10] H. J. Schoeps, *Theologie und Geschichte des Judenchristentums* (1949); *idem Aus frühchristlicher Zeit* (1950); *idem, Urgemeinde, Judenchristentum, Gnosis* (1956); S. G. F. Brandon, *The Fall of Jerusalem and the Christian Church* (1951).

[11] See the works cited above in footnote 1.

the older judgment of the existence of a Jewish Christian stratum in early Christianity, it is fair to say that they have revolutionized the treatment of the subject.

Basic to all that follows in the present study is the awareness of early Jewish Christianity as an entity able to be distinguished from both Judaism and Pauline Christianity (more, of course, from the former than the latter, as the name itself suggests), and the conviction that the nature of this distinctiveness in the area of christology needs to be more adequately explicated in the light of materials recently made available. In relation to Judaism, it was the allegiance of the earliest believers to Jesus, and the implications arising from their early commitment to him as Messiah and Lord, which set Jewish Christians apart as something more than just sectarians of or schismatics from the established faith. And this consciousness of distinction from their Jewish compatriots – even though there existed a feeling of affinity in much else – is signalled in the very existence of baptism and the Lord's Supper in the earliest period of the church, whether or not there will ever be a scholarly consensus as to the nature of these sacraments in the life of the early church. In relation to Pauline Christianity, the early Jewish believers were distinctive in at least three ways:

1. In their basically nonconformist Jewish background, which evidences itself in their patterns of thought and understanding of the Old Testament Scriptures, rather than the more official Jewish training and procedures reflected in Paul's writings.

2. In their temperamental tendencies, stemming from both background and circumstances, to think more in functional and historical terms than in speculative or metaphysical.

3. In their understanding of the implications involved in the church as the true Israel, which underlies much of their thought regarding the course of the Christian mission and the believer's relation to the Mosaic law.

Jerusalem Christianity to be understood in terms of both unity and diversity. Important also in the study of the formative period of the Christian faith is the recognition that early Jerusalem Christianity must be understood in terms of both unity and diversity. The common factor holding all together was that of devotion to Jesus as Messiah and Lord, from which stemmed a 'sense of centre' in doctrinal and practical matters – especially in the earliest days and on the part of the apostolic leadership. Walter Bauer's thesis that heresy stands at the beginning of new insight is important in understanding one element in the development of thought, but it is woefully inadequate as an explanation for the origin of the earliest Christian convictions.[12] Underlying all doctrinal advances, and overspreading all differences, was a unity of basic christological conviction.

But unity must not be construed to mean uniformity. There were definite variations and differences within the Jerusalem church; and these, for at least three reasons. In the first place, the early Christians had diverse backgrounds. No longer is it possible to view first-century Judaism as monolithically Pharisaic. Outside ideologies and alien outlooks were pressing in upon Palestine and, while not overwhelming, imperceptibly left their mark and were often unconsciously accepted in part. Palestinian Jews were not uniform in outlook, and thus Jewish Christians varied in their pre-conditioning. Secondly, a probable transfer of attitude characteristic in Judaism should be noted. While Judaism was based upon a theological foundation and built upon a basic kerygmatic core,[13] and while it took the *Shema* of Deut. 6.4ff. to be the quintessence of its faith, it has traditionally been more of an orthopraxy than an orthodoxy.[14] And this attitude was probably carried over

[12] For an excellent critique of W. Bauer's *Rechtgläubigkeit und Ketzerei im ältesten Christentum*, which, while recognizing the presence of many valuable insights and suggestions given along the way, faults the author on his over-simplification of issues, his ruthless treatment of evidence which fails to support his view, and his failure to appreciate the breadth of early orthodoxy, see H. E. W. Turner, *The Pattern of Christian Truth* (1954), pp. 39–80.

[13] Cf. e.g., Deut. 4.32–34; 6.20–25; 26.5–19; Josh. 24.1–28.

[14] W. D. Davies has aptly said: 'Now, this distinction between the two faiths cannot be pressed to the last degree. . . . There is a "dogma" or "creed" implicit, if not always explicit, in Judaism. . . . There are certain implicit, and sometimes explicit, basic principles to which we have already referred. But these apart, it is rightly, if humorously, asserted that where there are three Jews, there can be four opinions. For example, there is no one doctrine of the Messiah. It is easily possible for a Jew to claim to be the Messiah without incurring censure, provided he observes the *Miṣwot*. Herbert Danby is reported to have once said, playfully no doubt, that he once lectured in Jerusalem when there were six Messiahs in his audience. To observe the Law confers freedom for almost anything else and, to parody Augustine, a Jew might urge: "Observe the Law and believe what you like" ' ('Torah and Dogma: A Comment', *HTR*, LXI [1968], pp. 88–90). Davies further speaks of Judaism as retaining 'a kind of massive *halakic* simplicity, suspicious of speculation and uninterested in dogma', and insists that 'the actuality of obedience to the Torah, not theological interpretation of it, has been the hallmark of Judaism' (*ibid.*, p. 93).

in large measure into the early church, allowing for diversity within a oneness of basic commitment and fellowship. Thirdly, we must not overlook the elemental and functional nature of the early faith itself. Though all claimed a common Lord, many of the issues and implications of this allegiance had yet to be faced. And with the detailing of creed and practice yet to be spelled out, variation was inevitable. Thus, to speak of only the obvious, the church at Jerusalem in its early days was composed of *am-haaretz* believers, Pharisees, Hellenists, Zealots, probably Essenes, and perhaps some Sadducees; and beyond its immediate borders certain Samaritans, with at one time even a Roman centurion accepted as an equal.[15] Christologically, embryonic orthodoxy, incipient Ebionism, and probably proto-gnostic tendencies intermingled. In regard to the Law, there were tensions between the early Hellenists, those sympathetic to a Gentile mission but who felt personally obligated as Jews to the Law, and the Judaizers. There were incipient universalists and reactionary particularists, and evidently there was confusion in matters eschatological as well.

Jesus the source of early Christian tradition and the paradigm for interpretation. That the needs and circumstances of the church were factors in the preservation, selection, and shaping of the

[15] The thesis that there were really two churches in Palestine from the earliest days, a Galilean and a Jerusalem (cf. E. Lohmeyer, *Galiläa und Jerusalem*, 1936), has failed to convince. Our earliest evidence, that of the letters of Paul, takes only the Jerusalem community into account and associates the Galilean apostles with its leadership.

Much is made today of pre-Pauline hellenistic Christianity, whether pre-Pauline *hellenistic Jewish* or pre-Pauline *hellenistic Gentile*. To this category all concepts that manifestly antedate Paul but are judged too advanced for native Palestinians are assigned; and, to judge by modern pronouncements, most of the creative insights and distinctive features of the New Testament are to be credited. But has not 'pre-Pauline hellenistic Christianity' become a grab-bag for concepts which philosophic scepticism refuses to allow either to Jesus or to the earliest disciples? That there were hellenistic Christians, both Jewish and Gentile, in the church before Paul's distinctive ministry we may readily acknowledge. But that they were such a formative factor and creative influence as often asserted may well be questioned. In setting aside Jesus and the early Jerusalem apostles as foundational in the Christian faith, and favouring an anonymous group (or groups) of hellenistic Christians as the major creative factor in the New Testament, are we not engaging in an evasive type of action whereby our reconstruction of early Christianity finds its source primarily in *a priori* assumptions, its validation mainly in the consistency of the details in the portrayal presented, and its conviction solely in the profundity of argument. Rather than building hellenistic castles in the air, this work will centre its attention upon Palestinian foundations.

individual units in the gospel tradition seems to be the plain meaning of Luke 1.1-4 and John 20.30f.; and to be manifest in all four Gospels, as well as in the Acts of the Apostles. To this extent, of course, *Formgeschichte* has performed a service in reminding us of the kerygmatic nature of the New Testament materials, though we may question its extremely negative attitude towards questions of historical reliability. But neither catechetical, missionary, or polemic interests were sufficiently creative to originate that tradition. The powerful unity of thought from the very beginning presupposes, in addition to the activity of the Spirit, a similarly powerful creative personality. Jesus himself was for the earliest Christians both the source of their basic convictions and the paradigm in their interpretation of the Old Testament. Further, while the expectation of the approaching *parousia* undoubtedly suppressed many issues for a while in the early church, we cannot say that the delay of its fulfilment exercised any substantial influence on the earliest formulations of the church's faith. There is indeed a *Sitz im Leben Kirche*. But it must also be recognized that there is a *Sitz im Leben Jesu*. Both are proper and necessary considerations for the historian. But to understand the early church, that of Jesus must take priority over that of the church.

Early conviction to be understood in terms of both immediacy of revelation and providential development. Fourthly, it need be recognized that theological conviction on the part of early Jewish Christians was the product of both immediacy of relevation and providential development; that is, that both an initial consciousness and a process of gestation were involved in the formulation of early doctrine. This is not to deny a 'givenness' in the faith of the early church, or to minimize the uniqueness of Christian theology. Nor is it to suggest that an evolutionary scheme suffices to explain Christian thought. Rather, it is to point out, first, that while a distinctive appreciation of the 'Christ-event' (incarnation, ministry, passion, and resurrection) – as interpreted to an extent by Jesus himself and as illuminated by the Spirit – was common to all early Christians and basic to all genuinely Christian thought, early Jewish Christian conviction did not evidence the flowering of Chalcedon or even the fulness of Paul; and secondly, to insist that, though it was necessarily elemental and dominantly functional, the earliest Christian faith contained certain implicit metaphysical presuppositions and carried ontological overtones which were to receive clarification and explication in the continued ministry of the Spirit. This is what the church understood Jesus to have promised in the words: 'I have yet many things to say to you, but you cannot bear them now. But when the Spirit of truth comes, he will guide you into all truth.'[16] And this is what the Jerusalem Christians believed they were experiencing in the constant interaction of conviction and circumstances.

Further, this is not to imply that the theology of the early church is to be separated from the revelational events upon which it is based in such a manner as to be considered only a nominalistic response to these events, and thus to be distinguished from revelation. Nor is it, on the other hand, to suggest that all theology true to its revelational base is of the nature of revelation itself. The early church understood revelation as both event and its interpretation, but confined that authentic interpretation to the apostolic witness.[17] What our hypothesis does assert, however, is that our sources give no justification for reading back into early Jewish Christianity – particularly in its formative days – the fulness of later theological treatment. Here, too, as in previous times, God worked concursively with men in the expression of his will; and that, by a process of providential development of thought as well as by an immediacy of redemptive activity.[18]

Early expression to be understood in terms of both 'hard core' kerygma and circumstances. And finally, there will be advocated in the pages that follow the thesis that early Jewish Christian expression must be understood in terms of both 'hard core' kerygma and circumstances affecting the life of the church at given periods and in particular situations. Without denying theological development and diversity in the church, it is at bottom true that the New Testa-

[16] John 16.12f.; see also 14.26; 15.26; 16.14.

[17] Cf. F. J. A. Hort: 'Our faith rests first on the Gospel itself, the revelation of God and His redemption in His Only begotten Son, and secondly on the interpretation of that primary Gospel by the Apostles and Apostolic men to whom was Divinely committed the task of applying the revelation of Christ to the thoughts and deeds of their own time. That standard interpretation of theirs was ordained to be for the guidance of the Church in all after ages, in combination with the living guidance of the Spirit' (*Epistle of St. James,* p. ix). Note the consciousness of the centrality of the apostles as expressed in John 15.27; Acts 1.22; Eph. 2.20.

[18] Cf. W. Manson: 'The stream of thought flowed in an intense but narrow channel; carrying in its flood much that for the time remained in solution in the sub-conscious rather than in the conscious region of the Christian mentality' (*Jesus the Messiah* [1943], p. 52).

ment, as C. F. D. Moule has said, 'debates from a single platform, but from different corners of it;'[19] that is, that

each several explanation of the faith or defence of it is likely to run along rather particular lines, according to circumstances. In other words, it may be assumed that, although this activity, taken as a whole, has added considerably to the range of the Christian vocabulary, each separate manifestation of it is likely to be specialized and aimed at solving only one or two particular problems or meeting certain specific objections; and it is here that an explanation may reasonably be sought for some of the curious selectiveness of the N.T.[20]

This means that in dealing with various phrases and terms used in the Jewish Christian materials, attention must be given to such factors as (1) the demands of worship, (2) the requirements of preaching, teaching, and polemic, (3) concerns having to do with locality and specific situations encountered, and (4) circumstances arising from a distinctive ideological milieu. These, of course, are matters inherent in any real-life situation. And they must be taken into account at every point in our work if we are to be saved from treating early Jewish Christianity in a sterile or wooden fashion.

CRITICAL ASSUMPTIONS

Before dealing with specifics of identification and interpretation, some account must be given regarding the critical assumptions upon which this study is based. Space permits only a cursory treatment here, with the expectation that some matters will later be more fully developed where pertinent.

Noncanonical Jewish Materials. Most significant of the noncanonical Jewish materials of importance in the study of early Jewish Christianity are the Dead Sea Scrolls, which have, since their initial discovery in 1947, revolutionized much of New Testament research. Together with the vast majority of scholars in the field, I take the distinctive literature of Qumran to reflect one segment of the Essene mentality in Palestine and to have been written during the first century BC and early first century AD.[21]

---

[19] C. F. D. Moule, *The Birth of the New Testament* (1966), p. 167.

[20] C. F. D. Moule, 'The Influence of Circumstances on the Use of Christological Terms', *JTS*, X (1959), 255; see also *idem*, 'The Influence of Circumstances on the Use of Eschatological Terms', *JTS*, XV (1964), pp. 1–15.

[21] For an early, brief, and altogether reliable discussion of the evidence, see W. F. Albright, 'Postscript', *BASOR – Supplementary Studies*, Nos. 10–12

Admittedly, final judgments regarding the Qumran texts are impossible, since many have yet to be published (particularly from Caves 4 and 11, as well as the recently recovered Temple Scroll) and more may possibly come to light. Yet sufficient material has been made available to begin the tracing of the beliefs, expectations, and thought patterns of one prominent sectarian group within Judaism at a time roughly contemporary with the rise of early Christianity. And in that the Qumran community and early Jewish Christianity had much in common ideologically as well as being closely related temporally and geographically – though at the same time were quite distinct at crucial points theologically – the Dead Sea literature is of immense value as an external aid in understanding the subject at hand.

The conclusions reached in R. H. Charles' two-volume *magnum opus* regarding date and provenance of the Old Testament apocryphal writings I accept as generally reliable, though with these qualifications: (1) that to date there is no evidence for the pre-Christian nature of either the 'Similitudes' of Enoch (chs. 37–71 of Ethiopic Enoch) or the Greek version of the Testaments of the Twelve Patriarchs, and (2) that many of those writings labelled by Charles as 'Pharisaic' because of their opposition to Sadducean perspectives (I refer especially to Jubilees, the Greek and Aramaic portions of Enoch, and the Psalms of Solomon) must now be seen to be within an Essene cycle of influence, whether originally written by Essenes (or 'proto-Essenes') or taken over by them. British scholars have frequently questioned the pre-Christian origin of the Similitudes on the basis of their absence in the extant

---

(1951), pp. 57–60. Note also M. Burrows, *The Dead Sea Scrolls* (1955); J. T. Milik, *Ten Years of Discovery in the Wilderness of Judaea* (ET 1959); F. M. Cross, *The Ancient Library of Qumran* (1958). Expressing minority views are (1) C. Roth, *The Historical Background of the Dead Sea Scrolls* (1959), and G. R. Driver, *The Judaean Scrolls: The Problem and a Solution* (1965), who argue that the Qumran texts represent first-century Zealotism; (2) J. L. Teicher, 'The Dead Sea Scrolls—Documents of the Jewish-Christian Sect of Ebionites', *JJS* II (1951), pp. 67–99, and P. Kahle, *Die Hebräischen Handschriften aus der Hohle* (1951), pp. 56f., who claim that they reflect Ebionite circumstances and theology during the first four centuries of the Christian era; and (3) S. Zeitlin, ' "A Commentary on the Book of Habakkuk", Important Discovery or Hoax', *JQR*, XXXIX (1949), pp. 235–47, who asserts in this article and succeeding ones in *JQR* that the Scrolls come from Jewish authors in medieval times. The debate is probably most closely joined and clearly highlighted in R. de Vaux's review of Driver's work in 'Essenes or Zealots? Some Thoughts on a Recent Book' *New Blackfriars*, XLVII (1966), pp. 396–410.

Greek portions of the work,[22] though continental Europeans seem to have little trouble in accepting an early Jewish provenance for these chapters. But with the absence of this section in the Qumran discoveries to date – though with fragments of every other chapter of I Enoch found in those materials – it seems that there is further reason to question the traditionally ascribed provenance.[23] Probably the Similitudes represent a syncretistic Jewish Christianity of the first or second century AD.[24] But because of the difficulty of precise determination, they will be employed in this work only as a supplementary source and no interpretation will be labelled as possible if drawn from them alone. The Testaments of the Twelve Patriarchs presents us with a similar case. In the revised form of his thesis, Martin de Jonge has argued that they are a Jewish composition which has undergone extensive redaction so that the extant Greek version now expresses Christian theology throughout.[25] In the Qumran finds, only an Aramaic Testament of Levi and a portion of a Hebrew Testament of Naphtali have been identified to date – both longer than their Greek counterparts and both devoid of Christian emphases. It therefore may be postulated that this work in its final form is a Jewish Christian composition of the first or second century AD.[26] Its Christian author may have had an Essene background, either immediate or distant, and may have utilized two or more original Jewish Testaments as his models; or, of course, he may have only revised a full-blown Jewish work on the final words of the twelve

[22] Stemming principally from C. H. Dodd, *According to the Scriptures* (1952), pp. 116f.; *idem, The Interpretation of the Fourth Gospel* (1953), pp. 242f.

[23] For a survey of the problems involved in a pre-Christian provenance, though without committing myself necessarily to the solution proposed, see J. C. Hindley, 'Towards a Date for the Similitudes of Enoch. An Historical Approach', *NTS*, XIV (1968), pp. 551–65.

[24] Cf. J. T. Milik, *Ten Years of Discovery*, pp. 33f.; F. M. Cross, *Ancient Library of Qumran*, pp. 202f., n. 7.

[25] M. de Jonge, *The Testaments of the Twelve Patriarchs* (1953); *idem*, 'Christian Influence in the Testaments of the Twelve Patriarchs', *NovT*, IV (1960), pp. 182–235, and V (1962), pp. 311–19.

[26] This is the view of J. Daniélou, *The Dead Sea Scrolls and Primitive Christianity* (ET 1958), pp. 114–17, and J. T. Milik, *Ten Years of Discovery*, pp. 34f., which has been accepted by M. Burrows, *More Light on the Dead Sea Scrolls* (1958), pp. 179f., and J. van der Ploeg, *Excavations at Qumran* (ET 1958), pp. 205f. R. H. Fuller asserts that it is 'earlier than the Qumran literature' (*The Foundations of New Testament Christology*, 1965, p. 55 n.), but on little evidence. J. B. Lightfoot long ago argued that the work was definitely that of a Christian author, possibly from the Nazarene sect (*Galatians*, pp. 319–21).

patriarchs, the major portion of which is now lost. But in any case, as with the Similitudes of Enoch, we are unable to employ the Testaments of the Twelve Patriarchs in a study of early Jewish Christianity as anything more than supplementary material.

The rabbinic literature of the Talmud and its cognate codifications is also of aid in gaining impressions of Jewish thought and circumstances during the first Christian century,[27] though for the study of nonconformist Jewish Christianity its value is somewhat diminished. Its chief importance for the study at hand lies in its historical allusions, which aid in a reconstruction of the first-century period, and its reflection of hermeneutical procedures, which allow comparative studies of practices at Qumran, among Jewish Christians, and within Pharisaic Judaism.

Noncanonical Jewish Christian Materials. Of noncanonical Jewish Christian materials, probably the most important for our purpose is the Nag Hammadi collection of thirteen Coptic codices containing over 1,000 pages of approximately fifty Christian tractates. The discovery was made in 1945 or 1946 by peasants digging for topsoil in an old Graeco-Roman cemetery near the present city of Nag Hammadi in Upper Egypt (*c.* 300 miles south of Cairo) and in the vicinity of the remains of an ancient Pachomian monastery where the town of Chenoboskion once was.[28] While only a fraction of the material has been published to date, it seems from what has been studied that what we have here are writings representative to some extent of heterodox Jewish Christianity within which the incipient gnosticism of Judaism has blossomed under the stimulus of hellenic religious philosophy. The authors of the various tractates may not have been Jewish Christians themselves, or at least many of them probably were not.[29] But the traditions they draw upon and the conceptual

[27] See my *Paul, Apostle of Liberty* (1964), pp. 1–13, for a brief introduction to talmudic literature wherein a method for determining the earlier strata among the rabbinic traditions is proposed.

[28] For descriptions of the Nag Hammadi materials, see J. Doresse, *The Secret Books of the Egyptian Gnostics* (ET 1960); W. C. van Unnik, *Newly Discovered Gnostic Writings* (1960); H. C. Puech, *NT Apoc.*, I, pp. 231–8; A. K. Helmbold, *The Nag Hammadi Gnostic Texts and the Bible* (1967); R. McL. Wilson, *Gnosis and the New Testament* (1968); J. M. Robinson, 'The Coptic Gnostic Library Today', *NTS*, XIV (1968), pp. 356–401.

[29] Note, however, Gospel of Philip, Logion 6: 'When we were Hebrews, we were orphans and had [only] our mother; but when we became Christians we obtained a father and a mother.' See also Logion 102.

framework within which they work have definite Jewish Christian characteristics,[30] and the investigation of such features is of great importance for the study of early Jewish Christianity. We need not go so far as to claim a primitive Christian character for the theology of the Nag Hammadi texts, as some have asserted;[31] though, on the other hand, they are probably more than just revisions of canonical material.[32] Agreeing with Quispel in the main, I take the Nag Hammadi 'Gospels' (Thomas, Philip, and Truth) to be basically independent of at least the Synoptic Gospels and to represent adaptions of early hebraic Gospel materials – perhaps the Gospel to the Hebrews and a *Logia* (or *Logoi*) collection.[33] And this is probably the case with the rest of the writings in the Nag Hammadi codices as well, though less obviously so.

As to the many New Testament apocryphal books in addition to the tractates from Nag Hammadi, the second-century Gospels, Acts, Preachings, and Apocalypses associated with the names of Peter, James, John, Thomas, the Hebrews, and the Nazarenes (to name only the prominent representatives of the lot) are *prima facie* Jewish Christian, and may be taken to represent at least one segment of Jewish Christianity as it continued into the patristic period.[34] Probably from the same circles, though evidencing a greater degree of heterodoxy and featuring an anti-Paul polemic, are the Pseudo-Clementine writings. While very diverse evaluations

[30] See R. McL. Wilson, *Studies in the Gospel of Thomas* (1960), pp. 117–32, for a balanced discussion of 'The Jewish-Christian Element' in the Gospel of Thomas. The fact that the Nag Hammadi Gospels employ this underlying tradition in an anti-Jewish manner reflects more on their heterodox Christian stance than denies a Jewish Christian dependence.

[31] E.g., H. Koester, 'GNŌMAI DIAPHOROI: The Origin and Nature of Diversification in the History of Early Christianity', *HTR*, LVIII (1965), pp. 279–318.

[32] E.g., R. McL. Wilson, *Studies in the Gospel of Thomas* (1960), pp. 45–116; R. M. Grant and D. N. Freedman, *The Secret Sayings of Jesus* (1960); B. Gärtner, *The Theology of the Gospel according to Thomas* (ET 1961); H. E. W. Turner, 'The Gospel of Thomas: Its History, Transmission and Sources', *Thomas and the Evangelists* (1962), pp. 11–39.

[33] G. Quispel, 'The Gospel of Thomas and the New Testament', *VC*, XI (1957), pp. 189–207; *idem*, 'Some Remarks on the Gospel of Thomas', *NTS*, V (1959), pp. 276–90. Cf. H. Montefiore, 'A Comparison of the Parables of the Gospel according to Thomas and of the Synoptic Gospels', *Thomas and the Evangelists* (1962), pp. 40–78; C. F. D. Moule, *Birth of the New Testament*, p. 152.

[34] See E. Hennecke and W. Schneemelcher's two-volume *NTApoc.*, as edited and translated by R. McL. Wilson (1963–5), for introductions and English translations of the separate works.

of these works have been given in the past,[35] there seems to be a growing consensus today that the Clementine Homilies (late second century or early third) and the Clementine Recognitions (first half of the fourth century) probably continue in large measure certain beliefs and attitudes of at least one sector of early Jewish Christianity.[36] And possibly such views are continued to some extent in a tenth-century Arabic manuscript written by Abd al-Jabbār, which has recently been discovered.[37]

The early patristic writings are somewhat removed from our centre of interest, since all of the so-called Apostolic Fathers, the Apologists, and the historians whose works are either extant or known to us through quotations in Eusebius and others wrote from within Gentile Christianity; and none, with the possible exceptions of Clement of Rome and the author of the Shepherd of Hermas, can be claimed to have had any type of background in Judaism personally. But what is of significance in the patristic materials for our purpose is what has appeared to many to be a Jewish or Jewish Christian substratum of thought and expression. And while the use to which we can employ this underlying element in the patristic compositions must be limited to confirming and illuminating data drawn more directly from Jewish Christian sources themselves, it nevertheless cannot be ignored in our quest.

The prime example of a work which probably contains such a substratum of thought and expression is the Didache ('Teaching of the Twelve Apostles'), a handbook of church discipline dating from the late first or early second century, whose exposition of the

[35] E.g., in the works of F. C. Baur and H. J. Schoeps, they are considered foundational to a study of early Jewish Christianity, while in the treatments of H. Lietzmann and J. Munck, they are entirely discounted.

[36] See especially J. Daniélou, *Theology of Jewish Christianity,* p. 59; G. Quispel, 'The Discussion of Judaic Christianity', *VC*, XXII (1968), pp. 82–84. Also *NT Apoc.*, II, pp. 103–5, 532–5, and the bibliographies given there.

[37] S. Pines, 'The Jewish Christians of the Early Centuries of Christianity according to a New Source', *Proceedings of the Israel Academy of Science and Humanities* (in Hebrew), II (13, 1966), pp. 1–73. See, however, R. McL. Wilson, 'The New "Passion of Jesus" in the Light of the New Testament and Apocrypha', *Neotestamentica et Semitica,* ed. E. E. Ellis and M. Wilcox (Edinburgh: T. & T. Clark, 1969), pp. 264–71, for a survey of initial reactions to the new discovery and an appropriate word of caution regarding premature claims for its importance in the study of Christian origins. Note also E. Bammel, 'Excerpts from a New Gospel?', *NovT,* X (1968), pp. 1–9, who argues that the Islamic polemist's work rests solely on the Jewish *Toledoth Jeshu* traditions.

'Two Ways' in the first six chapters appears to be based upon Jewish ethical teaching. And there are further indications of such an underlying element in the rest of the book as well, whether it be considered Jewish or Jewish Christian.[38] Earlier, these archaisms were thought to be feigned. Recently, however, there has developed a general consensus that they are genuine and represent earlier materials incorporated by the author into his writing.[39] To a lesser extent, this seems to be true as well of I Clement (AD 95) and the Shepherd of Hermas (first half of the second century), especially in their liturgical and catechetical portions. And perhaps chs. 18–21 of the Epistle of Barnabas (first half of the second century), which have striking literary affinities to the Two Ways of the Didache, also reflect an earlier Jewish or Jewish Christian source, despite the marked antagonism of the work to Judaism generally.

Of the Apologists, only Justin Martyr is of importance here. A Gentile by birth and training, in his conversion to Christ he became very interested in the Old Testament and the Jewish basis of his faith. His earlier two-volume Apology is a typical defence of Christianity along Gentile Christian lines. But in his Dialogue with Trypho (AD 150–60) he manifests an attempt to understand Christianity from a Jewish perspective – though, admittedly, with anti-Judaistic bias. There is no question but that Justin possessed only an outsider's knowledge of Judaism itself, and a far from complete understanding of early Jewish Christianity. The arguments he places in Trypho's mouth and the answers he returns indicate no more. But it must be recognized, none the less, that Justin was very interested in speaking to Jewish interests as he understood them and in reproducing the primitive Christian apologetic as he believed it had been carried on. And for these reasons his work has some significance for our subject at hand.

Papias of Hierapolis, who wrote a treatise in five books on 'Explanations of the Sayings of the Lord' (AD 130) and is known to us through comments regarding him by Irenaeus, Eusebius, and Jerome, is also of some importance for our study. According to Irenaeus, Papias had heard the apostle John preach. And judging

[38] As J. R. Harris insisted: 'The Jewish character of the book is just as marked in the middle as at the beginning, and just as marked at the end as in the middle' (*The Teaching of the Apostles* [1887], p. 91).
[39] See F. L. Cross, *The Early Christian Fathers* (1960), pp. 10f., and the bibliography given there.

by views attributed to him, Papias seems to have incorporated into his teaching certain Jewish Christian emphases ('chiliasm', for example, was certainly no Gentile Christian invention). Mention must also be made of Hegesippus, a late second-century member of the church at Aelia (Gentile Jerusalem) who is known to us in quotations of his writings by Eusebius and Epiphanius. From him we have certain ecclesiastical traditions current in Palestine in his day, which, while obviously incorporating a degree of fanciful elaboration, undoubtedly preserve some genuine memories of the first-century Christian community on that site.

Canonical Jewish Christian Writings. In the New Testament, a number of writings have been seen of late to have closer ideological and conceptual affinities with a sectarian Judaism of the type seen at Qumran than to any other contemporary feature known to date. I refer to Matthew's Gospel, John's Gospel, the Letter to the Hebrews, James, the Johannine letters, I Peter, and perhaps also II Peter and Jude. These I take, along with the Apocalypse, to be 'Jewish Christian' writings in the sense that they both reflect a Jewish Christian background and are addressed to Jewish Christians or to potentially interested Jews, whether of Palestine-Syria or of the wider Diaspora.

Mark's Gospel, it is true, reflects 'the kind of Greek which an Aramaic-speaking Jew would write',[40] and has traditionally been associated with the preaching of Peter. Yet that same tradition, stemming from Papias *via* Eusebius,[41] considered it to have been written in Rome for a predominantly Gentile audience; and the work bears some traces of this fact. Luke's Gospel manifests an interest in Judaism, beginning and ending, for example, in the Jewish temple. But its author was probably a Gentile Christian who wrote for Gentiles. The intention of Matthew's Gospel, however, to judge from internal evidence, 'was to present the Christian dispensation in terms of Judaism'.[42] It appears to have been written at a time when the struggle between Judaism and Christianity was still *intra muros*, probably between AD 65 and 85,[43] and therefore,

---

[40] M. Black, *An Aramaic Approach to the Gospels and Acts* (1946), p. 206 (1967), p. 271.

[41] Eusebius, Eccles. Hist., III. 39.

[42] W. D. Davies, *The Setting of the Sermon on the Mount* (1964), p. 25.

[43] G. D. Kilpatrick represents critical opinion of the first half of the twentieth century in dating Matthew late in the first century (*The Origins of the Gospel according to Matthew* [1946]; cf. also W. G. Kümmel, *Introduction to the*

whether finally composed in Palestine or Syria, reflects one element of early Jewish Christian thought.[44] Likewise John's Gospel can rightly be classed as a Jewish Christian composition, and the recognition of its 'Jewishness' in both background and presentation is becoming established in contemporary criticism.[45]

New Testament [ET 1965], p. 84). Note, however, W. D. Davies' counter to a suggestion of a date after AD 85 ('Matthew', *Hastings Dictionary of the Bible,* rev. & ed. F. C. Grant and H. H. Rowley [1963], pp. 632f.), R. M. Grant's evaluation of the critical problems involved (*A Historical Introduction to the New Testament* [1963], p. 107), D. Guthrie's treatment of the predictive element in Jesus' message (*The Gospels and Acts* [1965], pp. 43f.), and C. F. D. Moule's suggestion of a pre-destruction provenance (*The Birth of the New Testament,* 2nd ed. [1966], pp. 121f.).

[44] The preponderance of critical opinion today favours Matthew as a Jewish Christian Gospel written for Jewish Christians or for Jews; though for contrary opinions, see: E. J. Goodspeed, *An Introduction to the New Testament* (1937), pp. 178f.; P. Nepper-Christensen, *Das Matthäusevangelium: ein judenchristliches Evangelium?* (1958); G. Hebert, 'The Problem of the Gospel according to Matthew', *SJT,* XIV (1961), pp. 403–13; W. Trilling, *Das Wahre Israel* (1964).

[45] That the Fourth Gospel has its roots in a Judean milieu of the pre-destruction period has become a growing conviction since the article by W. F. Albright in the *Festschrift* to C. H. Dodd ('Recent Discoveries in Palestine and the Gospel of St. John', *The Background of the New Testament and its Eschatology,* ed. W. D. Davies and D. Daube [1956], pp. 153–71). Earlier efforts to relate the Gospel to an early Palestinian background were heroic, but lacked demonstrable support of an external nature, at times were overstated, and seemingly had little effect on current criticism. J. B. Lightfoot and Israel Abrahams, for example, declared this Gospel to be 'the most Hebraic book in the New Testament, except perhaps the Apocalypse' (J. B. Lightfoot, *Biblical Essays* [1893], p. 135; on Abrahams' verbal comment, see S. Neill, *The Interpretation of the New Testament* [1964], p. 315). But that claim, though advanced by knowledgeable and competent scholars, the one Christian and the other Jewish, failed to carry conviction in the face of prevailing opinion to the contrary. C. F. Burney and C. C. Torrey argued for an Aramaic original (C. F. Burney, *The Aramaic Origin of the Fourth Gospel* [1922]; C. C. Torrey, 'The Aramaic Origin of the Gospel of John', *HTR,* XVI [1923], pp. 305–44). But within a decade, E. C. Colwell was able to show that the syntactical features relied upon to prove translation Greek could be paralleled in the vernacular papyri (*The Greek of the Fourth Gospel* [1931]). Erwin R. Goodenough demonstrated that the thought-world of the Fourth Gospel is not really comparable to that of the hellenistic world known from second-century sources, and that therefore there is the possibility that John reflects one element among many within early Palestinian Christianity ('John a Primitive Gospel', *JBL,* LXIV [1945], pp. 145–82). But he had no parallel material by which to compare the Gospel positively, and thus to establish his thesis as to provenance. It was only with the discovery of the Dead Sea materials that a credible case could be made for an early Palestinian background based on geographical correspondances, historical correlations,

The Letter to the Hebrews also deserves a place among the writings classed as Jewish Christian; if not demonstrably because of its author, at least because of its addresses and its author's attempt to speak to their interests.[46] Admittedly, however, the

---

ideological comparisons, and terminological peculiarities. Today, based primarily on the striking parallels which exist between the Fourth Gospel and the Dead Sea evidence, the assertion is rising from many quarters that 'the *Heimat* of the Johannine tradition, and the *milieu* in which it took shape, was the heart of southern Palestinian Judaism' (J. A. T. Robinson, 'The Destination and Purpose of St. John's Gospel', *NTS*, VI [1960], p. 124; cf. *idem.*, 'The New Look on the Fourth Gospel', *Studia Evangelica,* I, ed. K. Aland [1959], pp. 338–50, A. J. B. Higgins, *The Historicity of the Fourth Gospel* [1960], S. Neill, *Interpretation of the New Testament*, pp. 308–24, R. E. Brown, *The Gospel according to John,* I [1966], pp. xli–lxvi); though there are still expressions to the contrary (e.g., W. G. Kümmel, *Introduction to the New Testament,* pp. 156–61).

A correlative to an early Judean milieu is the rising insistence upon the Jewishness of the Fourth Gospel's addressees, whether exclusively or principally so (cf. W. C. van Unnik, 'The Purpose of St. John's Gospel', *Studia Evangelica,* I, ed. K. Aland [1959], pp. 382–411; J. A. T. Robinson, 'Destination and Purpose of St. John's Gospel', *NTS*, VI [1960], pp. 117–31; R. E. Brown, *John,* I, pp. lxxiii–lxxv). Probably the Gospel was written to those of the Diaspora, for scarcely would its explanations of terms and conditions be required for a Palestinian audience. Perhaps also it was directed to a community where Essene influence was prevalent (cf. L. Mowry, 'The Dead Sea Scrolls and the Background for the Gospel of John', *BA*, XVII [1954], pp. 78–97; though conversely, see H. M. Teeple, 'Qumran and the Origin of the Fourth Gospel', *NovT*, IV [1960], pp. 6–25). But whatever its specific destination and whatever its specific purpose, the Fourth Gospel, like the First, evidences patterns of thought, terminology, and emphases from at least one element within early Jewish Christianity – though to a degree unmatched in Matthew's Gospel, it seems to speak more to the sectarian mentality within Judaism.

[46] Earlier critical opinion vacillated between viewing its message as directed to Palestinian Jewish believers residing in or near Jerusalem (e.g., B. F. Westcott, *The Epistle to the Hebrews* [1889]; A. B. Bruce, *The Epistle to the Hebrews* [1899]) and Gentile Christians living somewhere in the empire (e.g., J. Moffatt, *The Epistle to the Hebrews* [1924]; H. Windisch, *Der Hebraerbrief* [1931]; E. F. Scott, *The Epistle to the Hebrews* [1922]; G. Vos, *The Teaching of the Epistle to the Hebrews* [1956]), though seemed finally to find direction in William Manson's carefully developed thesis of its recipients as being Jewish Christians in Rome (W. Manson, *The Epistle to the Hebrews* [1951]; cf. also G. Milligan, *The Theology of the Epistle to the Hebrews* [1899], pp. 34–52). But with the publication of the Qumran texts from the first caves, a whole new approach towards Hebrews set in. Y. Yadin inaugurated this new attitude in his 1958 article wherein he spelled out areas of reapproachment existing between the Letter to the Hebrews and the Dead Sea Scrolls, arguing that the addressees were Christians who had an Essene background (Y. Yadin, 'The Dead Sea Scrolls and the Epistle to the Hebrews', *Aspects of the Dead Sea*

letter also serves as something of a bridge between Jewish Christian interests and Gentile Christianity. The designation 'general'
or 'catholic' for the Letters of James, Peter, John, and Jude is an
exceedingly deceptive misnomer. The name originated on the
assumption that these writings were intended for Christians
generally, in contrast to those of Paul which were addressed to
individual congregations and persons.[47] But it is becoming increasingly evident, particularly as a result of their affinities to the
Qumran materials, that these letters are in reality Jewish Christian
compositions which at first circulated primarily within the Jewish
cycle of witness in the church.[48] That the book of Revelation
springs from a Jewish Christian milieu seems beyond doubt. In
form, it is comparable to the spate of Jewish apocalyptic works
associated with the names of Enoch, Abraham, Moses, Baruch,
and Ezra. In content, though without any formal quotations, the
vast majority of its verses evidence an extensive saturation in the
Old Testament. And in language, it, above all others in the canon,
is 'particularly stained by "Semitisms" ';[49] 'no New Testament
book', in fact, as Matthew Black reminds us, 'has a better claim to
be written in "Jews' Greek" than the Apocalypse'.[50]

Scrolls, ed. C. Rabin and Y. Yadin [1958], pp. 36–55). The change which
Yadin's thesis effected in critical thought is most apparent in the writings of
Ceslas Spicq, who, after publishing his excellent introductory volume on
Hebrews in 1952, found in 1959 that he had to modify his earlier position to
bring it into line with Yadin's evidence (cf. Spicq's 'L'Epître aux Hebreux,
Apollos, Jean-Baptiste, les Hellenistes et Qumran', *RQ*, I [1959], pp. 365–90,
with his earlier *L'Epître aux Hebreux,* I [1952]). Today, acceptance of a Jewish
Christian destination for the Letter to the Hebrews is widespread; whether it
be the earlier view of W. Manson, a position still highly respectable and
respected, or some form of the thesis of Yadin, which I personally favour.

[47] Eusebius, Eccles. Hist. II. 23, was the first to speak of these epistles
collectively as the 'seven catholic epistles', though individual letters had been
designated 'catholic' earlier.

[48] Cf. W. F. Albright: 'Each of the Catholic Epistles contains many
Essene reminiscences. . . . I must stress the fact that it is not necessary to
suppose that these reminiscences were exclusively Essene. They may also go
back to earlier Jewish sects whose literatures have been lost. We do know,
however, that little of this material appears in Rabbinic sources, which reflect
later Pharisaism in its development from the time of Christ onward' ('Retro-
spect and Prospect in New Testament Archaeology', *The Teacher's Yoke,* ed.
E. J. Vardeman and J. L. Garrett [1964], p. 41).

[49] M. Black, 'Second Thoughts—X. The Semitic Element in the New
Testament', *ExpT*, LXXVII (1965), p. 23.

[50] *Ibid.*

Paul has indicated in Gal. 2 that the early advance of the Christian gospel took place along two main lines of endeavour and within two major spheres of influence: the Jewish mission, in which James, Peter, and John were most prominent, and the Gentile mission, in which Paul himself took the lead. The writings which I have enumerated above I take to be reflective of this first mission, though with the important qualification that they represent varied aspects of that mission at various stages of its development and not a monolithic entity – for just as the Gentile centres of Paul's evangelization show diversity and development, so we should posit the same for the Jewish mission.

Paul and the Acts of the Apostles. But more significant than these for the identification of early Jewish Christian christological patterns – if for no other reason, because of the early date of the material in which they are contained – are portions found in the Pauline letters: (1) snatches of incorporated confessional and hymnodic material (certainly I Cor. 15.3–5, probably Phil. 2.6–11, and perhaps many others), and (2) polemic discourse where there is reason to believe a type of Jewish Christian argumentation is being countered (principally in Galatians and Colossians). Of these matters I must speak later where the issues are directly pertinent to the discussion. Suffice it here to say that in the New Testament the presence of both Judaizers and more orthodox Jewish believers 'can easily be discerned moving shadowily behind its pages, especially in the Pauline epistles'.[51] A study of these reflections in the letters of Paul furnishes valuable insight into the conceptual patterns, motifs, and emphases of at least certain elements within early Jewish Christianity. Likewise the first part of the Acts of the Apostles may be employed here, for whether its 'semitisms' are the phenomena of a translation, the result of a literary use of sources, the conscious or unconscious imitation of the LXX, or a combination of these factors, its author apparently is structuring his presentation according to these two cycles of early Christian advance and shows an interest in 'archaizing' in respect to the Jewish mission – whether that be judged as conscious or derivative.

PROCEDURES EMPLOYED

It has become usual of late to centre attention upon the christological titles of the New Testament in the historical study of first-

---

[51] W. D. Davies, 'Torah and Dogma', *HTR*, LXI (1968), p. 101.

century Christian thought regarding Jesus of Nazareth. And this procedure will be followed in the present study as well, emphasizing particularly the major groupings or clusters of appellatives as they appear in the materials of early Jewish Christianity. This is not to suggest that the titles, as fixed semantic counters, 'carry' the christology of the early faith. It is, rather, to acknowledge that the convictions of the earliest believers regarding Jesus were expressed through conceptual imagery and motifs at hand, and to believe that a study of such ascriptions in both their individual nuances and their interrelationships will significantly advance our understanding of early Jewish Christian convictions. Admittedly, as is true of any other single approach, the procedure must skim all too lightly over certain aspects of early belief, simply because the early Christians found themselves groping for ways in which to express what they had come to believe and the titles at hand were unable to contain fully their basic convictions. None the less, the insights which such a procedure affords are of such substance as to engender forgiveness for its faults and to encourage its employment.

A study of the titles ascribed to Jesus is especially rewarding when dealing with early Jewish Christianity. While many titles are employed in the writings of the Apostolic Fathers and early Apologists, they tend to become levelled or simply equated in the developing orthodoxy of the second century. Even Paul's christology, while full-orbed and many-sided, is not always best apprehended by way of the titles he employs, for in this area the apostle is much more limited than were his Christian predecessors; many early appellations are conspicuous by their absence in what we know of Paul, or appear in such veiled fashion as to make their presence debated. By far the dominant title for Jesus in the Pauline letters is that of 'Lord', and into it the apostle seems to have compressed most of the nuances of his christology. Early Jewish Christians, however, employed a great variety of christological titles, with nuances drawn from their background and with an evident awareness of differing connotations. Our proposed procedure is therefore most appropriate in dealing with the convictions of this stratum and sector of early Christian faith.

In such a study as here taken up, we are immediately faced with the question of methodology. Too often the issues have been determined by (1) evaluating the hellenistic contribution to the New Testament, subtracting this from the total, and acclaiming the residue to be semitic and primitive (oblivious to the intermingling of hebraic and hellenistic ideologies and terms in first-century Palestine), and (2) working from a predetermined set of convictions as to what was possible in a hebraic milieu. Now *a priori* assumptions can never be eliminated altogether from any study; and certainly should not be condemned *per se*, for without them one would never begin. But they must be checked both historically and critically.

This process of 'hellenistic subtraction' has been in large measure abetted in the past by the nature and paucity of extant materials with which the New Testament could be compared. But with the discoveries of the Dead Sea and Nag Hammadi texts, and the resultant re-evaluation of previously known noncanonical writings, material is now at hand for a new application of the old comparative-religion methodology which gives promise of more adequately based results. It is becoming increasingly evident today that in the scientific study of the New Testament, the Jewish backgrounds rather than the Grecian parallels offer the soundest basis of approach.

In the chapters that follow, it is this procedure and this method which will be followed: first treating those christological motifs and titles which appear to have been distinctive to early Jewish Christianity, then studying early conviction regarding the messiahship of Jesus and implications stemming from that commitment, and thirdly dealing with the consciousness of the early believers regarding the lordship of Jesus and concepts attendant to that perspective. Admittedly, the three groupings of ideas and expressions presented in chapters two through four overlap to some extent, forbidding any claim to completely separate provenances. Yet like strands of a single rope or elements of a compound, they may be profitably analysed individually. Finally, however, as in chapter five, it will be necessary to indicate something regarding the interrelationships of the themes and motifs from these three major strands or groupings of titles in an endeavour to understand the fusing or crystallization of christological thought in first-century Jewish Christianity.

II

DISTINCTIVE IMAGERY AND MOTIFS

EARLY JEWISH CHRISTIAN theology was 'almost exclusively Christology'.[1] Belief in a theistic God – the one true God, who is both Creator and Redeemer – was axiomatic. What concerned the earliest Christians, and that which they centred their attention upon, was the redemptive activity of God in the person and work of Jesus. No other consideration loomed so large in their thinking. And all others, whether advances in their apprehension of God, consciousness of their place in redemptive history, or developments in their ecclesiology, sprang from this source. It is therefore necessary in the study of early Jewish Christianity to start where they began, and to attempt by means of their expressions to gain an understanding of their basic christological convictions.

It is the thesis of the present chapter that certain portions of the New Testament, as delineated in chapter one, stand in direct ideological and conceptual continuity with the Dead Sea Scrolls and related Old Testament apocryphal materials, on the one hand, and the post-apostolic Jewish Christian writings and related Nag Hammadi texts, on the other; and that by tracing parallels of imagery and expression between these three bodies of material – with appropriate allowances for differences of theological outlook and the development of thought – there result some interesting identifications and conclusions regarding distinctive features in early Palestinian christology such as were not possible before. Following out the suggestions and work of others, it is my purpose here to isolate some distinctive Jewish Christian themes and conceptual patterns in the New Testament by reference to these earlier Jewish and later Jewish Christian writings – extrapolating both forward and backward in search of legitimate concurrences. In the

---

[1] O. Cullmann, *The Christology of the New Testament* (ET 1959), p. 3. Cf. *idem, The Earliest Christian Confessions* (ET 1949), pp. 38–41, 50–52; V. Taylor, *The Person of Christ in New Testament Teaching* (1958), p. viii.

following chapters additional themes and further developments in Jewish Christian christology will be considered.

ANGELOMORPHIC CHRISTOLOGY

Perhaps the methodology here invoked is most readily seen in a consideration of angelomorphic christology. Jean Daniélou has demonstrated that terms borrowed from the vocabulary of angelology were widely used by Jewish Christians up to the fourth century with reference to Christ and the Spirit, and that after this these expressions tended to disappear because of their ambiguity and the use made of them by the Arians.[2] Of the Ebionites, Tertullian says that they make of Christ a mere man, 'though more glorious than the prophets, in that they say that an angel was in him';[3] and Epiphanius reports that 'they say that he [Christ] was not begotten of God the Father, but created as one of the archangels . . . that he rules over the angels and all the creatures of the Almighty'.[4] In Test. Dan 6.2 there seems to be a transposition from the Jewish theme of the intercession of the angel Michael for the nation Israel to the Jewish Christian theme of the mediatorship of Christ along with the defense of Israel, in the exhortation: 'Draw near unto God and unto the angel that intercedeth for you, for he is a mediator between God and men, and for the peace of Israel shall he stand up against the kingdom of the enemy.'[5] Admittedly, the employment of such evidence here is dependent upon a Christian provenance for the Greek Testaments, which I believe to be probable. Similarly, and with the same critical problem, Test. Levi 5.6 makes this same transposition in Levi's dialogue with an angel and his identification of that angel as 'the angel who interceeds for the nation Israel *and* for all the righteous' (italics mine). In Clementine Homilies 18.4 and Recognitions 2.42 there is a comparable pattern in the representation of the seventy nations governed by seventy angels, over whom Christ rules as the greatest of the archangels and therefore is called 'God of gods'.

---

[2] J. Daniélou, 'Trinité et Angelologie dans la Theologie judéo-chrétienne', *RSR*, XLV (1957), pp. 5–41; *idem*, *Theology of Jewish Christianity*, pp. 117–46.
[3] De Carn. Christi 14.5; see entire fourteenth chapter.
[4] Haer. XXX. 16. 4.
[5] On the identification of Michael with Christ in early Christian angelomorphic christology, see, e.g., Hermas, Sim. VIII. 3. 3; II Enoch 22.4–9. On the correspondence of Melchizedek and Michael in Qumran thought, see 11QMelch.

The Shepherd of Hermas speaks frequently of the exalted Lord as the 'glorious angel', the 'most venerable angel', the 'holy angel', and the 'angel of the Lord', and distinguishes him quite clearly from other angels who are sent by him to guide Hermas.[6] Even Origen, though not himself a Jewish Christian, comes close to an angelomorphic christology in his identification of the two seraphim of Isa. 6.3 as being Christ and the Holy Spirit.[7] Interestingly, however, Origen claims to have received this interpretation from a Hebrew teacher; though whether he means that the germinal idea was received from a non-Christian Jew and he christianized it or that this was the interpretation of some Jewish Christian instructor is uncertain, and probably not vitally important here. It is sufficient to note that even in this moderate approach to angelomorphic christology a Jewish source is cited.

I am not suggesting from the citation of references to the Ebionites that I think all Jewish Christianity was Ebionite, either in patristic times or in the apostolic period, or that only Ebionites employed such imagery and expression. What I am proposing as probable is that the various groupings within what can be spoken of as Jewish Christianity in the patristic period shared a common body of conceptual imagery and expression, and that the portrayal of Jesus as an angel occurred in both heterodox formulations and more orthodox ones.

The fact that second-century Christian tradition included an angelomorphic representation of Christ is directly attested by Justin in the Dialogue:

But if you knew, Trypho, who He is that is called at one time the Angel of great counsel, and a Man by Ezekiel, and like the Son of man by Daniel, and a Child by Isaiah, and Christ and God to be worshipped by David, and Christ and a Stone by many, and Wisdom by Solomon, and Joseph and Judah and a Star by Moses, and the East by Zechariah, and the Suffering One and Jacob and Israel by Isaiah again, and a Rod, and Flower, and Cornerstone, and Son of God, you would not have blasphemed Him who has now come, and been born, and suffered, and ascended to heaven; who shall also come again, and then your twelve tribes shall mourn.[8]

[6] Cf. Hermas, Vis. V. 2; Com. V. 1. 7; Sim. V. 4. 4; VII. 1–3, 5; VIII. 1. 1–2, 2. 1; IX. 1. 3, 12. 7–8.

[7] Princ. I. 3. 4.

[8] Dial. 126.1–2. See also Dial. 55.10; 58.3; 126.4–5 on Justin's christological understanding of the 'angel of the Lord'.

Justin is here marshalling titles and giving a *précis* of the gospel as he believes pertinent for a Jewish audience and as he believes was commonly done by Jewish Christians. And it is significant that he begins by identifying Christ as 'the Angel of great counsel'. Likewise the Gospel of Thomas, while itself opting for a more esoteric evaluation of Jesus, acknowledges that angelomorphic christology was a prominent feature in certain Christian circles of the second century, as is indicated in the first part of Logion 13:

Jesus said to his disciples: Make a comparison to me, and tell me whom I am like. Simon Peter said to him: 'You are like a righteous angel.' Matthew said to him: 'You are like a wise philosopher.' Thomas said to him: 'Master, my mouth is not at all able to bear that I say whom you are like.'

It therefore seems well within the evidence to conclude that in the patristic period angelomorphic christology was a feature within Jewish Christian circles and even expressed itself to some extent in the writings of certain Gentile Christians who had been influenced by Jewish or Jewish Christian modes of thought.

Sources for an angelomorphic christology can, of course, be found in pre-Christian Judaism. In Isa. 63.9, God who grieves over the affliction of his people and 'the angel of his presence' who saves them are joined together: 'In all their affliction he was afflicted, and the angel of his presence saved them.' Here something of a Protoevangelium appears in that God's people are to be saved by the activity of the angel of his presence who is sent by the afflicted God.[9] The Old Testament speaks repeatedly of the theophanic presence as the 'Angel of God', the 'Angel of Yahweh', or simply 'the Angel',[10] and at times actually identifies such manifestations as deity;[11] thereby offering solid biblical support for the Christian

[9] Cf. M. Takahashi, 'An Oriental's Approach to the Problems of Angelology', *ZAW*, LXXVIII (1966), p. 346.

[10] 'Angel of God': Gen. 21.17; 31.11; Ex. 14.19; Judg. 6.20; 13.6, 9; 'Angel of Yahweh': Gen. 16.7–11; 22.11, 15; Ex. 3.2; Num. 22.22–35; Judg. 2.1, 4; 5.23; 6.11–22; 13.3–21; 'The Angel': Gen. 48.16.

[11] Note the cases of (1) the angels who appeared to Abraham by the oaks of Mamre in Gen. 18.1–33, where from v. 22b to the end it is Yahweh, not the angels, who holds conversation with Abraham; (2) the angels who appeared to Lot in Sodom in Gen. 19.1–22, where in vv. 17f. and 21f. the two angels are transformed in the narrative into a single personage who is addressed as deity; and (3) the angel who appeared to Gideon in Judg. 6.7–24, who from v. 14 to the end is identified as deity. Cf. M. Takahashi, *ZAW*, LXXVIII

attribution of angelomorphic categories to the Christ on the part
of even the most orthodox. The LXX indicates an interest in
angels in its translations of Deut. 32.8, reading 'the angels of the
nations' for 'the children of Israel', and Deut. 33.2, where 'at his
right hand were his angels with him' appears in place of 'at his
right hand was a fiery law for them'; and possibly also in Ps. 8.5,
where 'angels' is the translation of the possibly obscure 'gods' or
'God'.

In the Talmud, God is viewed as surrounded by his heavenly
courtiers, each with his proper rank and particular function. It
must be noted, however, that in talmudic Judaism 'angels, however abundant, have small religious importance'.[12] They serve in
communicating God's message to men. But the rabbinic attitude
towards their conveyance of men's prayers to God is far less positive, and even ambiguous. A Jerusalem Gemara explicitly forbids
prayer by means of angelic mediation.[13] The Babylonian Talmud,
however, seems to allow angelic mediation if one prays in biblical
Hebrew – the angels being ignorant of Aramaic.[14] But such a
restriction would seem to limit seriously the mediatorial value of
angels for the *am haaretz*, and practically speaking tends to substantiate G. F. Moore's judgment that 'in orthodox Judaism they
were not intermediaries between man and God'.[15]

Philo, too, has an angelology. For him, as with Judaism generally, angels serve in the administration of the cosmos and in the
communication of revelations. But in his attempt to bridge the gap
between the pure Being of God and the world of Becoming, angels
were 'a considerably vaguer category' than either Logos, who is
God's Thought or Reason, or Powers, which are manifestations
of divine activity.[16] Angels in the Philonic treatment are subsumed

---

(1966), pp. 346–8, on the 'fluctuation or fluidity between God and angels' in
the Old Testament.

[12] C. G. Montefiore and H. Loewe, *A Rabbinic Anthology* (1938), p. 23.
[13] J. Ber. 13a: 'If a man is in distress, let him not call on Michael or
Gabriel, but let him call direct on me, and I will hearken to him straightway.'
Cf. also IV Ezra 7.102–115, where mediation of any kind is explicitly denied.
[14] B. Shab. 12b, b. Sot. 33a. The prohibition against prayer in Aramaic
is ascribed to R. Judah the Prince and, as R. A. Stewart suggests, 'may be pro-
Hebraic rather than anti-angelic' (*Rabbinic Theology*, [1961], p. 57).
[15] G. F. Moore, *Judaism in the First Centuries of the Christian Era*, I (1927),
p. 411.
[16] H. A. A. Kennedy, *Philo's Contribution to Religion* (1919), p. 162.

under the broader concept of Powers; though, significantly, are ruled over by the Logos – the 'elder of the angels' (τὸν ἀγγέλων πρεσβύτατον), the 'archangel as it were' (ὡς ἂν ἀρχάγγελον).[17]

Of greatest significance for our purpose here, however, is the angelology of the Dead Sea Scrolls and related apocryphal writings. At the close of a lengthy description of an Essene candidate's initiatory rites, Josephus tells us that the sectarian proselyte was 'carefully to preserve the books of the sect and the names of the angels'.[18] And the material found at Qumran – both the distinctive sectarian literature and the works taken over by the group – evidence an elaborate angelology; particularly in the larger portions of 1QS, 1QH, 1QM and I Enoch 1–36, though also in the fragments. Especially important in this material, however, is the aspect of angelic ministration in the redemption of man. For not only are angels considered to superintend the created universe and to act as messengers of God to man, but they also aid men to be acceptable before God,[19] convey human prayers to the Almighty,[20] and act as intercessors for men as well.[21]

When these elements of redemptive angelic ministration and angelomorphic christology are extrapolated into the New Testament, interesting correspondences result. We need not dwell on the general angelology of the New Testament, for that is too common to be important here. Nor need we consider the common Jewish theme of the presence of angels in the giving of the Law in Acts 7.53; Gal. 3.19f.; and Heb. 2.2, though that is a bit more to the point. The wide dissemination of this idea by means of the LXX translation of Deut. 33.2 and rabbinic exposition on it, however, make it difficult to handle with any precision. What does seem significant is the association in certain New Testament passages of angels with Christ and redemption; and further, that the

[17] De Conf. Ling. 146.

[18] War II. 8. 7 (II. 142).

[19] Note, e.g., the discussions of the Angel of Truth or Light helping man to be acceptable in spite of all that the Angel of Darkness or Hostility can do to the contrary in 1QS 3.18ff.; 1QM 13.9f. Cf. also 11QMelch.

[20] E.g., 1QH 6.13; Tob. 12.12–15; III Bar. 11–17.

[21] E.g., I Enoch 9.10; 15.2; 99.3, 16; II Bar. 6.7 (also I Enoch 40.9; 47.2; Test. Levi 3.5; 5.6f.; though here methodologically ruled out as evidence). On the angelic liturgy and angels having priestly characteristics at Qumran, see J. Strugnell, 'The Angelic Liturgy at Qumran – 4Q Serek Sirot 'Olat Hassabbat', *VT S*, VII (1960), pp. 318–45. Only in Zech. 1.12 is there anything similar in the Old Testament.

clearest instances of this are to be found in polemical portions directed against certain contemporary Jewish Christian views.

Assuming a Jewish Christian identification for the troublers at Galatia (contra J. Munck, though not going to the other extreme of H. J. Schoeps and S. G. F. Brandon in equating them with the whole of the Jerusalem church), Paul's references to angels in that letter are interesting. In Gal. 1.8 he anathematizes even an angelic revelation if it conflicts with what he has proclaimed, and in Gal. 3.19f. he contrasts the angelic and Mosaic mediated covenant with that which is the better in Christ. Evidently, his converts were beginning to restructure their thinking along angelomorphic lines to the disparagement of the primacy and sufficiency of Christ – or at least Paul thought that there was this danger inherent in the heresy which enticed them; and the apostle speaks against it. And in Gal. 4.14, in probably a play on their reconstituted conceptual imagery, Paul seems to equate the 'angel of God' with 'Christ Jesus' in his reminder to them that they received him on his former visit 'as an angel of God, as Christ Jesus'. In Colossians, assuming some type of syncretistic Jewish Christian agitation behind the difficulties in the Lycus Valley, Paul speaks in 2.18 of the 'worshipping of angels'; by which he probably means, as in the Galatian letter, such prominence given to angelic manifestations and angelomorphic categories as to minimize the uniqueness of Christ.[22] And in the Letter to the Hebrews, assuming a Jewish Christian audience – whether in Palestine–Syria, Rome, or Corinth – for whom a return to Judaism was a live option, the opening argument of chapters one and two on the supremacy of the Son over angelic ministers seems to point to a distinctive doctrine of redemptive angelology held by the recipients.[23] Perhaps, also, inferences can be drawn from the frequency of angels in the Lucan birth narrative, if this can be related to translation phenomena or to a literary use of sources, as well as in the Matthean infancy account.

But whatever is thought regarding these latter cases in Luke and

[22] The assertion of the Preaching of Peter, as preserved by Clement of Alexandria and Origen, that the Jews worship angels (cf. *NT Apoc.*, II, pp. 100f.) probably stems entirely from Col. 2.18.

[23] As M. de Jonge and A. S. van der Woude point out, 11QMelch. 'illustrates the type of thinking about angels and other heavenly beings which the author of Hebrews is up against' ('11QMelchizedek and the New Testament', *NTS*, XII [1966], p. 317).

Matthew, it does seem from the polemic on the part of those in the
Gentile mission against certain antagonists and views held within
the Jewish mission that angelomorphic christology, or something
approaching it, was an element within Jewish Christianity in
apostolic times. For a number of Jewish believers, evidently, the
angelology of the Old Testament – particularly the angelic theo-
phanies – became a starting point in their christological understanding and expression. Again, this is not to claim that Gentile
Christianity and Jewish Christianity stood in opposition throughout (though, for the extremes in both groups this may very well
have been the case). It is only to assert the probability that just as
the Gentile mission operated within a body of conceptual imagery
and expression, though with various emphases evident within the
cycle, so the Jewish mission in its various manifestations shared
common patterns of thought and expression. There was undoubtedly a great deal of overlapping. But distinctives also seem
evident. And one of these for Jewish Christians was apparently
that of angelomorphic christology.[24]

THE ESCHATOLOGICAL MOSAIC PROPHET

Of significance as well for early Jewish Christians was the idea of
the eschatological Mosaic prophet, springing as it did from their
contemporary Jewish milieu and thus meaningful both to themselves and to their Jewish audience in the carrying out of the
Christian mission.

The literature of Judaism evidences an expectation that in the
Messianic Age the spirit of prophecy would be restored and
prophetic figures would be prominent in the life of the nation.
Ideas regarding the exact nature of this prophetic activity, however, were often loose and mixed; and there were differences concerning the identity of the expected figure or figures. I Maccabees
4.46 and 14.41, for instance, speak rather indefinitely of 'a faithful

[24] W. Michaelis has argued '*dass das Urchristentum keine Engelchristologie
gekannt hat*' (*Zur Engelchristologie im Urchristentum* [1942], p. 187, *passim*). But
that judgment was levelled against the very extreme thesis of M. Werner that
late Jewish apocalypticism (i.e., Dan. 7.13, Test. Levi and the Similitudes of
Enoch) had an angel-messianology, and that this was carried over into
Christianity so that the earliest christology was essentially an angel-christo-
logy (*Die Entstehung des christlichen Dogmas* [1941], pp. 302–49). Both methodologically and theologically, however, the material presented above finds little
parallel with Werner's treatment; and thus is not really affected by Michaelis'
wholly negative review.

prophet' who should 'come' or 'arise'.[25] Attention in Sir. 48.10f.
and Genesis Rabbah 71.9 and 99.11 is centred upon Elijah as the
coming prophet who would inaugurate the final age and be God's
restorer.[26] In other passages, notably IV Ezra 6.26 and 7.28, all the
men taken from the earth without dying – Enoch and Elijah, later
Moses, and possibly Ezra, Baruch, and Jeremiah[27] – are expected
to accompany the Messiah and to have prophetic functions in the
establishment of the eschatological period of salvation.

But while there was a measure of ambiguity within Israel regarding personages and relationships in future prophetic and
messianic activity, the view that the eschatological prophet and/or
coming Messiah would have Mosaic characteristics seems to have
been firmly embedded in Jewish expectations during the first
centuries BC and AD. The inclusion of Deut. 18.18f. in the testimonia fragment discovered at Qumran indicates that in certain
circles, at least, the appearance of a prophet 'like unto' Moses
was an important feature in messianic expectations. N. Wieder
has demonstrated on the basis of epithets bestowed on the Teacher
of Righteousness in the Manual of Discipline that (at least in its
early days) the Dead Sea community looked upon its founder and
teacher as a Second Moses, who was preparing God's elect
through his biblical interpretations for the coming of the Messiahs
of Aaron and Israel.[28] Later, however, with the death of the

---

[25] J. Klausner interprets these verses as having Elijah in mind (*The
Messianic Idea in Israel* [ET 1956], p. 260), and W. D. Davies understands
Moses as alluded to (*Torah in the Messianic Age and/or the Age to Come* [1952],
p. 44). Probably, however, the author of I Maccabees was unable to furnish a
precise identification, living as he did in the last quarter of the second century
BC before the issues relevant to the competing views had been spelled out
(cf. H. M. Teeple, *The Mosaic Eschatological Prophet* [1957], pp. 2f.).

[26] On the basis of Mal. 4.5f. (MT 3.23f.). Cf. Elijah's inclusion among the
'four craftsmen' (the eschatological חרשים) of b. Suk. 52b: 'The Messiah
the son of David, the Messiah the son of Joseph, Elijah and the Righteous
Priest.' In Deut. R. 3.17, Elijah and Moses are spoken of as coming together
'at one time'.

[27] Cf. *Ap. & Ps.*, II, pp. 576f. (on IV Ezra 6.26) for references on this list
of 'the immortal companions'.

[28] N. Wieder, 'The "Law-Interpreter" of the Sect of the Dead Sea Scrolls:
The Second Moses', *JJS*, IV (1953), pp. 158–75. Cf. W. H. Brownlee,
'Messianic Motifs of Qumran and the New Testament', *NTS*, III (1956), p. 17,
in agreement and for a bibliography of early interpreters taking this position.
Further, accepting the reconstruction of the lacuna in line 18 of 11QMelch.
as 'anointed of the Spirit', we have 'the first instance in the Qumran literature
of a singular use of the expression to denote a prophet'; and also, 'it is quite
possible that the "anointed by the Spirit" mentioned here is the same as the

Teacher and the rising importance of a Pharisaic element within the community, the second-Moses ascription was probably applied more to the coming Messiah; in line with the shift from the priestly hope of a prophet and two Messiahs, as in the earlier Manual of Discipline, to the more Pharisaically-influenced expectation of a single messianic figure who would incorporate in his person varied functions, as in the Damascus Document.[29] And in the Samaritan concept of the coming Messiah, who is called the 'Restorer' (the *Taheb* or the *Shaheb*), Deut. 18.15–18 is foundational. While much is vague in Samaritan eschatology, the Restorer's Mosaic character is set in bold relief; so much so, as to be a Moses *redivivus*.[30]

As J. Jeremias has pointed out, the degree to which the concept of a Mosaic Messiah was established in first-century Judaism is illustrated by the many claimants to messiahship who attempted to validate their claims by re-enacting the experiences of Moses.[31] This is not to assert the expectation of a second coming or a reincarnation of Moses himself in pre-Christian Judaism. What evidence there is for that in rabbinic and Jewish Christian sources is late.[32] But it is to insist that the Jewish populace generally thought of the personages of the future not just in terms of (1) the Messiah, and (2) Elijah, who would prepare men for the final day of the Lord in terms of Mal. 4.5f., but also of (3) a 'prophet like unto Moses' – *the* Prophet – who would bear some intimate relationship to the Messiah *or* in fact be the Messiah himself, as prophesied in Deut. 18.15–19.[33] Though not completely absent, the relative

---

"prophet like Moses" in 4Q Test' (M. de Jonge and A. S. van der Woude, '11QMelch. and the N.T.', *NTS*, XII [1966], pp. 306f.).

[29] Accepting the essentials of J. T. Milik's thesis of development and rising Pharisaic importance in the group, though without insisting upon differing geographical provenances for 1QS and CDC (cf. *Ten Years of Discovery*, pp. 124–8; note also W. H. Brownlee, 'John the Baptist in the New Light of Ancient Scrolls', *The Scrolls and the New Testament*, ed. K. Stendahl [1957], pp. 44f.; *idem*, 'Messianic Motifs', *NTS*, III [1957], p. 199). Note the three offices in the one descendant of Levi in Test. Levi 8.11–15.

[30] Cf. M. Gaster, *The Samaritans* (1925), pp. 90f.; J. MacDonald, *The Theology of the Samaritans* (1964), pp. 160, 198, 216f. 361–3.

[31] J. Jeremias, 'Μωυσῆς', *TWNT*, IV, p. 866 (ET, p. 862).

[32] Contra O. Cullmann, *Christology of the New Testament*, p. 16. On the rabbinic texts, see P. Volz, *Die Eschatologie der jüdischen Gemeinde im neutestamentlichen Zeitalter* (1934), p. 195.

[33] Philo seems to have had Deut. 18.15–18 in mind in speaking of Moses'

infrequency of a second-Moses motif in the earlier rabbinic materials should probably be accounted for on the basis of an anti-Christian polemic.[34]

The Gospels reflect these Jewish expectations, particularly in John's accounts of the questions put to the Baptist by delegates from Jerusalem and the Samaritan woman's response to Jesus.[35] And there are verses in the Gospels which state that Jesus was regarded by at least a segment of the populace as a prophet,[36] and that he encouraged this idea of himself.[37] Had we no more than this, we would yet be in touch with something meaningful. For, as Cullmann points out, the acclamation of Jesus as a prophet is not the same as the attribution of the honorific title rabbi; in days when the restoration of prophecy was viewed as signalling the beginning of the last days, such an acclamation was fraught with eschatological significance.[38] In addition, the Gospels record instances where others referred to Jesus as *the* prophet.[39] And there is the suggestion in two passages that even Jesus' critics understood his claim to messiahship to include the concept of being a prophet like unto Moses. The first is in the account in Mark 14.65, where at his trial Jesus was blind-folded and called upon to prophesy – possibly taunting him with the accusation that in his silence he is not like the veiled Moses but like the veiled Balaam.[40] The second appears in Luke 7.39 (accepting the reading of B) in the objection of the Pharisee that Jesus was certainly not *the* prophet because he allowed a woman of the street to touch him.

But of greater importance for our purpose here is the evidence in the New Testament for an early Jewish Christian consciousness regarding Jesus as the eschatological Mosaic Prophet. Whether

---

promise of 'full knowledge of the future' and saying that a 'prophet possessed by God will suddenly appear and give prophetic oracles' (De Spec. Leg. I. 64f.).

[34] Cf. N. Wieder, 'The Idea of a Second Coming of Moses', *JQR*, LXVI (1956), pp. 356–66; though opposed by S. Zeitlin in an appended note to Wieder's article.

[35] John 1.19–27; 4.25.

[36] Mark 6.15; 8.28; Luke 7.16; 9.8; 24.19; John 4.19.

[37] Mark 6.4; Luke 4.24; 13.33.

[38] O. Cullmann, *Christology of the New Testament*, pp. 13–15.

[39] Certainly John 6.14; probably John 7.52 (according to P66, cf. John 7.40); and possibly Luke 7.39 (according to B, *et. al.*) and Matt. 21.11.

[40] See Num. 24.3. Cf. C. H. Dodd, 'Jesus as Teacher and Prophet', *Mysterium Christi*, ed. G. K. A. Bell and A. Deissmann (1930), p. 57.

Jesus ever thought of himself or was considered by others an eschatological prophet 'like unto' Elijah may be debated.[41] But that he was considered the eschatological prophet 'like unto' Moses seems to be fairly clear in the Gospels of Matthew and John, the first part of the Acts, and the letter to the Hebrews.

Deuteronomy 18.15, 18 are directly referred to as being fulfilled in Jesus in Acts 3.22 (Peter's address) and 7.37 (Stephen's defence). And it is probable that we should understand the 'hear ye him!' of the heavenly voice in Mark 9.7 (par.) as an allusion to the 'him shall ye hear' of Deut. 18.15 as well.[42] Matthew's Gospel has been often interpreted along 'New Moses' lines.[43] But while a Moses typology is certainly a feature in the presentation of the First Gospel, the Evangelist seems to be invoking primarily an Israel typology wherein Jesus is represented as the embodiment of the nation and the antitype of Israel's experiences – and within which larger framework the elements of a Moses typology come to expression. Thus, while parallels between Jesus and Moses undoubtedly exist, they coexist with other emphases. Only in the Sermon on the Mount of chs. 5–7 and, to a lesser extent, in the transfiguration narrative of 17.1–9 are the parallels in the First Gospel clearly enough drawn to warrant the definite ascription of a new-Moses understanding. It is in these two portions that the Mosaic prophet theme indeed comes to the fore, though, it must be noted, not to the exclusion of other imagery and not just as 'a second edition of Moses, as it were, on a grand scale, but one who supersedes him'.[44]

This same combination of similarity to, yet contrast with, Moses is also a feature in the Gospel of John, where, as one aspect in the portrayal, 'there can be little doubt that the way in which Christ is presented in the Fourth Gospel is intended to indicate that he is the fulfilment of Deut. 18.15–19'.[45] The narrative of Jesus' feeding of the multitude and his subsequent address to the people in John 6, together with such words of Jesus as found in 1.17;

[41] See J. A. T. Robinson, 'Elijah, John and Jesus', *NTS*, IV (1958), pp. 263–81 (also in *Twelve New Testament Studies* [1962], pp. 28–52), for an answer in the affirmative.

[42] Cf. W. D. Davies, *The Setting of the Sermon on the Mount* (1964), pp. 53f.

[43] Note a recent marshalling of parallels in H. M. Teeple, *Mosaic Eschatological Prophet*, pp. 74–85.

[44] W. D. Davies, *Setting of the Sermon on the Mount*, p. 92.

[45] T. F. Glasson, *Moses in the Fourth Gospel* (1963), p. 30.

5.39–47; and 14.6, explicitly make the point. And while Miss Guilding has undoubtedly gone beyond the evidence in constructing her lectionary thesis for John's Gospel,[46] and T. F. Glasson tends to construct the typology too closely to a Mosaic theme,[47] many of the allusions to Moses in the Fourth Gospel which they have pointed out are none the less significant. Likewise the opening words of the Letter to the Hebrews, while not explicitly Mosaic, are clearly based on a view of Jesus as the Prophet of eschatological consummation: 'In many and various ways God spoke of old to our fathers by the prophets, but in these last days he has spoken to us by his Son.' (Heb. 1.1f.) Even the anti-Mosaic polemic of Heb. 3.1–6; 7.22; 8.6; and 9.15–22 is not essentially different from that in Matthew and John in its insistence that while Jesus can be paralleled with Moses he yet supersedes him by far; for, as Glasson has aptly remarked, 'it is impossible to contrast two objects or persons unless they have much in common'.[48]

It has often been observed that a new-Moses motif comes to expression in the New Testament only in certain writings, being entirely absent in others. And it has been suggested that this is due to the fact that either (1) 'only a portion of Judaism entertained this expectation, and therefore it is not surprising that there were also many Jewish Christians who did *not* interpret Jesus in that manner',[49] or (2) a Mosaic prophet christology was too limited and deficient to be valuable in the development of Christian theology.[50] But the first explanation is not true; and the second, without qualification, is insufficient to account for the phenomenon. Rather, this selectivity of imagery seems to be related to conceptual and expressional differences between early Jewish Christianity and the Gentile mission. Whereas Paul proclaimed Abraham as the true symbol of Israel and laid no stress on a Mosaic prophet christology, the Jerusalem Christians as portrayed in the first part of Acts and the writers in the Jewish Christian cycle of witness interpreted Jesus along the lines of the eschatological Mosaic Prophet.

[46] A. Guilding, *The Fourth Gospel and Jewish Worship* (1960). In reply, see L. Morris, *The New Testament and the Jewish Lectionaries* (1964).
[47] T. F. Glasson, *Moses in the Fourth Gospel, passim.*
[48] T. F. Glasson, *Moses in the Fourth Gospel*, p. 25n.
[49] H. M. Teeple, *Mosaic Eschatological Prophet*, p. 74.
[50] O. Cullmann, *Christology of the New Testament*, p. 49.

That Jewish Christianity continued to employ a Mosaic prophet christology following the apostolic period can be seen in the second-century Preaching of Peter, where the central theme seems to have been 'the true prophet' who conveys divine revelation.[51] And this concept of the true Mosaic prophet is carried on in the Pseudo-Clementine Homilies and Recognitions of the late second through the fourth centuries.[52] The second-century Gospel of Thomas associates Jesus with the prophetic message of old, yet asserts a higher validation of his ministry: 'His disciples said to him: Twenty-four prophets spoke in Israel, and they all spoke concerning you. He said to them: You have neglected him who is alive before you, and have spoken about the dead.'[53] Jerome, in commenting on Isa. 11.2, reports that in the Gospel of the Hebrews the Spirit is represented as saying to Jesus: 'My Son, in all the prophets was I waiting for thee that thou shouldest come and I might rest in thee.'[54] And Test. Levi 8.14f. is of significance here as well, assuming a Jewish Christian provenance or redaction for the Testaments, in that it speaks of the third office of Levi's seed as being 'a prophet of the Most High'.

There is admittedly a shift of emphasis from the *eschatological* Mosaic prophet of the canonical writings to the *true* prophet, who is at times spoken of as being Mosaic, in the noncanonical Jewish Christian literature. This is obvious in the Preaching of Peter, the Pseudo-Clementines, and finds its final expression in the prophetology of Islam. Gnosticism undoubtedly played a large part in this shift from an historical to a more static understanding of the title.[55] But the evidence drawn from later Jewish Christian materials in no way sets aside the importance of the eschatological Mosaic prophet motif in early Jewish Christian christology. It only reveals that this concept, as is true of every other, had its own ideological matrix and could be developed in either orthodox or heterodox fashion.

[51] Cf. *NT Apoc.*, II, pp. 107f., 115f.

[52] E.g., Hom. 1. 40–41, 49; Recogn. 1. 43.

[53] Logion 52. Perhaps Matthew's purported comparison of Jesus to a 'wise man of understanding' (philosopher) in Logion 13 is also of pertinence here.

[54] See *NT Apoc.*, I, pp. 163f., on Comm. on Isa. IV.

[55] Perhaps, in part, capitalizing on the twenty-three uses of 'true' in the Johannine literature (nine in the Gospel, four in I John, and ten in the Apocalypse; whereas the word occurs only once in Paul, once in the Synoptic Gospels, and three times in Hebrews).

THE NEW EXODUS AND NEW TORAH

In his 1952 monograph on rabbinic and sectarian expectations regarding messianology and the Law, W. D. Davies concluded quite temperately in saying: 'We can at least affirm that there were elements inchoate in the Messianic hope of Judaism, which could make it possible for some to regard the Messianic Age as marked by a New Torah.'[56] In his recent *The Setting of the Sermon on the Mount*, having available the literature from Qumran, there is less reserve in affirming such a position.[57] And in the opening paragraph of his invaluable section on the 'New Exodus and New Moses' in that latter work, he makes the observation and claim:

Before the discovery of the Dead Sea Scrolls, the enthusiasm with which the theme of a New Exodus was often discovered in pre-Christian Judaism, and employed in the elucidation of the New Testament, may have been over-confident and slightly uncritical, in view of the sparse evidence for the motif in the sources available. But there can no longer be any doubt, since that event, that the ideal future of Jewish expectation was conceived, in some circles at least, in terms of a New Exodus.[58]

Without attempting to reproduce Davies' extensive and detailed argument, three points need to be stressed: (1) that 'the members of the [Dead Sea] community conceive[d] of themselves as repeating in a later age the experience of their remote fathers in the days of Moses';[59] (2) that the activities of the revolutionary Messiahs from Hezekiah through Simeon ben Kosebah in marshalling their forces in the wilderness evidence how firmly a New Exodus concept was connected with messiahship;[60] and (3) that 'the ease with which New Testament writers interpreted the Christian dispensation in terms of the Exodus is explicable only on the supposition that such a procedure was readily comprehensible'.[61] In regard to the theme of a New Torah, it need only

---

[56] W. D. Davies, *Torah in the Messianic Age*, p. 85.

[57] In regard to Qumran's understanding of the Messiah as God's Torah in 1QIs[a] 51.4, 7 and 26.8, see J. V. Chamberlain, 'The Functions of God as Messianic Titles in the Complete Qumran Isaiah Scroll', *VT*, V (1955), pp. 366–72.

[58] W. D. Davies, *Setting of the Sermon on the Mount*, p. 26.

[59] T. H. Gaster, *The Dead Sea Scriptures* (1964), p. 4; without, however, understanding 'repeating in a later age' as implying a cyclical view of history.

[60] Cf. J. Jeremias, 'Μωυσῆς', *TWNT*, IV, p. 866 (ET, p. 862).

[61] W. D. Davies, *Setting of the Sermon on the Mount*, p. 116.

be added that (1) Clement of Alexandria three times cites the early second-century Preaching of Peter as calling the Lord both 'Law and Word';[62] (2) Justin refers a number of times to Jesus as 'another Law', 'the eternal and final Law', 'another Covenant', 'the new Covenant for the whole world', and 'God's Covenant';[63] and (3) the Shepherd of Hermas explicitly equates the 'Law of God' with the 'Son of God'.[64] The silence of earlier talmudic materials on these motifs must be considered a result of anti-Christian polemic.

While salvation in Jesus is formulated in various places in the New Testament in terms of the Exodus,[65] nowhere is there so concentrated an effort to relate the Christian community with the people of God (ἐκκλησία) in the wilderness than in Matt. 2.13–7.29; Acts 7.17–46; and Heb. 3.7–4.11.[66] While Paul spoke of 'the Law of Christ' (ὁ νόμος τοῦ Χριστοῦ), being 'in-lawed to Christ' (ἔννομος Χριστοῦ), and related himself to the words and example of Jesus,[67] the literature of the Jewish Christian mission presents Jesus himself as in some sense a new Torah. Paul indicates in I Cor. 11.25 that the idea of Jesus as establishing in his person and redemptive work a 'new covenant' was alive in early Christian tradition. And the use of the new covenant theme in Hebrews reveals something of its meaningfulness to a Jewish audience. But John's Gospel goes further than this in actually setting forth Jesus' own person as the new Torah: (1) in the Prologue, presenting the divine Logos as the counterpart to Jewish ideas regarding the Torah; (2) in symbolic fashion, presenting Jesus as the true manna, water and light (perhaps also wine and well), in counterdistinction to contemporary claims for the Torah; and (3) in directly asserting his centricity in opposition to the exclusivist Torah-centricity of Judaism in John 14.6 and 5.39–47.[68] Matthew's presentation of the Sermon on the Mount

---

[62] Strom. I. 29; II. 15; Ecl. Proph. 58.

[63] Dial. 11.2, 4; 24.1; 43.1; 51.3; 112.4; 118.3; 122.5.

[64] Hermas, Sim. VIII. 3. 2.

[65] Cf. H. Sahlin, 'The New Exodus of Salvation', *The Root of the Vine*, A. Fridrichsen, *et al.* (1953), pp. 81–95; P. Minear, *Images of the Church in the New Testament* (1960), p. 78.

[66] I Cor. 10.1–15 employs the Exodus theme more illustratively than typologically, in accordance with the rabbinic argument that 'that has relevance to this'.

[67] Cf. Gal. 6.2; I Cor. 9.21, and my *Paul, Apostle of Liberty*, pp. 187–96.

[68] Cf. C. H. Dodd, *Fourth Gospel*, pp. 82–6; T. F. Glasson, *Moses in the Fourth Gospel*, pp. 45–64, 86–94, *passim*.

and James' echoing of it indicate a similar understanding as pre-supposed.

There is admittedly an overlapping here between the canonical literature of the Jewish Christian mission and Paul. But it seems that whereas Paul employed the history of the nation in its exodus from bondage more illustratively and based his teaching in large measure on what he knew Jesus to have said and done, the early Jewish Christians went further and to some extent developed a new-Exodus redemptive typology and a new-Torah christology.

In the new-Exodus and new-Torah cluster of concepts, the Jewish believers were employing motifs which sprang from their contemporary ideological milieu, and thus were meaningful both to themselves and to their Jewish compatriots. Yet, while the terminology provided an important bridge for meaningful com-munication within the Jewish Christian cycle of witness, there was a decided and vital difference between Judaism and early Jewish Christianity in the use of this imagery. As Davies rightly observes:

> Whereas in the complex referred to as the Exodus, at which Israel's redemption was wrought, Judaism came to place more and more emphasis on the Torah, that is, the demand uttered on Sinai, which was itself a gift, the figure of Moses being a colossus because he mediated the Torah, the Church as it looked back to the new Exodus wrought in Christ, first remembered not the demand but the person of Jesus Christ, through whom the New Exodus was wrought, and who thus came to have for the Church the significance of Torah. This is why ultimately the tradition of Judaism culminates in the Mishnah, a code of *halakoth*, and in Christianity in the Gospels, where all is subservient to Jesus as Lord.[69]

THE NAME

In the Valentinian Gospel of Truth, the theme of the Son as the Name of the Father is explicitly developed at some length.[70] The passage begins:

> The Name of the Father is the Son. It is He who, in the beginning, gave a name to Him who came forth from Him and who was Himself, and whom He engendered as a Son. He gave Him His Name which be-longed to Him – He, the Father, to whom belong all things which

---

[69] W. D. Davies, *Setting of the Sermon on the Mount*, p. 480, crediting D. Daube in large measure; see also *idem*, 'Torah and Dogma', *HTR*, LXI (1968), p. 98.

[70] Gospel of Truth 38.6–41.3.

exist around Him. He possesses the Name; He has the Son. . . . One does not pronounce the Name of the Father; but He reveals Himself through a Son. Thus, then, the Name is great.

The Gospel of Philip also speaks of 'the Name which the Father gave to the Son, which is above all things, which is the Name of the Father'.[71] Jean Daniélou has argued that already in I Clement and the Shepherd of Hermas, especially in liturgical sections reflecting traditional material, there are echoes of such an earlier christological attribution; though not anywhere as strong as it appears in the Nag Hammadi Gospels.[72] G. Quispel has shown that speculations on the divine name as a quasi-hypostatic entity active in the mediation of revelation can be observed in pre-Christian esoteric Judaism and in Jewish Christian heterodoxy of the third to sixth centuries.[73] And G. Scholem, following out the work of H. Odeberg, points out that in later Jewish mystical writings there appear similar speculations on the angel of the Lord in whom is the name of the Lord, who is the bearer of all the divine attributes and who is to guide men before the throne of God.[74]

The *locus classicus* for this concept is Ex. 23.20f., where God promises to send an angel before the people and warns them to take heed to him for 'my name is in him'. And it finds support in the many Old Testament passages where the divine name (שֵׁם) signals the presence of God.[75] In the alteration of the first person singular suffix to that of the third person masculine in 1QIs^a 51.5, there is the hint that the Dead Sea sectarians understood God's ethical qualities and attributes in the eschatological portions of Isaiah to be descriptive names for the Messiah.[76] Thus

---

[71] Gospel of Philip, Logion 12; cf. also 19.

[72] J. Daniélou, *Theology of Jewish Christianity*, pp. 151–7.

[73] G. Quispel, 'The Jung Codex and its Significance', *The Jung Codex*, trans. and ed. F. L. Cross (1955), pp. 68–78. The question of provenance is important in regard to I Enoch 69.14, where the 'hidden Name' of God is requested for inclusion in an oath in order to add authority to the oath. But whether this reference is Jewish or Jewish Christian, or both, its Jewish basis is undisputed.

[74] G. Scholem, *Major Trends in Jewish Mysticism* (1941), pp. 212–17; cf. H. Odeberg, *3 Enoch or the Hebrew Book of Enoch* (1928), p. 144.

[75] E.g., Deut. 12.11, 21; 14.23f.; 16.2, 11; 26.2; Neh. 1.9; Ps. 74.7; Isa. 18.7; Jer. 3.17; 7.10–14, 30.

[76] Cf. D. Barthélemy, 'Le grand rouleau d'Isaïe trouvé près de la Mer Morte', *RB*, LVII (1950), p. 548n; J. V. Chamberlain, 'Functions of God as Messianic Titles', *VT*, V (1955), pp. 369f.

the 'O Lord, we await your name' of 1QIs^a 26.8 was probably read at Qumran with messianic import. And it is possible that we should understand the profaning of 'the name' and references to God's 'great name' in the other scrolls as having among the sectarians messianic significance as well.[77] It is also significant that Philo, evidencing his Jewish background while at the same time blending into it extraneous elements, employs τὸ ὄνομα as one of the names of the Logos.[78]

Extrapolating into the New Testament, instances of the use of 'the name' take on greater significance. And interestingly, it is the Jewish Christian materials of the New Testament which evidence both a greater interest in the name of Jesus generally and an almost exclusive use of 'the name' as a christological designation.

In the Gospel of Matthew there is an emphasis upon the name of Jesus such as is not found in the other Synoptists. While both Matthew and Luke tell of the circumstances in the naming of Jesus, only Matthew speaks of the significance of the name.[79] Also, only Matthew records Jesus' promise of his presence in any gathering, however small, that meets 'in my name' (εἰς τὸ ἐμὸν ὄνομα).[80] All three Synoptic Gospels recount Jesus' words regarding leaving everything, house, family, and relatives for his sake and the purpose of the gospel. But whereas Mark's account reads 'for my sake and for the gospel',[81] and Luke's 'for the sake of the kingdom of God',[82] Matthew's wording is 'for my name's sake'.[83] In the sending out of the twelve to evangelize the country-side, only Matthew records the apocalyptic portion that includes the warning: 'And you will be hated of all men because of my name' (διὰ τὸ ὄνομά μου).[84] Matthew alone describes pseudo-

---

[77] CDC 15.3 (19.4); T. H. Gaster fills in the lacuna of line two to read: 'for the name of God is spelled out in that law' (*Dead Sea Scriptures*, p. 95). See also 1QM 11.2–3; 18.6, 8; 1QH 11.6; 12.3.

[78] Of the Logos, Philo says: 'And many names are his, for he is called the Beginning (ἀρχή), and the Name of God (ὄνομα θεοῦ), and His Word (λόγος), and the Man after His image (ὁ κατ᾽ εἰκόνα ἄνθρωπος), and he that sees (ὁ ὁρῶν), that is Israel' (De Conf. Ling. 146).

[79] Matt. 1.21–25; cf. Luke 1.31; 2.21.

[80] Matt. 18.20.

[81] Mark 10.29.

[82] Luke 18.29.

[83] Matt. 19.29.

[84] Matt. 10.22; though in a later apocalyptic section the warning is repeated and all three Gospels include διὰ τὸ ὄνομά μου (Matt. 24.9; Mark 13.13; Luke 21.17; cf. Luke 21.12).

Christians rejected by Jesus as those preaching and working wonders 'in your [Jesus'] name' (thrice: τῷ σῷ ὀνόματι).[85] And in the last three verses of Matthew's Gospel, it is the name of the triune God, together with the authority of Jesus, that is central.[86] John's Gospel stresses believing 'in his name' (εἰς τὸ ὄνομα αὐτοῦ),[87] life 'in his name' (ἐν τῷ ὀνόματι αὐτοῦ),[88] and Jesus' invitation to ask 'in my name' (ἐν τῷ ὀνόματί μου).[89] The Acts of the Apostles speaks of Jewish exorcists who wanted to profit by the power of the name of Jesus,[90] and of the Jewish Christian Ananias telling Saul to call 'on his name' (ἐπὶ . . . τὸ ὄνομα αὐτοῦ).[91] The Apocalypse as well evidences an interest in the concept of a name, referring to 'a new name' and 'the name of my God' given to believers.[92] Paul, of course, also refers to the name of Jesus: in appeal to the Corinthians 'by (διά) the name of our Lord Jesus Christ',[93] in alluding to his converts' baptism in Jesus' name,[94] in reference to their gathering together in judgment of sin within the church,[95] in exorcising an evil spirit,[96] and in teaching on prayer and diligence.[97] But his use is largely traditional, and relatively infrequent.

As a christological designation, 'the name' appears almost exclusively in materials that reflect the Jewish Christian mission and Jewish Christian interests. The three uses of Joel 2.32 (MT 3.5) in Acts 2.21; 4.12; and Rom. 10.13, where the calling on the 'name of the Lord' refers to God in the Old Testament and the exalted Jesus in the New, are all within a Jewish Christian context – even the latter, set as it is in Paul's treatment of the 'Jewish question' in Rom. 9–11.[98] The strange wording of Acts 3.16,

---

[85] Matt. 7.21–23; cf. Luke 6.46.

[86] Matt. 28.18–20. Cf. H. Kosmala, 'The Conclusion of Matthew', *Annual of the Swedish Theological Institute*, IV (1965), pp. 140f., though without accepting his exclusively christological treatment of the passage.

[87] John 1.12; 2.23; 3.18.

[88] John 20.31.

[89] John 14.13f.; 15.16; 16.23–26.

[90] Acts 19.13–17.

[91] Acts 22.16.

[92] Rev. 2.17; 3.12.

[93] I Cor. 1.10; cf. also II Thess. 1.12; 3.6.

[94] I Cor. 1.13; 6.11.

[95] I Cor. 5.3–5, though with which clause 'in the name of the Lord Jesus Christ' is to be associated is problematic.

[96] Acts 16.18.

[97] Col. 3.17; Eph. 5.20; cf. I Cor. 1.2.

[98] Perhaps T. W. Manson's suggestion of a wider destination for the

'his name, through faith in his name (ἐπὶ τῇ πίστει τοῦ ὀνόματος
αὐτοῦ . . . τὸ ὄνομα αὐτοῦ), has made this man strong' – which
has often been declared a mistranslation on the part of the
author of Acts[99] – is probably to be explained as an archaic rem-
nant of an early Jewish Christian christology. Likewise James'
reference to the rich who blaspheme 'the good name (τὸ καλὸν
ὄνομα) by which you are called', which plainly has reference to
blaspheming the name of Jesus.[100] And the opening lines in the
second half of the christological hymn reproduced by Paul in
Phil. 2 carry similar significance: 'Wherefore God also has highly
exalted him, and given him a name which is above every name; that
at the name of Jesus every knee should bow.'[101] In John's Gospel,
Jesus' prayers regarding declaring, manifesting, and glorifying
God's name have christological import as well, for the Evangelist's intention is clearly to demonstrate that in the person and
redemptive ministry of Jesus exactly this was accomplished.[102]
And this archaic understanding of the significance of 'the name'
is probably the basis for Jesus' statement in John 8.58 that 'before
Abraham was, *I am*' (ἐγὼ εἰμί); as well as for the 'I am' analogies
of the Fourth Gospel – whether we take these as themselves
dominical or as later expressions of an earlier consciousness.[103]

Just as 'the name' was a pious Jewish surrogate for God, so for
the early Jewish Christians it became a designation for Jesus, the
Lord's Christ. And as in its earlier usage, so with the Christians it

---

Letter to the Romans may be invoked here as well; cf. 'St. Paul's Letter to the
Romans – and Others', *Studies in the Gospels and Epistles* (1962), pp. 225–41.

[99] E.g., C. C. Torrey, *The Composition and Date of Acts* (1916), pp. 14–16;
F. J. Foakes Jackson, *Beginnings*, II, p. 42.

[100] James 2.7.

[101] Phil. 2.9–10a.

[102] John 12.28; 17.6, 26.

[103] John 6.35; 8.12; 10.7, 9, 11, 14; 11.25; 14.6; 15.1; cf. also 8.23f., 28;
13.19. For a denial of dominical status set in a context of a high view of
Johannine historicity generally, see A. J. B. Higgins, *The Historicity of the
Fourth Gospel* (1960), pp. 73f. In defence of the absolute 'I am' on the lips of
Jesus and its correlation with the divine name, see H. Zimmermann, 'Das
absolute "Ich bin" in der Redeweise Jesu', *Trierer Theologische Zeitschrift*,
LXIX (1960), pp. 1–20; *idem*, 'Das absolute *ego eimi* als die neutestamentliche
Offenbarungsformel', *Biblische Zeitschrift*, IV (1960), pp. 54–69, 266–76. In
explication of the expression 'I am' as a divine self-affirmation of Jesus – in
fact, 'Jesus's boldest declaration about himself' – see E. Stauffer, *Jesus and His
Story* (ET 1960), pp. 149–59.

connoted the divine presence and power.[104] It had a definite history; and while used more widely and combined with other emphases as the Christian message spread, it was originally employed meaningfully in a Jewish Christian context.[105] When divorced from its Jewish moorings, it seems to have either suffered subordinationistic interpretations or been considered equivalent to the Greek οὐσία.

THE RIGHTEOUS ONE

In the Similitudes of Enoch, the expression 'the Righteous One' (ὁ δίκαιος) appears as a messianic title. I Enoch 38.2 reads:

And when the Righteous One shall appear before the eyes of the elect righteous whose works are wrought in dependence on the Lord of Spirits, and light will appear to the righteous and the elect who dwell on the earth – where then will be the dwelling of the sinners, and where the resting place of those who have denied the Lord of Spirits?

And I Enoch 53.6 states:

And after this the Righteous and Elect One will cause the house of his congregation to appear: henceforth they will no more be hindered, in the name of the Lord of Spirits.[106]

The alteration of the first person singular suffix to the third person singular suffix in the Qumran text of Isa. 51.5 suggests that possibly the Qumran sectarians understood the expression 'my righteousness' in the passage more as a messianic title than merely a divine attribute.[107] Neither the Similitudes of Enoch nor the text of Isa. 51.5 at Qumran, however, offer a firm basis for asserting that 'the Righteous One' was definitely a pre-Christian messianic title in the Jewish world; the first because of doubts as to its provenance, and the second because of its failure to be fully explicit.

Whatever be thought of its pre-Christian titular appearance, the eventual employment of 'the Righteous One' as a messianic appellation was undoubtedly based in large measure on the common messianic predicates of 'righteous' and 'righteousness' in

---

[104] E.g., Acts 3.16; 4.7, 10; 16.18; 19.13–17.
[105] Contra R. Bultmann, *Theology of the New Testament* (ET 1952), I, p. 40.
[106] Perhaps also 'the blood of the righteous' (ὁ δίκαιος) of I Enoch 47.1–4, in distinction to 'the prayer of the righteous' (οἱ δίκαιοι) in the same passage.
[107] 1QIsᵃ 51.5. See below, p. 100, for text and bibliography.

late Judaism. The rabbis spoke of the righteous Messiah on the basis of 'the righteous branch' of Jer. 23.5f.; 33.15, and the description in Zech. 9.9,[108] and the Psalms of Solomon laid great emphasis upon the anointed Son of David as being a righteous king who would establish righteousness and direct men in the works of righteousness.[109]

This background of usage is pertinent for the New Testament in that the canonical Jewish Christian materials employ δίκαιος not only as an attribute of Jesus[110] but also in substantival adjective form as a christological title.[111] In Acts, Jesus is called 'the Righteous One' (ὁ δίκαιος) by (1) Peter before the Sanhedrin;[112] (2) Stephen before the Council;[113] and (3) Paul in addressing the Jerusalem crowd from the steps of the Antonian fortress.[114] James speaks of the rich who 'condemned' and 'killed the Righteous One' of whom it is further said that 'he did not resist you'.[115] And probably δίκαιος should be understood as a quasi-title, at least, in I Peter 3.18 ('Christ suffered once for sins, the righteous for the unrighteous'), and in I John 2.1 ('We have an advocate with the Father, Jesus Christ the righteous'). Some have suggested on the basis of a comparison between Acts 22.13f. (ὁ δίκαιος) and Acts 9.17 (ὁ κύριος) that 'the Righteous One' is an older title for Jesus than 'the Lord',[116] which may very well be the case. At least there is no evidence that it should be directly tied in with the ascription 'Lord', nor any clear evidence that it was used as a messianic title in pre-Christian Judaism. While later associated with concepts of messiahship, it seems to have had its own history in Jewish thought. As such, it was most appropriate in the Christian mission to Jews; and, to judge by the New Testament distribution of the title, was distinctive to early Jewish Christianity.

---

[108] Cf. G. Schrenk, 'δίκαιος', *TWNT*, II, p. 188 (ET, pp. 186f.), for talmudic passages to this effect.

[109] Pss. Sol. 17.23–51; 18.8f. Perhaps also Wisd. Sol. 2.18: 'For if the righteous man is God's son, he will uphold him; and he will deliver him out of the hand of his adversaries.'

[110] E.g., I John 1.9; 2.29; 3.7; Rev. 16.5.

[111] Cf. J. Jeremias, *The Servant of God* (ET 1957), p. 91.

[112] Acts 3.14.

[113] Acts 7.52.

[114] Acts 22.14.

[115] James 5.6.

[116] See, e.g., F. J. Foakes Jackson and K. Lake, *Beginnings*, I, p. 4.

THE SHEPHERD AND THE LAMB

In the Old Testament, the relation between both (1) God and his people, and (2) a human leader and his subjects, is repeatedly portrayed in terms of a shepherd and his flock. The imagery of Ps. 23.1–6 and the title 'Shepherd of Israel' in Ps. 80.1 immediately come to mind with reference to God; while with reference to God's appointed agents, Ps. 77.20, for example, reads: 'Thou didst lead thy people like a flock by the hand of Moses and Aaron'; and Isa. 63.11, recalling the same exodus experience, asks: 'Where is he who brought up out of the sea the shepherds (or, shepherd) of his flock?' Whether the Isaiah passage should read 'shepherds' (MT) or 'shepherd' (LXX), both psalmists and prophets spoke of God, to whom the flock belongs, and his vicegerents, to whom was entrusted the care of the flock, as shepherds over their sheep; the one the supreme Shepherd and the others undershepherds. And such representations of leadership, whether human or divine, seem to have been common in the ancient world,[117] and were continued in the intertestamental period among the Jews.[118]

Of greater significance for our purpose here, however, are the Old Testament passages which describe the promised Messiah in terms of a shepherd over God's people. Micah 5.4, with reference to the 'ruler in Israel' who shall come from Bethlehem Ephrathah, says: 'He shall stand and feed his flock in the strength of Yahweh, in the majesty of the name of Yahweh his God.' Ezekiel 34.23 presents God as promising: 'I will set up over them one shepherd, my servant David, and he shall feed them; he shall feed them and be their shepherd.' And Zech. 13.7, at the close of an extended homily on the various shepherds of Israel's history, speaks of God's final shepherd over his people as follows:

Awake, O sword, against my shepherd, against the man who stands next to me, says Yahweh of hosts.
Strike the shepherd, that the sheep may be scattered; and I will turn my hand against the little ones.[119]

That the shepherd of Zech. 13.7 was understood by the Qumran

---

[117] Ipuwer, an Egyptian sage of *c.* 2000 BC, described the ideal king as 'the herdsman of all men' (trans. J. A. Wilson, *Ancient Near Eastern Texts Relating to the Old Testament*, ed. J. B. Pritchard [1955], pp. 441f.), and Homer spoke of Agamemnon as 'the shepherd of the peoples' (ποιμένα λαῶν) (Iliad II. 243).

[118] E.g., I Enoch 89f., CDC 13.9 (16.3).

[119] Cf. Isa. 40.11; Ezek. 37.24; Jer. 23.1–6.

covenanters to be an eschatological figure, whether the Messiah himself or not, is directly stated in manuscript B of the Zadokite fragments:

But all the despisers of the commandments and of the ordinances shall be visited with extinction when God visits the earth to cause the recompense of the wicked to return upon them, when the word comes to pass which is written by the prophet Zechariah: 'Awake, O sword, against my shepherd, against the man who stands next to me, says God; strike the shepherd, that the sheep may be scattered; I will turn my hand against the little ones.' And they that give heed unto Him are 'the poor of the flock'.[120]

And in Pss. Sol. 17.45, the coming Messiah is explicitly pictured as 'shepherding the flock of the Lord faithfully and righteously'. The use of the title in regard to Jesus seems to have stemmed from Jesus himself, for it appears as a self-designation in all the Gospel strata. Matthew and Mark report that Jesus applied the words of Zech. 13.7, 'I will strike the shepherd, and the sheep will be scattered', directly to himself and his approaching passion.[121] Luke, in his special Perean material, presents Jesus as alluding to the language and sentiment of Zech. 13.7–9 in saying: 'Fear not, little flock (τὸ μικρὸν ποίμνιον), for it is your Father's good pleasure to give you the kingdom.'[122] And John, of course, incorporates into his portrayal the parable of the Good Shepherd and his sheep.[123] In the light of such a background within Judaism and the precedent set by Jesus himself, Jewish Christians continued to speak of Jesus as 'the Shepherd' (ὁ ποιμήν),[124] 'the Chief Shepherd' (ὁ ἀρχιποίμην),[125] and 'the Great Shepherd of the sheep' (ὁ ποιμὴν τῶν προβάτων ὁ μέγας).[126] And this was continued in certain circles of the second century AD, as most prominently seen in the Shepherd of Hermas – especially in the 'Commandments', where Hermas receives his teaching from the 'Angel of Penance' who appeared to him in the form of a shepherd.

The title 'the Lamb' as applied to Jesus appears in John 1.29, 36; Acts 8.32; and I Peter 1.19, in all four instances employing the

---

120 CDC 19.5–9 (9.2f.).
121 Matt. 26.31; Mark 14.27.
122 Luke 12.32.
123 John 10.1–18, 26–30.
124 I Peter 2.25.
125 I Peter 5.4.
126 Heb. 13.20.

term ὁ ἀμνός, and twenty-eight times in the Apocalypse, always by τὸ ἀρνίον. The difference in the terms employed is of some interest, and probably reflects the different sources from which the concept stems and the differing nuances meant to be suggested.

The LXX uses ἀμνός about a hundred times to mean lambs for sacrifice, and it is the word that appears in Isa. 53.7 to describe the Lord's afflicted and oppressed servant who bears 'the iniquity of us all'. The quotation of Isa. 53.7 in Acts 8.32 indicates that it is in this sense we should understand the application of the title to Jesus wherever ἀμνός is employed; that is, by John the Baptist and by Peter as well as in the identification by Philip. I Enoch 89f., however, uses ἀρήν (of which ἀρνίον is a variant, diminutive in form though probably not in the *koine* period in meaning) for the eschatological and victorious horned lambs of the Messianic Age. And it is in this sense that the title should probably be understood in the Apocalypse.[127] In so handling the title, the Jewish Christians seem to have been attempting, whether consciously or not, to signal both aspects of their Lord's ministry: the sacrificial suffering (ἀμνός) and the triumphant glory (ἀρνίον) – though of this suffering-and-glory motif I must speak more fully later.

There is a degree of fluidity and imprecision in the christological titles 'Shepherd' and 'Lamb'. Both have some associations with messiahship in pre-Christian Judaism, yet both also evidence a degree of independence and separate backgrounds. As christological titles, however, both seem to have been rather unique to the Jewish Christian sector of the early church and were employed within that cycle of interest to signify the authority, care, suffering, and future glory of their Lord.

THE REJECTED STONE – COPESTONE

The Christian conviction regarding the primacy and priority of Jesus in the redemptive activity of God comes to expression in the Jewish Christian materials of the New Testament in various ways and forms. At times, the language of Old Testament devotion is employed; at times, motifs drawn from Israel's wisdom literature are invoked; and at times, terms in common coin from the hellenistic world are used. While lines are not clearly drawn, there are features that should be noted as being fairly distinctive.

[127] Contra T. Holtz, *Die Christologie der Apokalypse des Johannes* (1962), pp. 39–47, who interprets ἀρνίον as 'das Passalamm'.

In the first place, there is the imagery of 'the stone' – especially the 'rejected stone – copestone' motif. All three Synoptic Gospels record that Jesus applied Ps. 118.22 to himself: 'The stone which the builders rejected has become the "head of the corner".'[128] And the New Testament evidences three christological variations on the stone theme, with three different Old Testament texts used in support: (1) the 'rejected stone which has become the head of the corner' (ὁ λίθος ὁ ἐξουθενηθείς . . ., ὁ γενόμενος εἰς κεφαλὴν γωνίας) based on Ps. 118.22; (2) the 'foundational cornerstone' (λίθος ἀκρογωνιαῖος) based on Isa. 28.16; and (3) the 'stone of stumbling and rock of offence' (λίθος προσκόμματος καὶ πέτρα σκανδάλου) based on Isa. 8.14. The first is confined to Jewish Christian materials: Acts 4.11 and I Peter 2.4, 7, both instances credited to Peter. The second is implicit in I Cor. 3.11, and comes to expression in Eph. 2.20 and I Peter 2.5f. The third is found in Rom. 9.33; Luke 20.18; and I Peter 2.8.

J. Jeremias has argued that both 'cornerstone' (λίθος ἀκρο- γωνιαῖος) and 'a stone at the head of the corner' (λίθος . . . κεφαλὴ γωνίας) should be understood as a 'copestone', or 'topstone' (*Abschlussstein*), and not as a 'foundation stone' (*Grundstein*).[129] And he has marshalled a number of texts in support; most significant of which is the first-century AD Jewish Testament of Solomon 22.7–23.4, where both λίθος ἀκρογωνιαῖος and λίθος . . . κεφαλὴ γωνίας unambiguously refer to the final copestone at the summit of the Jerusalem temple and Ps. 118.22 is explicitly quoted.[130] New Testament scholarship largely follows Jeremias here, with many interpreters even going beyond him in under- standing the reference to be to a keystone of an archway which serves as a locking stone for the whole structure.[131] It need be noted, however, that the 'stone' imagery and Isa. 28.16 are also

---

[128] Matt. 21.42; Mark 12.10f.; Luke 20.17f.

[129] J. Jeremias, 'Κεφαλὴ γωνίας – Ἀκρογωνιαῖος', *ZNW*, X XIX (1930), pp. 264–80; *idem*, 'Eckstein – Schlussstein', *ZNW*, XXXVI (1937), pp. 154–7; *idem*, 'γωνία, ἀκρογωνιαῖος, κεφαλὴ γωνίας', *TWNT*, I, pp. 792f. (ET, pp. 791–3); *idem*, 'λίθος', *TWNT*, IV, pp. 275–83 (ET, pp. 271–80).

[130] Cf. Symmachus' translation of II Kings 25.17 (ἀκρογωνιαῖος), and the Peshitta rendering of Isa. 28.16 as 'head of the wall'.

[131] See bibliography in R. J. McKelvey, 'Christ the Cornerstone', *NTS*, VIII (1962), pp. 352f., which is reprinted in Appendix C of *The New Temple: The Church in the New Testament* (1969), pp. 196f. Note the translation of 'keystone' in the Jerusalem Bible at Acts 4.11 and I Peter 2.7, and in the NEB in the text of Acts 4.11 and the footnote to Eph. 2.20.

used in Jewish literature with reference to a foundation stone
(אבן שתיה) upon which a building is erected, as is clear in Manual
of Discipline 8.4 and Babylonian Yoma 54a.[132] It therefore seems
that while Jeremias has demonstrated a very important point,
especially in regard to the understanding of the figure in Ps.
118.22 during the first century, his conclusion cannot be rigidly
applied in every instance where λίθος appears as a christological
ascription in the New Testament, particularly when based upon
Isa. 28.16. Variations existed within contemporary Judaism on
the stone theme, and a precise understanding of its use in various
New Testament passages must depend upon the individual
contexts.

In Jesus' usage of Ps. 118.22 and in its employment in Acts
4.11 and I Peter 2.4, 7, it is probable that the idea of the rejected
stone which has become the copestone or topstone of the building
– consummating all previous building activity and standing
supreme over the whole structure – is in mind. And very likely
this 'rejected stone – copestone' motif, finding its basis in the
teaching of Jesus and having pertinence to the fulfilment message
of the earliest Christians, was the original theme in the Jerusalem
church, to which were added the 'foundational' and 'stumbling'
motifs. The inclusion of all three in I Peter 2.4–8 probably indicates a later development; possibly under Pauline influence, which
may be partially explained by the acknowledgment in I Peter 5.12
of Silas' hand in the composition, though just as possibly due to
variations on the theme current in Jewish Christian circles. But
even here it should be noted that the 'rejected stone – copestone
(head of the corner)' motif is dominant in the passage, as witness
both the order of listing and the relative frequency of occurrence.
Paul's development in I Cor. 10.4 of the rabbinic legend of the
accompanying rock in the wilderness, which he calls a 'spiritual
rock' and identifies with Christ, may have been inspired to some
extent by an early Christian 'stone' theme; though it evidences no

---

[132] See R. J. McKelvey, 'The Foundation-Stone in Zion', Appendix A of
The New Temple, pp. 188–94. Note also *idem*, 'Christ the Cornerstone', *NTS*,
VIII (1962), pp. 352–9 (also Appendix C of *The New Temple*, pp. 195–204)
as a corrective of Jeremias. In fairness, however, Jeremias' one paragraph
qualification on Isa. 28.16 should be noted (*TWNT*, IV, p. 279, ET, p. 275),
though it is much too reserved. On the foundational rock motif in Jewish
thought, cf. also 1QH 6.25–27; 7.8–9; 1QS 5.6; 9.5f.; j. Sanh. 29a; Exod. R.
15.7; Lev. R. 20.4.

necessary connection. But however this may be, his allusion points to a contemporary Jewish tendency to conceptualize the divine presence in terms of a rock or stone.[133]

In the second century Christ is spoken of as a 'stone', 'rock', and 'cornerstone' by Justin, the Shepherd of Hermas, and the Epistle of Barnabas.[134] Here are witnesses to 'stone' as an early christological ascription; though it is also evident that by the time of these second-century Fathers the earlier variations in that designation had either vanished or become amalgamated. Logion 66 of the Gospel of Thomas reads: 'Jesus said: Show me the stone which the builders have rejected; it is the cornerstone.' Though set in a gnostic framework and perhaps not meant to be a christological affirmation in that context, this saying seems more than any other to have carried into the second century elements of the original Jewish Christian identification of Jesus as the 're-jected stone who has become the copestone' – thus preserving to some extent the dual emphases of (1) rejection, and (2) primacy, as found in the earliest christological stone ascriptions.

Ἀρχή, Πρωτότοκος, AND COGNATES

In writings of the patristic period, Christ is also often designated by such terms as ἀρχή and πρωτότοκος, and their cognates. For example, to cite some significant second-century instances, Theophilus of Antioch appealed to the LXX of Gen. 1.1 (ἐν ἀρχῇ ἐποίησεν ὁ θεός) in support of ἀρχή as a christological ascription;[135] and this was the usual proof-text, though Justin had earlier also used Prov. 8.22, 'the Lord created me in the beginning (ἀρχή) of his way'.[136] Clement of Alexandria calls Christ the ἀρχή and πρωτότοκος, crediting the early second-century Preaching of Peter as his source and attributing to Peter's 'accurate understanding' of Gen. 1.1 the origin of these ascriptions.[137] Similarly, Jerome speaks of 'the Gospel written in the Hebrew speech which the Nazarenes read' as calling Christ the Spirit's 'firstborn Son that reignest forever'.[138] Not only Theophilus of Antioch's geographical

---

[133] On the rabbinic legend, see E. E. Ellis, *Paul's Use of the Old Testament* (1957), pp. 66–70.

[134] Dial. 126.1–2; Sim. IX, esp. 12.1ff.; Barn. 6.2ff.

[135] Ad Autolycus II. 10.

[136] Dial. 61.1; 62.4.

[137] Strom. VI. 7. 58.

[138] Comm. on Isa. IV (on Isa. 11.2); cf. *NTApoc.*, I, pp. 163f.

proximity to Jewish Christian centres, and Justin's evident acquaintance with Jewish Christian motifs, but also the direct assertions of Clement of Alexandria and Jerome as to their source lend credence to the idea that the connection of ἀρχή, πρωτότοκος, and their cognates with Christ took place first in Jewish Christian circles, and then spread more widely.

There are a number of expressions of this type denoting primacy and priority which are applied to Jesus in the New Testament. I refer especially to ἀρχή (beginning), ἀρχηγός (chief one, leader, prince, founder, originator, pioneer), πρωτότοκος (firstborn), μονογενής (only, favoured, chosen, unique), κεφαλή (head), μορφή (form), and εἰκών (image, likeness, form). And, interestingly, the majority occur in material which is either Jewish Christian in nature or polemical against certain Jewish Christian errors; the only exceptions being the use of πρωτότοκος in Rom. 8.29, εἰκών in II Cor. 4.4, and κεφαλή in Ephesians.[139] Omitting consideration of the much discussed Col. 1.15–20 for the moment, Peter is recorded as speaking of the exalted Jesus as 'the ἀρχηγός of life' in Acts 3.15, 'ἀρχηγός and saviour' at God's right hand in Acts 5.31, and 'κεφαλή of the corner' in Acts 4.11 and I Peter 2.7. In the hymn of Phil. 2.6–11, Jesus is spoken of as 'in μορφή of God' and exalted. He is the πρωτότοκος worthy of angelic worship in Heb. 1.6, the ἀρχηγός of the believer's salvation in Heb. 2.10, and the ἀρχηγός of faith in Heb. 12.2.[140] He is the μονογενής Son of God the Father in John 1.14; 3.16, 18; and I John 4.9 – perhaps even the μονογενής θεός in John 1.18. He is 'the ἀρχή and the end' in Rev. 21.6; 22.13 (also Sinaiticus Rev. 1.8) and 'the ἀρχή of the creation of God' in Rev. 3.14. Perhaps also 'the Alpha and

---

[139] Even these might not prove too significant in rebuttal to our thesis, especially if the body of the Letter to the Romans be viewed in light of a wider destination than just Rome, the problems of II Corinthians recalled for Paul an earlier judaizing conflict, and Ephesians can be associated temporally and logically with Colossians.

[140] The similarity of terms in Hebrews and Luke-Acts (particularly the first half of Acts) has often been noted, and is frequently employed as an argument for identity of authorship and post-Pauline Gentile provenance (e.g., C. P. M. Jones, 'The Epistle to the Hebrews and the Lucan Writings', *Studies in the Gospels*, ed. D. E. Nineham [Oxford: Blackwell, 1957], pp. 113–43. What is not sufficiently appreciated in contemporary evaluations, however, is that this phenomenon of similarity in language (as the use of ἀρχηγός here noted) may also be due to a common set of terms being used in early Jewish Christianity which is reported in the first half of the Acts of the Apostles and reflected in the Letter to the Hebrews.

Omega' of Rev. 1.8; 21.6 and 22.13 should be joined to these expressions.[141] And the description in Heb. 1.3 of the Son as 'the effulgence (ἀπαύγασμα) of the glory [of God] and the very stamp of his nature (χαρακτὴρ τῆς ὑποστάσεως αὐτοῦ)' is only a paraphrase of the concept of 'image' (εἰκών).

It is commonly asserted that since these terms originated in a hellenistic milieu, their presence in the New Testament indicates the hellenistic Christian character of those portions in which they are found.[142] But to this it must be said: (1) that these are terms which, though first coined in the cosmological speculations of Greek philosophy, were in common circulation in the first centuries BC and AD;[143] (2) that the presence of these terms in the LXX and the popular literature of pre-Christian Judaism would have afforded their wide dissemination in Palestine (as well, of course, as in the Diaspora), should they have needed such aid in propagation;[144] and (3) that their transference to the status of christological ascriptions in the early church was motivated chiefly by religious rather than cosmological interests.

Where these terms do seem to evidence gnostic or proto-gnostic influence, however, is in Col. 1.15–20; though that influence should probably be described differently than is usually the case.[145] Assuming (1) a Jewish sectarian basis for the heresy at

---

[141] W. H. Brownlee has suggested that the *Aleph* of 1QS 10.1 should be understood as an abbreviation for Elohim, forming an acrostic with the *Mem* and the *Nun* of the following lines (*The Dead Sea Manual of Discipline*, *BASOR* Supplementary Studies Nos. 10–12 [1951], pp. 50f.; *idem*, 'Messianic Motifs', *NTS*, III [1957], pp. 201–3). Cf. also T. H. Gaster's translation at this point (*Dead Sea Scriptures*, p. 126). If this be true, the use of *Alpha* for Christ in the Apocalypse has a Palestinian foundation as well as hellenistic parallels. The major problem in reading 1QS 10.1 in this manner is that the *Aleph* has no space before it, thus possibly connecting it to the preceding word as a third person singular suffix.

[142] E.g., R. Bultmann, *Theology of the New Testament*, I, pp. 132f., 177f.

[143] They are common to Philo in his descriptions of the Word; cf. De Conf. Ling. 146. Similarly, I Enoch 15.9 speaks of evil spirits born of men and the Holy Watchers as 'the beginning of creation and primal origin' (ἡ ἀρχὴ τῆς κτίσεως [cf. Rev. 3.14] καὶ ἀρχὴ θεμελίου) – a tautology, employing ἀρχή twice. Wisd. Sol. 7.22–26 attributes to wisdom the terms 'unique', (μονογενής), 'effulgence' (ἀπαύγασμα), and 'image' (εἰκών). Cf. also I Enoch 106.10 on the use of εἰκών in connection with an awesome apocalyptic figure.

[144] Note, e.g., Ex. 4.22; Jer. 38.9 (MT 31.9); I Enoch 15.9; 106.10; Wisd. Sol. 7.22–26.

[145] On the treatment of Col. 1.15–20 by German scholars, who (in company with many others today) usually view the passage as a pre-Pauline hymn of the hellenistic Christian community and understand its christology as

Colosse, as comparison with the Qumran material reveals, (2) incipient gnostic elements to have been incorporated into the heresy during its syncretistic development, and (3) Paul's use of some of the heretics' own terminology in dealing with their thought (perhaps even to the recasting of a hymnodic portion employed by them), it is plausible to view the basic problem in the Colossian church as that of the harmonization of a primarily religious conviction with an interest that is dominantly cosmological. It was the problem of reconciling the Christian conviction of the primacy and priority of Jesus – which hitherto had been considered mainly in religious and historical terms, but without any real thought given to questions of cosmology – with a Grecian understanding of gradations and relative orders of primacy in the universe.[146] Inherent in the problem was the conflict of differing *Weltanschauungen*: the one religious and historical, the other philosophic and cosmological. And it was a conflict that probably became exceedingly confused, for undoubtedly many of the same terms were used in the expression of these differing orientations. It was this commonness of terminology, in fact, which probably facilitated the submerging of the religiously based conviction of the primacy of Jesus into the maze of cosmological stratification in hellenistic thought, and made the heresy so difficult to treat at Colosse.

Paul's response to this challenge was the insistence that if one is to think philosophically as well as religiously, then indeed the primacy and priority of Jesus must be asserted in the cosmological sphere as well. No speculation, whatever its merits (and Paul seems to have had little inclination to enter into a discussion of relative merits on a philosophic basis), must be allowed to detract from the absolute supremacy of Jesus Christ. While the primacy of Jesus had hitherto been asserted in contexts primarily religious and historical, it had legitimate import for cosmology as well. Thus, in this context of thought, Paul insisted that Jesus is 'the

---

expressive of the hellenistic church, see H. Hegermann, *Die Vorstellung vom Schöpfungsmittler im hellenistischen Judentum und Urchristentum* (1961), pp. 88–137.

[146] For gnostic discussions of such related themes as divine plurality, angelology, and εἰκὼν τοῦ θεοῦ, pointing out that these 'appear to derive their origin from Jewish speculation', see R. McL. Wilson, 'The Early History of the Exegesis of Gen. 1:26', *Studia Patristica*, I, ed. F. L. Cross (1957), pp. 427–37.

εἰκών of the invisible God', 'the πρωτότοκος of all creation' and 'from the dead', 'the κεφαλή of the body', and 'the ἀρχή'. Furthermore, in him 'are hid all the treasures of wisdom (σοφία) and knowledge (γνῶσις)', in him 'dwells the whole fulness (πᾶν τὸ πλήρωμα) of deity bodily', and he is 'the head (κεφαλή) of all rule and authority (πάσης ἀρχῆς καὶ ἐξουσίας)', as the apostle goes on to say in Col. 2.1–10 in answer to the specifically gnostic features of the heresy.[147]

In the Letter to the Colossians, Paul is not originating new christological designations. These, in the main, had been used of Jesus by Jewish Christians before him. What he is doing is extending their reference to the field of cosmological speculation. In response to tendencies that would qualify the supremacy of Jesus by the imposition of a system of emanated and graduated primacies, Paul asserts the absolute primacy and priority of his Lord over all that may be envisaged. That his argument is circumstantially evoked is evidenced by the Letter to the Ephesians, where, assuming Pauline authorship, the apostle continues to use κεφαλή of Jesus but has turned from cosmology to ecclesiology in accordance with his addressees' concerns.

That this extension from categories of religious and historical primacy to that of cosmic supremacy was considered legitimate within the cycle of Jewish Christianity is seen in the somewhat similar treatment of the opening sentences of Hebrews and the Prologue to the Fourth Gospel. In Heb. 1.2f., the fact that the Son is 'heir of all things' gives rise to the accompanying claim that he was *also* (note the extension of thought implied in the καί) involved in the creation of all that exists (τοὺς αἰῶνας), and since he is 'the effulgence of the glory [of God] and the very stamp of his nature' it follows that he is involved in the sustaining of the universe 'by the word of his power'. The Prologue of John's Gospel, which is conceptually subsequent to the body of the Gospel and may very well have been added later, speaks of Jesus

---

[147] C. F. Burney has argued that in Col. 1.16–18 Paul is giving an elaborate midrashic exposition of the first word of Genesis, *bereshith*, and interpreting the *reshith* of Gen. 1.1 and Prov. 8.22 as referring to Christ ('Christ as the *APXH* of Creation', *JTS*, XXVII [1926], pp. 160–77; cf. also W. D. Davies, *Paul and Rabbinic Judaism* [1955], pp. 150–2). What is said above is not meant to oppose Burney's highly significant thesis, but only to point out in addition that Paul's argument, while possibly following a rabbinic pattern exegetically, was circumstantially evoked.

as a pre-existent cosmic figure and connects him with the wisdom motif of the Logos.[148] It is significant that in both these cases the addressees have a similar background and seem to be influenced by similar ideas as expressed in the heresy at Colosse; and in both there is a similar extension of the ascriptions of primacy and priority as in Paul's Colossian response. But it should also be noted that all of these extensions into the cosmological sphere presuppose earlier christological attributions of religious primacy and historical priority. And while they were originally coined in the context of hellenistic philosophy, there is good reason to believe that such terms as ἀρχή, ἀρχηγός, πρωτότοκος, μονογενής, κεφαλή, μορφή, and εἰκών were early used of Jesus by Jewish Christians as well.

THE Κατάβασις–ἀνάβασις THEME

A further feature of early Jewish Christianity appears to have been the description of Jesus and the redemption accomplished by him in terms of the κατάβασις (descent)–ἀνάβασις (ascent) motif. The hymn of Phil. 2.6–11, which because of its structure, style, and non-Pauline expressions has been viewed during the past half-century to reflect the convictions and piety of early Palestinian Christians,[149] begins with Christ as 'in the form of God', goes on to develop details of his humiliation ('form of a servant', 'likeness of

---

[148] As has been often pointed out, the ascription λόγος in the Prologue differs from the rest of the Gospel. Probably, as V. Taylor suggests, 'if we infer that the Prologue was written last, as a summary of St John's apprehension of the significance of the incarnation of the Son of God, we account better for the traditional element combined with interpretation present in the Gospel. The same inference is warranted if, as some have thought, he took over and adapted in i. 1–18 a pre-Johannine hymn' (*Person of Christ in New Testament Teaching*, p. 21). This connection of ἀρχή and its cognates with λόγος and its cognates is continued in such passages as Justin, Dial. 61.1, and Clement of Alexandria, Strom. VI. 7. 58.

[149] Cf., e.g., E. Lohmeyer, *Der Briefe an die Philipper* (1930), pp. 90–9; A. M. Hunter, *Paul and his Predecessors* (1961), pp. 39–44; R. P. Martin, *An Early Christian Confession: Philippians II. 5–11 in Recent Interpretation* (1960); *idem, Carmen Christi* (1968). On the criteria for establishing early hymnodic and catechetical formulae in the New Testament letters, see particularly E. Norden, *Agnostos Theos* (1912), pp. 380–7; E. Stauffer, *New Testament Theology* (ET 1955), pp. 338f.; R. P. Martin, *Worship in the Early Church* (1964), pp. 48–51; R. H. Fuller, *Foundations of New Testament Christology*, p. 21. Since the work of Lohmeyer, the semitic cast of at least the first half of the hymn has been generally recognized; though beyond this, there is little to locate it more exactly. It will not do, however, as many Bultmannians attempt, to appeal to the theology of the hymn in determination of its provenance, for that is begging the question and entirely dependent upon *a priori* assumptions. On

men', 'obedient unto death', 'the death of a cross'[150]), and concludes with an acclamation of his exaltation. Underlying the whole hymn, of course, is a κατάβασις–ἀνάβασις understanding of the person and work of Christ. In the Fourth Gospel, κατάβασις–ἀνάβασις christology comes to definite expression in two 'son-of-man' sayings of Jesus: (1) 'No one has ascended (οὐδεὶς ἀναβέβηκεν) into heaven except he who descended (ὁ καταβάς) from heaven, the Son of Man', of John 3.13, and (2) 'What if you were to see the Son of Man ascending (ἀναβαίνοντα) where he was before?' of John 6.62. The first half of the motif underlies the Prologue of John's Gospel, speaking as it does of pre-existence, divinity, and incarnation. And the second half is basic to the portrayal of the exalted Jesus throughout the book of the Revelation. The letter to the Hebrews indicates familiarity with this conceptual pattern in its presentation of the lowering, obedience, and temptations of the Son in chapters two and five, and in its doctrine of the heavenly high priesthood of Jesus in 4.14–10.8. And it is basic as well in the argument of I Peter 3.18–22, though the difficulties involved in interpreting 3.19f. and 4.6 defy delineation here as to precisely how the aspect of descent was conceptualized.[151]

---

the basis of its semitic cast, it seems reasonable to conclude that the hymn took form originally in Palestine – whether composed first in Aramaic or in Greek by Jews whose thought patterns were semitic; though the fact that it treats *Christos* as a proper name and was quoted to the Philippians seems to indicate that it circulated more widely in Grecian dress as well (cf. J. Jeremias, 'Zur Gedankenführung in den paulinischen Briefen: Der Christushymnus, Phil. 2.6–11', *Studia Paulina*, ed. G. Sevenster and W. C. van Unnik [1953], p. 154; O. Cullmann, *The Earliest Christian Confessions*, p. 22; *idem, Christology of the New Testament*, pp. 174–81).

[150] Though probably θανάτου δὲ σταυροῦ of v. 8b is a Pauline interjection into the hymn, since it fails to fit into most strophe reconstructions and is typically Pauline.

[151] On Pauline, Augustinian, Catholic, Reformation, and modern Protestant interpretations, with a detailed treatment of considerable merit in advocacy of the view that I Peter 3.18–20 teaches Christ's proclamation of triumph to spirits in the transcendental sphere, see Bo Reicke, *The Disobedient Spirits and Christian Baptism* (1945). For treatments coming to similar conclusions, see E. G. Selwyn, *The First Epistle of St. Peter* (1946), pp. 314–62; J. Jeremias, 'Zwischen Karfreitag und Ostern', *ZNW*, XLII (1949), pp. 194–201; J. Daniélou, *Theology of Jewish Christianity*, pp. 233–5; A. M. Stibbs, *The First Epistle General of Peter* (1959), pp. 138–52. I must confess, however, that Christ's proclamation to departed and imprisoned *human* spirits seems to me most exegetically founded (basically Augustinian); though without espousing Augustine's dualistic view that the prison is human flesh and without asserting the fulness of a *descensus ad inferos* doctrine.

In the letters of Paul, Eph. 4.8–10 probably incorporates a traditional understanding among Christians, for both the citation of Ps. 68.18 and the parenthetical comment which follows it are given in such a manner as though commonly assumed.[152] Evidently, to judge by the apostle's manner in these verses and the broader context, a statement of the obvious is made in order to bridge the gap in the argument from the 'gift of Christ' in v. 7 to a discussion of Christ's 'gifts' in vv. 11ff. And thus, probably, the references to Christ's descent (κατέβη, ὁ καταβάς) and ascent (ἀνέβη, ὁ ἀναβάς) reflect an earlier Christian tradition rather than being original with Paul. In Rom. 10.5f., the apostle evidences acquaintance with a κατάβασις–ἀνάβασις christological ascription in his quotation, with comments, of Deut. 31.12f.: 'Do not say in your heart, "Who will ascend (τίς ἀναβήσεται) into heaven?" – that is, to bring Christ down – or "Who will descend (τίς καταβήσεται) into the abyss?" – that is, to bring Christ up from the dead.' But, interestingly, he directly leaves it – even disparages it – in favour of an emphasis upon the presence of 'the word of faith', as based upon Deut. 30.14. Evidently, he feared that a κατάβασις–ἀνάβασις understanding of Christ could lead in this particular circumstance to a concept of remoteness; and he wanted to forestall any such false inference. In so doing, however, he indicates the pre-Pauline nature of the theme in question. The traditional nature of κατάβασις–ἀνάβασις christology is also indicated in the confession of I Tim. 3.16.[153]

It is commonly asserted of late that κατάβασις–ἀνάβασις christology arose under the influence of gnostic mythology in a hellenistic ideological milieu, and was 'completely foreign' to

---

[152] Possibly the text-form of Ps. 68.18, as well, was traditional within pre-Pauline circles.

[153] Other portions in the Pauline corpus where this theme is sometimes found cannot with sufficient certainty be so credited. I Cor. 15.3–5 may fit in and reflect an earlier consciousness, but its limited correspondence is probably incidental. I Cor. 2.8 and Col. 2.15 can be credited only by first classing κατάβασις–ἀνάβασις as a distinctly gnostic theme, and then identifying any terminology that remotely savours of gnosticism as based on a κατάβασις–ἀνάβασις concept. I have already indicated a circumstantial rationale for the gnostic features of Colossians, and would deny that 'ignorance' (as in I Cor. 2.8) is an exclusively gnostic note. The polarity of 'richness' and 'poverty' in II Cor. 8.9 may reflect an earlier 'descent' and 'ascent' conceptualization. But if so, it also indicates a reworking of the theme in the Pauline message. The work of E. Best on the Marcan soteriology tends to negate any discovery of a κατάβασις–ἀνάβασις theme in Mark (*The Temptation and the Passion* [1965]).

early Palestinian Christianity.[154] But while a case can be made for such a view, it should also be noted:

1. That chs. 12–16 of I Enoch offer a plausible prototype for certain elements of this biblical motif. And this is true, whether the descent in particular New Testament passages is understood as a *descensus ad inferos*, a penetration into the transcendental sphere of spirits, the Incarnation, or Pentecost – though, admittedly, easier for the former two positions than those of the latter. In I Enoch 12–16, Enoch is sent to the Watchers (fallen angels of Gen. 6) to proclaim to them their judgment. Terror-stricken, they implore him to draw up a petition on their behalf asking for forgiveness. Enoch is then lifted up to heaven and appears in the fiery courts of God, where he is given the terrible words to convey to his petitioners: 'You will have no peace.' The theology differs considerably, but the apocalyptic imagery – at least in the local aspect – bears a resemblance to features in certain passages where this theme appears in the New Testament. And this portion of I Enoch was sufficiently well known in Palestine to warrant our keeping chs. 12–16 in mind when dealing with the motif in the New Testament.

2. That the κατάβασις–ἀνάβασις theme – both in its earlier form of the descent of Christ from heaven to earth and in its developed form of descent from earth to hades – was prominent in Jewish Christianity of the second and third centuries. Jean Daniélou has collected the passages of pertinence here, and adequately demonstrated this point.[155] Representative is the Gospel of Peter 10.41f., where, after a description of two heavenly creatures coming out of the tomb sustaining a third whose head reached to heaven (the resurrected Jesus), 'a cross following them', it is said: 'And they heard a voice out of heaven saying, "Hast thou preached to them that sleep?" And from the cross there was heard the answer, "Yes." '[156]

---

[154] E.g., R. Bultmann, *Theology of the New Testament*, I, pp. 175–7; F. Hahn, *Christologische Hoheitstitel* (1963), pp. 126–32; R. H. Fuller, *Foundations of New Testament Christology*, pp. 234–57.

[155] J. Daniélou, *Theology of Jewish Christianity*, pp. 205–63.

[156] Note also Irenaeus' citation of traditional material from the teaching of 'the Elder' in Adv. Haer. IV. 27. 2; the passage from the Apocryphon of Jeremiah quoted by Justin in Dial. 72.4 and by Irenaeus in Adv. Haer. III. 20. 4; IV. 22. 1; IV. 33. 1; V. 31. 1; Similitude IX. 16. 5–7 of Hermas; and Test. Levi 4.1.

3. That κατάβασις–ἀνάβασις christology appears prominently
in Jewish Christian canonical materials, and that where it appears
in Paul it is with the suggestion of its pre-Pauline character. This I
have attempted to demonstrate above.[157]

In the canonical κατάβασις–ἀνάβασις passages there is, on the
one hand, an ambivalence which defies precise designation of the
nature of the descent involved, and, on the other, a comprehensive-
ness which allows for the amalgamation of the two aspects of a
descent from heaven to earth and a descent from earth to hades –
and for the development of the latter.[158] Probably the original
motif had to do only with the humiliation of incarnation, servi-
tude, temptation, and death, as seen in Phil. 2.6–11; John 1.1–18;
3.13; 6.62; Heb. 2; 5; and probably Eph. 4.8–10. Very soon, however, it appears to have been extended to include a *descensus ad
inferos*, as it was in the second century if not already in I Peter 3.19
and 4.6.[159] But however these two elements are to be related, there
is good reason for believing that κατάβασις–ἀνάβασις christology
was a distinctive feature of early Palestinian Jewish Christianity.

[157] Mention could also be made of the 'humiliation-exaltation' theme in
Jewish thought regarding the pious man (cf. E. Schweizer, *Lordship and
Discipleship* [1960], pp. 23–8 and passim); though, while evidencing a similar
pattern and lending some support to the above thesis, the 'humiliation-
exaltation' of the pious is not as far-reaching as κατάβασις–ἀνάβασις christology.

[158] Esp. note Phil. 2.10: 'That at the name of Jesus every knee should bow,
in heaven and on earth and *under the earth.*'

[159] 'There is no need to assign this teaching to a late date; it is the kind of
reflection which might arise at any time in the first generation of Christianity
when questions connected with Christ's resurrection and ascension were considered and when baptism, which is expressly mentioned in [I Peter] iii. 21
in connexion with the deluge and the story of Noah, was in mind' (V. Taylor,
Person of Christ in New Testament Teaching, pp. 87f.). In response to the problem
of the fate of pre-Christian worthies, which question undoubtedly concerned
the earlier generations of Christians, evidently some Jewish believers developed a doctrine of a pre-incarnation proclamation or of a proclamation
in hades. Gentile Christians, on the other hand, tended to employ the
Johannine Prologue in substantiation of a pre-Christian Logos-enlightenment
theme.

III

MESSIAHSHIP AND ITS IMPLICATIONS

BASIC TO THE christology of the earliest Jewish Christians was the conviction of Jesus as the Messiah. Subject as it was to political and nationalistic connotations, and requiring redefinition in order to be serviceable, it was the application of this title to Jesus which laid the foundation for the church's continuing thought about, and further acclamation of, the Man from Nazareth. So basic and central, in fact, was the messiahship of Jesus in the consciousness of early believers that it was the Greek word for Messiah, χριστός, and not another, which became uniquely associated with the person of Jesus, first as an appellative and then as a proper name, and which became the basis for their own cognomen in the ancient world as well.

In the ferment of present-day christological discussion, there is little hope of such an assertion going unchallenged. It is therefore the purpose of the present chapter to marshal the evidence for such a claim and to spell out the immediate implications of such a commitment. The following chapter will consider the parallel feature of lordship with its attendant concepts, and a further chapter will explore the relationships between these major strands of thought.

THE MESSIAH-CHRIST

Jewish Expectation. The literature of Judaism, both biblical and post-biblical, evidences a much greater interest in the Messianic Age itself and the activity of God during the Age than in the person or persons whom God would use to bring it about and to accomplish his purposes.[1] The semitic mind thinks more in terms

---

[1] One has only to scan the Old Testament passages which look towards the distant future to note that the greater emphasis is given to a description of the Age itself than to God's anointed instrument who will usher in that Age. While sections and chapters are devoted to the former (e.g., Isa. 26–29; 40ff.; Ezek. 40–48; Dan. 12; Joel 2.28–3.21), definite references to the latter are confined, in the main, to a few specific verses (e.g., Isa. 9.6f.; Micah 5.2; Zech. 9.9).

of ultimates than secondary agency and of functions than persons, resulting in an emphasis upon the fact and character of the coming Age more than in the nature or personality of God's anointed instrument to bring it about. Yet, while it does not come to frequent expression in those writings which are demonstrably pre-Christian, the concept of a personal Messiah appears to some extent in early Jewish materials and was inevitably connected with speculations regarding the Final Age. And in the days preceding the ministry of Jesus, the idea of the Messiah as God's deliverer in the eschatological consummation was becoming fixed in the expectations of many.[2]

The Hebrew משיח is used in the Old Testament and other early Jewish literature of a person or persons to whom God has extended a special call and assigned a special mission; principally of the anointed king ruling over the people of God,[3] but also of priests,[4] prophets,[5] and patriarchs[6] – and even of a foreign monarch carrying out a specific task in the divine economy.[7] But by the first century BC, if not earlier in 'the anointed one, the prince' (משיח נגיד) of Dan. 9.25–26a, the term 'Messiah' had come to be something of a *terminus technicus* for the Anointed One who would be God's deliverer in days of eschatological consummation.[8] Psalms of Solomon 17 and 18 speak of 'the Lord's Anointed' (χριστὸς κυρίου)[9] or 'his Anointed' (χριστὸς αὐτοῦ),[10] and in the title

[2] Sadducean redefinitions of the Messianic Age as a process rather than an event and of messiahship as an ideal rather than a person, while distinctly modern in that day and coming to expression again in Reformed Judaism of the last century and a half, seem to have had little appeal in the first century outside the circles of the 'sophisticated' landed gentry and those more politically orientated.

[3] E.g., I Sam. 2.10, 35; 24.6; 26.9, 11, 16, 23.

[4] E.g., Lev. 4.3, 5, 16; 8.12; Ps. 84.10.

[5] E.g., I Kings 19.16; CDC 2.12 (2.10); 6.1 (8.2); 1QM 11.7.

[6] E.g., Ps. 105.15; I Chron. 16.22.

[7] Isa. 45.1, with reference to Cyrus.

[8] M. de Jonge's denial of any fixed content to the idea of Messiah in the century preceding the Christian era and his argument for 'the relative unimportance of the term in the context of Jewish expectations concerning the future, at least in the Jewish sources at our disposal for this period' ('The Use of the Word "Anointed" in the Time of Jesus', *NovT*, VIII [1966], p. 134; cf. also pp. 132–48 and the article on χριστός in *TWNT*), is based on the relative infrequency of the appearance of the term in pre-Christian Jewish writings and thereby fails to take into account the semitic habit of stressing functions over persons.

[9] Pss. Sol. 17.32; 18.7.

[10] Pss. Sol. 18.5.

to Ps. 18 employs χριστός with the article to mean 'the Messiah of the Lord' (Ψαλμὸς τῷ Σαλωμών. ἔτι τοῦ χριστοῦ κυρίου). In the Qumran materials, reference is made to 'the Anointed Ones of Israel and Aaron',[11] 'the Anointed One of Israel',[12] 'the Anointed One of Righteousness/the Righteous' (משיח הצדק),[13] 'the Anointed One of Aaron and Israel',[14] and, in what appears to be an absolute usage, 'the Messiah' (המשיח).[15] It appears as well in a technical sense in Benediction 14 of the Shemoneh Esreh, the Targums,[16] IV Ezra 12.32, II Bar. 29.3; 30.1, and I Enoch 48.10; 52.4, though the extent to which each of these writings reflects pre-Christian Jewish usage is variously debated. The fact that no rabbi before AD 70 can be cited as using משיח in an absolute sense, or that Josephus does not employ the term, are probably not too significant, since material directly attributable to specific pre-destruction rabbis is itself very scarce and Josephus desired to play down this element before his Roman audience. Nor can it be said that the tendency on the part of the Sadducees to look back on the days of Maccabean dominance as the inauguration of the 'Golden' or 'Messianic Age' – which Age, from their perspective, was being perpetuated in their own titular authority in Israel – gained any great hearing or diminished to any real extent the hope of a future Messiah among the populace.

But while the concept of personal messiahship was a vital factor in the expectations of pre-Christian Judaism, conceptions regarding the nature and function of the coming Messiah (or Messiahs) varied considerably. In circles where a quietistic priestly emphasis was strong, the levitical character of the Messiah dominated.[17] Where Pharisaic influence was felt, legal and prophetic elements were stressed.[18] And popular imagination clothed the messianic hope in dress conformable to the varied apocalyptic images and

---

[11] 1QS 9.11.

[12] 1QSᵃ 2.14, 20.

[13] 4QPatr. 3.

[14] CDC 19.10f. (9.10); 20.1 (9.29); 12.23f. (15.4); 14.19 (18.8).

[15] 11QMelch. 18; though, of course, the mutilation of the text forbids certainty as to the article or to what follows the term. Cf. also such locutions as 'The Scion of David' and 'the Prince of all the Congregation' in 4QFlor. 11, 18–19; 1QSᵇ 11.4–5; 1QM 5.1.

[16] Targ. Palest. Gen. 3.15; 49.1, 10, 11; Ex. 40.9, 11; Num. 23.21; Targ. Jon. Isa. 16.1; 42.1.

[17] Cf., e.g., 1QS 9.11; also Test. Levi 8.11–15.

[18] Cf., e.g., Assump. Moses 9f.; also IV Ezra 14.

political conditions of the day.[19] Both spiritual and national features were intermingled in pre-Christian Jewish messianic expectations, though what seems to have captured the peoples' fancy was that the Messiah would be a political and nationalistic ruler – even a military leader. And to this idea was wedded the title 'Son of David'. While other elements vied for recognition, this political and nationalistic conception came to take the place of ascendancy in Jewish thought.[20] And in Jesus' day, this son-of-David understanding of messiahship was dominant.

Jesus' Consciousness. It was William Wrede who in 1901 first established the thesis that the reticence of Jesus to declare himself openly as the Messiah is a Marcan device, which was continued in the Gospels of Matthew and Luke and which appears in the Fourth Gospel as a doctrine of 'veiled glory'. And it was Wrede who christened his discovery with the paradoxical, yet aptly descriptive, name of the 'messianic secret'.[21]

Liberal biblical scholarship has generally followed Wrede at this point, insisting that, though he awakened messianic expectations in others, Jesus himself did not think of his person or his ministry in messianic terms at all – and that what evidence there is to the contrary is the product of later *Gemeindetheologie* and appears in the records through the impetus of Mark's ingenuity. To cite only one contemporary and representative example, Günther Bornkamm, in his widely read *Jesus of Nazareth*, asserts:

The idea of the Messianic secret in Mark so obviously presupposes the experience of Good Friday and Easter, and betrays itself as a theological and literary device of the evangelist, especially where we recognise the hand of the author, that it is impossible to treat it forthwith as a teaching of the historical Jesus. . . . Behind the doctrinal teaching concerning the Messianic secret there still dimly emerges the fact that Jesus' history was originally a non-Messianic history, which was portrayed in the light of the Messianic faith of the Church only after Easter.[22]

What differences there are among advocates of this position have

---

[19] While F. J. Foakes Jackson and K. Lake were a bit extreme in asserting of the messianic doctrine that only 'the thing itself was of faith, all the rest was free field for imagination' (*Beginnings*, I, p. 356), they were nevertheless generally correct.

[20] Cf., e.g., Pss. Sol. 17.23–51; 1QM.

[21] W. Wrede, *Das Messiasgeheimnis in den Evangelien* (1901).

[22] G. Bornkamm, *Jesus of Nazareth* (ET 1960), pp. 171f.

to do mainly with refinements of Wrede's thought regarding the purpose of Mark's fabrication: (1) Was it to impose a christology upon the non-christological tradition of early Palestinian Christianity, as Wrede himself and most have insisted?, or (2) Was it to tone down a 'divine man' epiphany christology which had arisen within a pre-Marcan hellenistic Christian faith, as many Bultmannians assert?[23]

Even in circles where a less radical solution is proposed, the portrayal in the Gospels of the secrecy of Jesus regarding his messiahship and of his hesitancy as to the title itself poses a real problem. And it is this feature which properly has been seen to demand some explanation in any discussion of early christology.

Repeatedly in the Gospels Jesus is presented as both reticent to declare himself Messiah and actually demanding silence on the part of those who would. The demons, for example, are not allowed to speak 'because they knew that he was the Christ (the Messiah)'.[24] Those healed by Jesus are enjoined to remain silent.[25] John the Baptist's direct inquiry regarding Jesus' messiahship is answered rather opaquely by reference to what was being done.[26] And the disciples are commanded not to tell what they had seen on the Mount of Transfiguration until after the resurrection.[27]

Three passages, however, are usually seen as bringing us to the heart of the problem: (1) Peter's declaration 'You are the Christ (the Messiah)!' and Jesus' response;[28] (2) Caiaphas' query 'Are you the Christ (the Messiah)?' and Jesus' response;[29] and (3) Pilate's question 'Are you the King of the Jews?' and Jesus' response.[30] In the first, Matthew's account records that Peter is commended for the appropriateness of his confession; though all three Synoptic writers conclude the vignette with the statement that Jesus urged secrecy upon his disciples regarding his messiahship. In Jesus' answer to Caiaphas, Mark has Jesus answering directly in the affirmative, though only after being asked twice, and

---

[23] E.g., H. Conzelmann, 'Gegenwart und Zukunft in der synoptischen Tradition', *ZTK*, LIV (1957), pp. 293–5.

[24] Luke 4.41; accepting also the reading of B for Mark 1.34.

[25] Mark 1.44; 5.43; 7.36; 8.26, and par.

[26] Matt. 11.2–6; Luke 7.18–23.

[27] Matt. 17.9; Mark 9.9f.; cf. Luke 9.36.

[28] Matt. 16.13–20; Mark 8.27–30; Luke 9.18–21.

[29] Matt. 26.57–66; Mark 14.53–64.

[30] Matt. 27.11–14; Mark 15.2–5; Luke 23.3; John 18.33–38.

Matthew presents him as responding somewhat enigmatically after being adjured by the high priest. And in both Matthew and Mark, Jesus' reply goes on to speak in terms of the 'Son of Man' and not messiahship, though the question was specifically directed to the latter. Jesus' response to Pilate may not have direct bearing on the issue at hand, though it does indicate at least that Jesus did not understand his messiahship in political terms.

By more conservative scholars, the contexts of these passages are understood as laden with nationalistic overtones, and thus the varied reporting of Jesus' answers to indicate (1) his rejection of a Jewish concept of political messiahship, (2) his reserve towards the title itself due to a very different view of its essential nature, yet (3) his willingness to accept the ascription when given in a more spiritual setting or when authoritatively demanded of him.[31] In substantial agreement, though with significant divergence, Oscar Cullmann has argued for Jesus' absolute rejection of a Jewish concept of messiahship coupled with his extreme reserve towards the title itself because of its contemporary connotations – in fact, his conscious avoidance of the designation rather than even any occasional acceptance of it.[32] In the interview with Pilate, there is an implicit rejection of that affirmed; and in the replies to Caiaphas' question and Peter's acclamation, as Cullmann understands them, Jesus remained non-committal.[33] Cullmann believes Jesus to have been the Messiah. And further, he believes Jesus to have been conscious of this status – his awareness of continuity with the Old Testament as expressed in his claim to fulfilment would make this inevitable. But Cullmann understands Jesus to have consciously avoided the title Messiah since political kingship was so firmly wedded to it. Bultmannians (including the so-called 'post-Bultmannians') assert Jesus' denial of the title *per se*, alleging that he viewed himself only as 'Messiah-designate' in his ministry and believed that full messiahship awaited the future coming of

[31] E.g., V. Taylor, *The Names of Jesus* (1953), p. 20; *idem, Person of Christ in New Testament Teaching* (1958), p. 4; V. H. Neufeld, *The Earliest Christian Confessions* (1963), pp. 112f.; A. J. B. Higgins, *Jesus and the Son of Man* (1964), pp. 18f.

[32] O. Cullmann, *Peter: Disciple-Apostle-Martyr* (ET 1953), pp. 170–84; *idem, Christology of the New Testament*, pp. 117–27. Cf. also G. S. Duncan, *Jesus, Son of Man* (1947), pp. 125f.

[33] Cullmann discounts the statement of John 4.26 as more the nomenclature of the Fourth Evangelist than that of Jesus (*Christology of the New Testament*, p. 125n.).

the Son of Man at the *parousia*.[34] Thus these passages are understood as Jesus' absolute rejection of both the Jewish idea of
Messiah and the title itself being properly ascribed to him,
messiahship being recognized by Jesus as 'a diabolical temptation'.[35]

Bultmann conveniently classes every Synoptic passage which
could be used in support of a messianic self-consciousness on the
part of Jesus as either (1) an Easter story projected back into the
life of Jesus, or (2) a legend.[36] Thus he rules out of court both
Peter's confession and the transfiguration narrative on the first
count, and the accounts of Jesus' baptism, messianic temptations
in the wilderness, challenge to the Pharisees regarding the nature
of messiahship, and entry into Jerusalem on the second. And after
deleting these portions from consideration, he triumphantly asserts
that he finds nowhere in the Synoptic records any hint that Jesus
challenged or attempted to reinterpret the contemporary Jewish
concept of Messiah;[37] and proposes without fear of rebuttal that
Jesus' self-consciousness was entirely non-messianic.[38] In distinction from Bultmann, Cullmann accepts these narratives as sub-
stantially accurate and interprets Jesus as possessing a messianic
consciousness. But he insists that a proper reading of Jesus' express statements on the subject of messiahship indicates at best a
non-committal attitude on his part to the acceptance of the ascription as given by others, and that Jesus' designation of himself as
Messiah before the Samaritan woman is to be attributed more to
the Evangelist than to Jesus himself.[39] Despite, however, the
Bultmannian denial of any messianic self-consciousness and the

---

[34] R. Bultmann, *Theology of the New Testament*, I, pp. 26f.; F. Hahn, *Christologische Hoheitstitel*, pp. 159–79; R. H. Fuller, *Foundations of New Testament Christology*, pp. 109–11.

[35] R. H. Fuller, *Foundations of New Testament Christology*, pp. 109, 150. Fuller cites Cullmann in support here; but Cullmann's point is that 'Jesus saw the hand of Satan at work in the contemporary Jewish concept of the Messiah', not in the title *per se* (*Christology of the New Testament*, p. 124; *Peter*, p. 178).

[36] R. Bultmann, *Theology of the New Testament*, I, pp. 26f.

[37] *Ibid.*, p. 28. See, however, E. G. Jay, *Son of Man, Son of God* (1965), pp. 25–7, on Jesus' answer to the query of John the Baptist and the passages in which Jesus predicts his sufferings and death as revealing 'precisely what Bultmann implies is absent – a correction of current ideas about the Messiah'.

[38] R. Bultmann, *Theology of the New Testament*, I, pp. 26–32. For a pertinent and brief evaluation of Bultmann at this point, see E. G. Jay, *Son of Man, Son of God*, pp. 24–31.

[39] O. Cullmann, *Christology of the New Testament*, p. 125n.

Cullmannian insistence on a conscious avoidance of the title, Jesus was crucified as a messianic pretender. This is indeed a fact of significance in the later use of the title in the church, as Ferdinand Hahn insists.[40] But has it no importance in our understanding of Jesus himself?

One is bound to wonder how a man who made no explicit messianic claim for himself, as Cullmann insists, or who absolutely rejected the ascription and did so little that was out of the ordinary, as the Bultmannians assert, could have aroused the intense opposition of Judaism to himself along messianic lines that culminated in his death. Of course 'misunderstanding' may be appealed to in explanation, as is so often done. But is this not too easy a way out of the difficulty? Perhaps Jesus' enemies were more perceptive than we credit them. And perhaps lack of insight in this case should be laid at doors more modern. One becomes highly suspicious that such is the case when evidence is hustled out of court on basically theological grounds in order to prove that there is no evidence, whether it be the allocating of passages to a later time in order to demonstrate the lack of a messianic self-consciousness on the part of Jesus or the emending of a text in order to dispute its *prima facie* meaning as to Jesus' occasional acceptance of the title.

That Jesus understood his ministry in terms of messiahship is the underlying presupposition in the narratives concerning the baptism, the temptation in the wilderness, the transfiguration, and the triumphal entry; and it is implicit in his controversy with the Pharisees regarding the nature of messiahship.[41] And if we are not permitted to appeal to the responses of Jesus to Peter and the high priest – both of which I personally consider valid appeals, though to varying degrees[42] – at least in John 4.26 there is the account of Jesus' acceptance of the title in the statement to the Samaritan woman, 'I that speak to you am he.' Despite the fact that he absolutely refused to associate himself with the contemporary idea of a political Messiah, even to the point of withdrawing from his followers when they attempted to foist it upon him,[43] Jesus could

[40] F. Hahn, *Christologische Hoheitstitel*, pp. 178f.

[41] Matt. 22.41–46; Mark 12.35–37; Luke 20.41–44.

[42] Cf. E. G. Jay, *Son of Man, Son of God*, pp. 14–18; B. H. Branscomb, *The Gospel of Mark* (1937), pp. 150–3; V. H. Neufeld, *Earliest Christian Confessions*, pp. 112f.

[43] John 6.15.

none the less hardly have claimed to be the fulfilment of Old Testament prophecy without at least implying that he was in some sense the Messiah of Israel's hope. For, at the very least, 'the idea of the Messiah is important to the extent that it establishes a continuity between the work of Jesus and the mission of the chosen people of Israel'.[44] · *See Harnack*

[The portrait of Jesus in the Gospels in regard to messiahship is indeed rather baffling, composed as it is of such elements as, on the one hand, (1) a radical rejection of the current Jewish idea of the Messiah, (2) an extreme reserve towards the title itself, and (3) explicit commands to his disciples and others not to speak of him in messianic terms, while, on the other hand, (4) a messianic consciousness underlying many of his actions and statements, (5) the acclaim of others as to his messiahship, (6) an occasional acceptance of this appellative, and (7) the express explication of his ministry in messianic terms after the resurrection, as presented in Luke 24. For those unwilling to solve the dilemma by setting aside any of the factors, the explanation has usually centred on the fact that contemporary Jewish messianology was so wedded to nationalistic concepts as to offer no fit vehicle of communication for Jesus' message in most cases – though where he could accept certain elements within that messianic hope and where he could heighten others, Jesus did so. And certainly this explanation is as good as any, and more historically founded than most.]

In 1959, however, David Flusser, in an article dealing with the treatment of II Sam. 7 in 4Q Florilegium, suggested, almost in passing, that the data comprising the heart of the messianic secret in the Gospels can be paralleled to a great extent in material found at Qumran and at Murabba'at, and that behind the hesitancy of Jesus, the Qumran Teacher of Righteousness, and Simeon ben Kosebah to more positively assert their claims lies a common motif of basic importance in Jewish thought.[45] It is this suggestion which I believe needs further explication and which I propose goes far towards resolving more adequately this most vexing problem.

It is widely accepted that behind the sectarian group represented

---

[44] As Cullmann says in defence of Jesus' messianic consciousness (*Christology of the New Testament*, pp. 126f.), though, of course, according to Cullmann, Jesus refused to accept the title because of its associations.

[45] D. Flusser, 'Two Notes on the Midrash on 2 Sam. vii', *IEJ*, IX (1959), pp. 107–9.

by the Dead Sea Scrolls stood an historical figure – probably the founder, though certainly the inspiration and guiding light of the group – who is highly extolled in the literature of the community. What is not so often realized is that in the *Hodayot*, which may reasonably be assumed to have been written by this personage himself, the laudatory epithets used elsewhere in the writings from Qumran are not employed, though the consciousness signalled in the titles underlies the whole of the Thanksgiving Hymns. In the Zadokite Document and in the pesher comments on Ps. 37 and Hab. 1f., for example, he is identified as the 'Teacher of Righteousness',[46] whereas the *Hodayot* contains no instance of the use of this title. The consciousness underlying the title, however, is echoed in the Hymns relatively frequently; for instance, in such a statement as: 'And thou, O my God, hast placed in my mouth rain [divine teaching] as an early shower of rain.'[47] And it is reflected in the claim of the writer: 'Thou hast set me as a banner to the elect of righteousness, as one who interprets with knowledge deep, mysterious things; as a touchstone for them that seek the truth, a standard for them that love correction.'[48] In addition, in the Manual of Discipline the Teacher seems to be accepted as a Second Moses,[49] and in the Zadokite Fragments and the Habakkuk Commentary as the Giver of the Covenant,[50] which ascriptions find their counterparts less directly in the Hymns in such words as: 'I do thank thee, O Lord, for my face thou hast enlightened for thy covenant's sake. Yea, from evening until morning do I seek thee; and as the sure dawn for perfect illumination hast thou appeared to me.'[51] And throughout the literature of Qumran there is evidence that the Teacher was understood in messianic terms, probably as the Prophet who was to prepare the way for the com-

[46] CDC 1.11 (1.7); 6.11 (8.10); 20.1 (9.29); 20.28 (9.50); 20.32 (9.53); 4QPs. 37 at 2.14–16 (on 37.24); 1QHab. 1.13 (on 1.4); 2.2 (on 1.4f.); 5.10 (on 1.13); 7.4 (on 2.2); 8.3 (on 2.4); 9.10 (on 2.8); 9.5 (on 2.15). Cf. also 1QMic. 2.5 (on 1.5).

[47] 1QH 8.16. See also 8.17–26 where this figure of rain (divine teaching given through the teacher at Qumran) is continued. Cf. also 5.9–12; 7.20–27; 11.3–18; 12.3, 11–23.

[48] 1QH 2.13f.

[49] Cf. N. Wieder, 'The "Law-Interpreter" of the Sect of the Dead Sea Scrolls: The Second Moses', *JJS*, IV (1953), pp. 158–75; see also W. H. Brownlee, 'Messianic Motifs', *NTS*, III (1956), p. 17, in agreement and for a bibliography of early interpreters taking this position.

[50] CDC 6.19 (8.15); 19.33f. (9.28); 20.12 (9.37); 1QHab. 2.7f. (on 1.5).

[51] 1QH 4.5f. Cf. also 1.21; 4.22–28; 7.10, 20–27.

ing of the Messiah or Messiahs;[52] which association allusively comes to expression in the *Hodayot via* the frequent employment of terminology drawn from the Isaian Servant Songs.[53]

This same phenomenon of (1) external acclamation, (2) reticence on the part of the individual to speak of himself in the terms others were using, yet (3) a consciousness on that person's part of the ultimate validity of the titles employed, seems to be true as well of Simeon ben Kosebah, the leader of the Jewish revolt against Hadrian, and of the materials from his desert headquarters at Wadi Murrabba'at. We know from rabbinic sources that with his initial victories over Roman power there arose a wild enthusiasm among the Jewish populace as to Simeon's messiahship and kingship, and that this enthusiasm engulfed even the leading rabbi of the day, Rabbi Akiba.[54] But what must be noted here is that from the few remains of his letters at Murabba'at, there is evidence only that Simeon ben Kosebah called himself Prince (*Nasi*), and not King or Messiah, even though he undoubtedly expected to fulfil the messianic expectations of his people as he understood them.[55]

What is the explanation of such data? To this, citing what he asserts to be a common Jewish pattern of thought, David Flusser pertinently observes: 'From the strictly theological point of view no man can be defined as a messiah before he has accomplished the task of the anointed.'[56] In the Jewish view, that is, the function and work must be accomplished first before the title may be right-fully claimed.[57] And in this, Jesus, the Qumran Teacher of Righteousness, and Simeon ben Kosebah seem to be in agreement, though their concepts of messiahship and each's understanding of his own place in the Messianic Age differed radically.

It is both interesting and illuminating to observe that only in Luke 24.26 and 24.46, accounts of the post-resurrection

---

[52] Cf. W. H. Brownlee, 'Messianic Motifs', *NTS*, III (1956), pp. 18–20, 26, 195–8.

[53] E.g., 1QH 7.6f.; 8.26f., 35f.; 9.29–32; 13.18f.; 14.25; 17.26; 18.14.

[54] Cf. L. Finkelstein, *Akiba* (1962), p. 269. Of course not everyone acclaimed him Messiah and King, as indicated in the Aramaic play on the name ranging from Bar Kokbah ('Son of the Star') to Bar Kozebah ('Son of the Lie').

[55] D. Flusser, 'Two Notes on the Midrash on 2 Sam. vii', *IEJ*, IX (1959), p. 107.

[56] *Ibid*.

[57] Cf. Jacob's words of Gen. 28.20–22, which are not so much a case of bargaining with God as a semitic response of this type.

appearances, is Jesus presented as directly initiating the discussion regarding his messiahship and as relating the Old Testament to himself in explicit messianic terms. But then he was able to re-interpret the title by reference to the immediately past events. And then he had accomplished the messianic task which he came to perform, thus allowing him to speak so openly. Thus, though in a certain sense he could be called 'Messiah-elect' (even 'Messiah-designate', if that term be thoroughly disinfected) during his ministry, Jesus was acknowledged Messiah in fact not just *after* his passion and resurrection but *because of* his passion and resur-rection – and, it must be insisted, in continuity with his own self-consciousness during the ministry.

Early Christian Conviction. The book of Acts asserts that a pro-minent element in early Christian proclamation was the demonstra-tion that Jesus was the promised Messiah; and this, in spite of the facts that he did not conform to the dominant messianic expecta-tion in contemporary Judaism and that he used the title with reference to himself only with great reserve. Peter is presented as preaching that David spoke of the resurrection of 'the Christ' (τοῦ χριστοῦ) and that 'all the prophets' foretold that God's Anointed One (τὸν χριστὸν αὐτοῦ) should suffer.[58] And Acts con-cludes its series of vignettes on the earliest days of the Jerusalem church with the remark: 'And every day in the temple and at home they did not cease teaching and preaching "Jesus as the Christ",' (τὸν χριστὸν, Ἰησοῦν).[59] In the advance of the gospel beyond Jeru-salem, Philip preached 'the Christ' (τὸν χριστόν) to Samaritans;[60] Paul proclaimed that Jesus was 'the Christ' (ὁ χριστός, τόν χριστόν) to Jews of Damascus, Thessalonica, and Corinth;[61] and Apollos is recorded as likewise very effectively 'showing from the Scrip-tures Jesus to be the Christ' (εἶναι τόν χριστόν, Ἰησοῦν) before a Jewish audience at Corinth.[62] In every case in the Acts of the Apostles where χριστός is used singly, it is as an appellative; and in every case where it appears as an appellative, it is in address to a Jewish audience. The only possible exceptions are in Philip's preaching to Samaritans and Paul's argument before Agrippa II

[58] Acts 2.31; 3.18; cf. 2.36; 3.20.
[59] Acts 5.42; cf. 4.26.
[60] Acts 8.5.
[61] Acts 9.22; 17.3; 18.5.
[62] Acts 18.28.

that the Old Testament prophesied that 'the Christ' (ὁ χριστός) must suffer.[63] In these two cases, however, though highly diverse, both blood lines and contact with Mosaic religion were sufficient to justify our view of the persons addressed as broadly speaking possessing a Jewish background and understanding; though, of course, other influences were present as well. Altogether, χριστός as a title appears in Acts at least twelve times. And even where the combination 'Jesus Christ' or 'Christ Jesus' appears, the original appellative idea seems still to be reflected in the usage. Henry J. Cadbury is probably overstating the case in saying: 'The result of the evidence in Acts concerning χριστός is certainly to compel us to acknowledge that for this author it is not a proper name.'[64] But certainly the evidence supports the view that its usual employment in the book of the Acts is as a title.

This same usage of χριστός as a title when addressed to a Jewish audience is found elsewhere in the New Testament. With the possible exception of 'Jesus Christ' in the introductions to the genealogy and the birth account,[65] every one of the remaining twelve instances of χριστός in Matthew's Gospel carries the idea of a title or designation rather than a name: nine times ὁ χριστός is employed,[66] once the crowd at the Jewish inquisition of Jesus is represented as mockingly called him χριστέ (vocative),[67] and twice Pilate refers to him as 'the one called Christ' (᾿Ιησοῦν τὸν λεγόμενον χριστόν).[68] Throughout the Johannine literature, without exception, wherever χριστός is used singly it is in an appellative fashion. In addition to the approximately one dozen instances where the word occurs in this manner in the Fourth Gospel,[69] the Evangelist declares quite plainly that his point in writing is to engender faith

---

[63] Acts 26.23.

[64] H. J. Cadbury, *Beginnings*, V. 358; cf., e.g., Acts 15.26.

[65] Matt. 1.1, 18. The omission of ᾿Ιησοῦ in the Latin tradition, early Syriac manuscripts, and Irenaeus suggests the possibility that Matt. 1.18 was originally read 'of the Christ'.

[66] Matt. 1.17; 2.4; 11.2; 16.16, 20; 22.42; 24.5, 23; 26.63 (rejecting the reading χριστός in Matt. 16.21 on textual grounds). Cf. also the use of 'Emmanuel' in Matt. 1.23, which appears more as a title than as a name.

[67] Matt. 26.68.

[68] Matt. 27.17, 22.

[69] John 1.41; 4.25, 29; 7.26, 27, 31, 41, 42; 9.22; 10.24; 11.27; 12.34. In John 1.17 and 17.3 the name 'Jesus Christ' appears, though the context indicates plainly that the author meant by this name 'the Messiah' (cf. W. C. van Unnik, 'The Purpose of St. John's Gospel', *Studia Evangelica*, I, ed. K. Aland [1959], p. 387).

in Jesus as 'the Christ, the Son of God' (ὁ χριστὸς ὁ υἱὸς τοῦ θεοῦ).[70] And interestingly, the only two places in the New Testament where the Hebrew משׁיח is simply transliterated Μεσσίας rather than translated – though in an explanatory aside also translated by χριστός in each case – are both in John's Gospel; the first credited to Andrew and the second on the part of the Samaritan woman.[71] The Johannine letters speak of denying that Jesus is 'the Christ', believing that Jesus is 'the Christ' and abiding 'in the doctrine of the Christ' (ἐν τῇ διδαχῇ τοῦ χριστοῦ).[72] The Apocalypse represents the voices from heaven as announcing 'the kingdom of our Lord/God and of his Christ' (τοῦ χριστοῦ αὐτοῦ),[73] and speaks of the blessed dead as reigning with and being priests of 'the Christ'.[74] The Letter to the Hebrews, excluding its two uses of the combination 'Jesus Christ',[75] employs χριστός as a designation rather than a name in six of its nine occurrences.[76]

When we turn from the Jewish Christian materials in the New Testament to those writings more representative of the Gentile cycle of the Christian mission, a difference in the use of χριστός can be noted. As E. Best points out: 'This title does not appear to have great significance for Mark. . . . Mark leaves the title, so far as we know, in the material as it comes to him; he does not deny that Jesus is the Christ, nor' – and this I would emphasize – 'does he stress it.'[77] The solitary instance in the Synoptics of the anarthrous use of χριστός employed singly occurs among Mark's relatively infrequent uses of the term.[78] And the one instance of χριστός which is assuredly Marcan, as distinguished from traditional, is not treated as a title but as a proper name: 'Ιησοῦ Χριστοῦ.[79] Luke uses the title more frequently than Mark, adding it to

[70] John 20.31.
[71] John 1.41; 4.25.
[72] I John 2.22; 5.1; II John 9.
[73] Rev. 11.15; 12.10.
[74] Rev. 20.4, 6.
[75] Heb. 10.10; 13.8.
[76] Heb. 3.14; 5.5; 6.1; 9.14, 28; 11.26. Cf. Heb. 3.6; 9.11, 24. It need be noted, however, that Hebrews is here considered to be 'Jewish Christian' primarily because of its audience and the conditioning of its argument to the interests of that audience. In many ways, of course, it is also a bridge between Jewish Christianity and that of the larger catholic Gentile church.

[77] E. Best, *Temptation and Passion*, pp. 165f.

[78] Mark 9.41. The other uses of χριστός in Mark's Gospel where it is employed singly, though all with the article, appear in 8.29; 12.35; 13.21; 14.61 and 15.32.

[79] Mark 1.1.

Marcan material at Luke 4.41;[80] though his emphasis upon Jesus as a 'Saviour, who is Christ the Lord', treating χριστός strictly as a proper name and subsuming it under σωτήρ, signals a break from rather fixed Jewish moorings and an association with motifs more common in the Gentile mission.[81] Similarly in the Pauline letters there is a definite awareness of an earlier appellative use of the term,[82] though it is used more frequently as a name.

The situation in I Peter is somewhat ambiguous, for while the letter gives *prima facie* evidence of reflecting Jewish Christian interests it expresses itself in terms more reminiscent of the Gentile mission. Thus χριστός appears in I Peter 1.1–4.11 exclusively as a proper name while in the latter section of 4.12–5.14 also as a title.[83] This may be due in part to Silas as the amanuensis. Or it may be employed in support of a late date for the letter; or as an argument for the lack of distinction in expression between the Jewish and the Gentile missions of the early church. I would suggest, however, that it may also illustrate the thesis that I Peter 4.12–5.11 reflects the situation which called forth the letter, and that the apostle incorporated catechetical or liturgical material – which may have received certain refinements in that usage – for the first portion of his letter. If so, the appearance of χριστός as a title in I Peter 4.13 and 5.1 could strengthen the case for the appellative use of the term in the Jewish Christian mission. Perhaps here we are witnessing Peter's willingness to use the term as a name, especially when incorporating ecclesiastical materials (which he may have had a part in constructing himself, though which probably suffered certain changes of expression in use), but also his unconscious habit of employing χριστός as a title – since it is that usage with which he is most accustomed from the earliest days of the church.

J. A. T. Robinson, explicating a Bultmannian viewpoint, has suggested that all of these applications of messiahship to Jesus in Acts and the Jewish Christian materials, while reflective of one stage in early Christian conviction, are really secondary to 'the most primitive Christology of all' as embedded in Acts 3.19–21:

[80] See also Luke 2.11, 26; 9.20; 20.41; 22.67; 23.2, 35, 39; 24.26, 46. Matthew adds the title to Mark's narrative in Matt. 16.20; 24.5; 26.68; 27.17, 22.

[81] Luke 2.11.

[82] Rom. 7.4; 8.35; 14.18; 15.3, 7, 18–20; 16.16; I Cor. 1.6, 13, 17; *passim*.

[83] I Peter 1.11, 19; 2.21; 3.16, 18; 4.1, 13, 14; 5.1, 10, 14.

'Repent, therefore, and turn again, that your sins may be blotted out, that times of refreshing may come from the presence of the Lord and that he may send the foreordained Messiah (τὸν προκεχειρισμένον χριστόν) to you, Jesus, whom heaven must receive until the time for establishing all that God spoke by the mouth of his holy prophets of old.'[84] As Robinson understands the participial phrase in its immediate context, here is an affirmation that Jesus has not as yet entered into messiahship but that that honour has been reserved for him in the counsels of God *for the future*. Presently, of course, Jesus is 'Messiah-designate' awaiting the future *parousia* of the Son of Man; and then he shall be Messiah in fact. And in Acts 3.19–21, according to Robinson, we have an outcropping of the earliest stratum of christological speculation, which very quickly faded away and was replaced by the christology of Acts 2 and the attribution of present messiahship to Jesus as seen throughout the rest of the New Testament. In fact, however, Jesus was first considered as Messiah-designate in the earliest Jewish church, and only later was he elevated in the thought of Christians to the rank of Messiah.

Robinson's view presents two exegetical problems. First, there is imposed on the passage a rigid chronological structure such as is unwarranted from the text itself. That Jesus is identified as 'the foreordained Messiah' is clear. But the temporal question as to when that messianic ordination was revealed or is to be revealed is not treated. One could just as well read the verse as 'that he may send the foreordained Messiah *again* (understanding πάλιν to be in mind) to you', as 'that he may send the foreordained and *future* (as Robinson reads it) Messiah to you'. Secondly, such an interpretation as Robinson proposes makes Luke appear incredibly naïve in placing two distinct and differing christologies side by side; for in Acts 3.18, the Messiah of God (τὸν χριστὸν αὐτοῦ) is identified as the one who suffered, whereas Robinson would have us believe that in Acts 3.19–21 Luke also inserts an affirmation

---

84 J. A. T. Robinson, 'The Most Primitive Christology of All?', *JTS*, VII (1956), pp. 177–89 (also in *Twelve New Testament Studies* [1962], pp. 139–53). Bultmann argued that 'in the earliest Church, Jesus' Messiahship was dated from the resurrection' (*Theology of the New Testament*, I, p. 27); though it was only 'as the coming Messiah' that he was originally so ascribed (*ibid.*, I, pp. 33–7). F. Hahn has gone further in asserting that originally Messiahship had nothing to do with Easter but only with the delay of the *parousia* (*Christologische Hoheitstitel*, pp. 179–89).

that messiahship is only to be looked for in the future. To argue that Luke included Acts 3.19–21 only to refute it by the preface of Acts 3.18 is absurd. He could better have done that by omitting it. And to say that he did not recognize the discrepancy is to make him astonishingly gullible. Robinson has detached Acts 3.19–21 from its context, and thus feels at liberty to impose temporal strictures upon it at that point where it is ambiguous when detached from its context. But Luke intended it to be read in context. And when read in context, the passage sets up no contradictory messianology – though it may not be as precise of itself as we might wish.

We must therefore conclude that conviction regarding the present messiahship of Jesus stems from the earliest stratum of Christian understanding. The evidence indicates that Jesus was considered by the earliest believers to be the Messiah promised of old, and that he was proclaimed as such by the earliest Jewish Christians.

In so concluding, we are faced with the question of how the earliest Christians came to this conviction when Jesus did not conform to current messianic expectations and when he had himself evidenced a real reserve on a number of occasions in regard to the title. W. C. van Unnik suggests that Luke gives us the key to the answer in 4.18ff. of his Gospel and Acts 10.38 wherein Jesus is identified as the one anointed by God with the Spirit; that is, that the disciples took their cue as to Jesus' character from his application of Isa. 61.1f. to himself and the evident anointing of the Spirit upon him during his ministry.[85] And as a minimal statement this seems beyond dispute. More, however, can be said than this. For while the reserve of Jesus to the title is pronounced in the Gospel portrayals, these same narratives, as I have argued above, also present Jesus as being conscious of his own messiahship during his ministry, having given some hints of it in his actions and teachings, and on a few occasions implicitly, at least, accepting the ascription. Along with E. G. Jay, 'we find it too great a psychological improbability to suppose that the early Church, or any member, or group of members of it, invented a christology which attributed to Jesus a status of which he had given them no hint and had even denied'.[86] The evidence from the New

---

[85] W. C. van Unnik, 'Jesus the Christ', *NTS*, VIII (1962), pp. 113–16.
[86] E. G. Jay, *Son of Man, Son of God,* p. 31.

Testament gives reason to believe, in fact, that Jesus' teaching about his person and mission had provided something for the resurrection to authenticate.

Most important in the establishment of Jesus as Messiah in the consciousness of the earliest Christians, however, was the fact that God raised Jesus from the dead. In Acts 2.22–35, while acknowledging heavenly attestation during his earthly ministry, Peter is reported as centring his attention upon the fact that God 'raised him up', with the conclusion being: 'Therefore, let all the house of Israel know assuredly that God has made (ἐποίησεν) him both Lord and Christ.'[87] In I John 5.6, this pattern of an open declaration only after the completion of the redemptive task is reflected in the words: 'This is he who came by water and blood, Jesus Christ; not in the water only, but in the water and the blood.'[88] A closely connected concept to that of Messiah is that of God's 'Son', or the 'Son of God', as is now clearly seen from the pesher comment on II Sam. 7.14 in 4Q Florilegium.[89] In Acts 13.33–37, quoting particularly Ps. 2.7, and in the pre-Pauline portion of Rom. 1.3f., the sonship of Jesus is proclaimed as having been 'declared' by the resurrection from the dead,[90] which, because of this association of concepts, has an obvious bearing on the theme of the messiahship of Jesus.

Christian conviction regarding Jesus as the Messiah arose, therefore, from a number of lines of converging evidence climaxing in the testimony of an event: (1) Jesus' application of Isa. 61.1f. to himself and his ministry (Luke 4.18ff.), (2) the manifestation of the Spirit's working in the earthly life of Jesus (e.g., Acts 2.22; 10.38), (3) the witness of the Spirit to the character of Jesus as the Anointed One of God (e.g., Matt. 16.17), (4) the

---

[87] Acts 2.36, understanding ἐποίησεν as an open avowal of the fact now that the function had been accomplished.

[88] Somewhat less direct, though still of significance here, are certain christological affirmations in the Letter to the Hebrews. In Heb. 2.10 it is stated that the 'pioneer of salvation' was made 'perfect through suffering'; and in Heb. 5.8f. the picture is of a Son who 'learned obedience through what he suffered', and thus was 'made perfect' and has become 'the source of eternal salvation'. And this thought of the necessity of suffering and the fulfilment of his assigned task in order in some way to bring about the complete perfection of Jesus seems to be reflected in Heb. 2.14; 4.15; and I Peter 4.1 as well.

[89] See below, p. 95

[90] Understanding τοῦ ὁρισθέντος υἱοῦ θεοῦ as 'defined', 'marked out', 'designated', or 'declared' the Son of God, not 'became'.

qualified acceptance of the title Messiah by Jesus on certain occasions (e.g., Matt. 16.17; John 4.26), (5) explicit messianic identifications in the post-resurrection ministry (Luke 24.26, 46) and, pre-eminently, (6) the resurrection of Jesus from the dead (Acts 2.24–26; 13.33ff.; Rom. 1.4).

Jesus as Messiah was a conviction shared by all Christians of the first century and, as will be seen in what follows, 'became more or less the crystallization point of all New Testament Christological views'.[91] It cannot be labelled as distinctive to early Jewish Christianity alone, for χριστός as a title as well as a name was carried on in the Gentile mission of the first century as well. But it must be noted that while 'Messiah' was not a term unique to the Christian community of Jerusalem and Palestine, it was stressed in early Jewish Christian circles in a manner which finds no parallel in Paul's letters, Mark's Gospel, or Luke's writings where not reporting the Jewish Christian ministry. As noted above, the titular use of χριστός is dominant in the book of the Acts, the First Gospel, the Fourth Gospel, and to a lesser extent is strong in the Letter to the Hebrews and the second part of I Peter. Evidently the rationale for this emphasis upon Jesus as the Messiah in only certain portions of the New Testament is because it was in the circles reflected or addressed in these writings that the title could be understood, and only there that it really mattered. The relative primitiveness of nomenclature, of course, has no necessary implications for the relative priority of date for the writings in question; at least, not for their chronological relation to other writings of the first century. But it does indicate a cycle of interest and outlook: a Jewish Christian milieu for which the title Messiah-Christ was highly significant.

Logion 47 of the Gospel of Philip is interesting in this regard:

The apostles who were before us called him thus: Jesus the Nazorean, the Messiah; that is, Jesus the Nazorean, the Christ. The last name is Christ, the first is Jesus, that in the midst is the Nazarene. Messiah has two meanings, both Christ and the measured. Jesus in Hebrew is the redemption. Nazara is the truth. The Nazarene accordingly is the truth. Christ is measured. The Nazarene and Jesus are they who have been measured.[92]

[91] O. Cullmann, *Christology of the New Testament,* p. 111.
[92] Cf. also Logion 19.

In a Greek milieu the title Messiah-Christ very soon became unintelligible, and under gnostic influence Jesus as the revealer of truth received exclusive emphasis. But the Gospel of Philip, rooted as it is in a Jewish subsoil and probably independent of the canonical Gospels, still preserves the memory of what χριστός originally meant – even though it does it in very garbled fashion and even though it prefers to use it as a name and present for it a decidedly secondary etymology.

DISPLACEMENT OF SON OF MAN

There has been a good deal of discussion in scholarly circles of late regarding the expression 'Son of Man' in the New Testament.[93] And while many different proposals have been made, two opinions on the subject have become dominant:

1. That there existed in pre-Christian Jewish thought a generally well-defined concept of a transcendent redeemer figure, spoken of as the Son of Man, whose coming to earth as Judge would be a feature of the drama of the End Time.

2. That the title Son of Man was not a self-designation of Jesus, but was applied to him by the early church through a series of misconceptions and became the foundational motif in the various early christologies; the few authentically dominical son-of-man sayings in the Gospels refer not to Jesus but to a future apocalyptic figure.

Despite the widespread propagation of these views, however, much can be said to the contrary and needs to be said by way of clarification.

In Pre-Christian Jewish Thought. In dealing with the Son of Man in Jewish thought, the first question of importance has to do with the identification of pre-Christian source materials, particularly with the relation of Dan. 7, I Enoch 37–71 and IV Ezra 13 to the subject at hand. The monographs of Oscar Cullmann, H. E. Tödt, A. J. B. Higgins, Ferdinand C. Hahn, and Reginald H. Fuller, together with articles by P. Vielhauer and Eduard Schweizer – to name only a prominent and representative few of recent vintage – begin on the premiss that I Enoch 37–71 (the 'Similitudes' or 'Parables') and IV Ezra 13, together with Dan. 7,

---

[93] For surveys of current discussion, see I. H. Marshall, 'The Synoptic Son of Man Sayings in Recent Discussion', *NTS*, XII (1966), pp. 327–51 and F. H. Borsch, *The Son of Man in Myth and History* (1967), pp. 21–54.

represent pre-Christian Jewish expectations regarding the Son of Man as the eschatological agent of redemption.[94]

A major difficulty with such a view is that to date there is no evidence for the pre-Christian nature of Book II (chs. 37–71) of Ethiopic Enoch, and it is precarious to deduce the existence of a firm son-of-man concept in the intertestamental period from Dan. 7 and IV Ezra 13 alone. As J. Y. Campbell points out, 'most of the extant manuscripts of the Ethiopic Enoch belong to the eighteenth century; none can be confidently dated earlier than the sixteenth' – and even if R. H. Charles' guess be accepted that the Ethiopic version was translated in the sixth or seventh centuries, or F. C. Burkitt's that this occurred as early as the fourth, we are still centuries removed from pre-Christian times.[95] It is for this reason that C. H. Dodd and a few British scholars influenced by him at this point have refused to erect any arguments on evidence drawn from the Similitudes,[96] though there seems to be little reticence in accepting an early Jewish provenance for these chapters on the Continent and in the United States. In addition, the caves of Qumran, while producing portions corresponding to every other chapter in Ethiopic Enoch, have yielded no fragments from the Similitudes themselves (i.e., I Enoch 37–71).[97]

---

[94] O. Cullmann, *Christology of the New Testament*, pp. 139–44; H. E. Tödt, *The Son of Man in the Synoptic Tradition* (ET 1965); A. J. B. Higgins, *Jesus and the Son of Man;* F. Hahn, *Christologische Hoheitstitel*, pp. 13–53; R. H. Fuller, *Foundations of New Testament Christology*, pp. 34–43; P. Vielhauer, 'Gottesreich und Menschensohn', *Festschrift für Günther Dehn*, ed. W. Schneemelcher (1957), pp. 51–79; *idem*, 'Jesus und der Menschensohn', *ZTK*, LX (1963), pp. 133–77; *idem*, 'Ein Weg der neutestamentlichen Theologie. Prüfung der Thesen Ferdinand Hahns', *EvangT*, XXV (1965), pp. 24–72; E. Schweizer, 'Der Menschensohn', *ZNW*, L (1959), pp. 185–209; *idem*, 'The Son of Man', *JBL*, LXXIX (1960), pp. 119–29; *idem*, 'The Son of Man Again', *NTS*, IX (1963), pp. 256–61. This is also the position of F. H. Borsch, *The Son of Man in Myth and History*, though expressed more guardedly and hesitantly.

[95] J. Y. Campbell, 'The Origin and Meaning of the Term Son of Man', *JTS*, XLVIII (1947), p. 146.

[96] C. H. Dodd, *According to the Scriptures*, pp. 116f.; *idem*, *Fourth Gospel*, pp. 242f. A variation on Dodd's thesis appears in Miss M. D. Hooker's, *The Son of Man in Mark* (1967), where the Jewish provenance and early date of the Similitudes is maintained (pp. 47f.), parallel ideas to Son of Man in other pre-Christian Jewish writings are traced (pp. 49–74), yet the supremacy of the corporate figure in Dan. 7 as the background for Jesus' usage is insisted upon (esp. pp. 11–32, 189–98).

[97] J. T. Milik, *Ten Years of Discovery*, p. 33; J. C. Hindley, 'Towards a Date for the Similitudes of Enoch', *NTS*, XIV (1968), pp. 553f., citing a private communication from Matthew Black.

This fact has compelled some to suggest a first- or second-century AD date for the composition of the Enochian Similitudes and to view them as representative of some facet of early Jewish Christianity.[98]

Admittedly, to argue from (1) omissions in the extant Greek portions and (2) the absence of these chapters in the evidence to date from the Dead Sea materials is to argue only negatively. Such a negative argument, of course, suffers from the inability of positive demonstration. It is also a tenuous argument in the sense that a great amount of material from Qumran has yet to be identified and published, some of which may present evidence to the contrary. But as matters stand today, it is a negative argument of sufficient import as to be highly significant. And it should give pause and cause for concern to those who erect upon the basis of the Similitudes such imposing son-of-man christologies as are becoming fashionable today (though, sadly, it seems to have had only minimal effect). It is not sufficient to say, as does Reginald Fuller, that 'while . . . we cannot be sure that the Similitudes themselves antedate the Christian era, we may treat them with some degree of confidence as evidence for a tradition in Jewish apocalyptic which is pre-Christian';[99] or to argue that since it cannot be definitely proved that they are not pre-Christian, we may continue to use them as such, as does A. J. B. Higgins.[100] The evidence to date is of such a nature as to make the employment of I Enoch 37–71 in reconstructing pre-Christian thought precarious indeed, and to suggest that the confidence with which these chapters are employed in current discussion as representing early Jewish apocalypticism is supported more by dogmatic assertion than critical judgment. In fact, of the three alleged sources commonly employed today in explication of the term Son of Man (I Enoch 37–71; IV Ezra 13; Dan. 7), only Dan. 7 is demon-

[98] E.g., J. T. Milik, *Ten Years of Discovery*, pp. 33f.; F. M. Cross, Jr., *Ancient Library of Qumran*, pp. 202f.

[99] R. H. Fuller, *Foundations of New Testament Christology*, pp. 37f. F. H. Borsch, *Son of Man in Myth and History*, also takes this attitude towards the Enochian Similitudes – and extends it to a host of other materials from differing times and localities, which is a major methodological fault. Conversely, R. Leivestad, 'Der Apokalyptische Menschensohn ein Theologisches Phantom', *Annual of the Swedish Theological Institute*, VI (1968), pp. 49–105, finds no apocalyptic son-of-man concept in pre-Christian Jewish thought, not even in Dan. 7.13 – which is certainly a case of 'overkill'.

[100] A. J. B. Higgins, *Jesus and the Son of Man*, pp. 15f., 198f.

strably pre-Christian. Written by a quietistic Pharisee, IV Ezra almost certainly stems from the latter part of the first Christian century. And the Similitudes of Enoch was probably written about the same time, or even later; possibly by a Jewish Christian with roots of some type in Jewish Essenism.

The second question of significance in dealing with the Son of Man in the thought of pre-Christian Judaism has to do with the use of the expression in rabbinic circles of the day; for since the cumbersome and rather inelegant ὁ υἱὸς τοῦ ἀνθρώπου hardly gives indication of having been coined in a Greek milieu, its basis must be sought in its Aramaic parallel בר אנש or the definite form בר נשא (though the determinate aleph is weak in Aramaic). While a great deal of effort has been expended on the use of בר אנש and בר נשא in the Targums and rabbinic writings, with often quite varied results, Géza Vermès' treatment is to date most comprehensive and convincing.[101] Picking up from Matthew Black's citation of Genesis Rabbah 7.2, Vermès goes on to quote a number of passages from the Jerusalem and Babylonian Gamaras, the Midrashim, the Targums, and 1Q Genesis Apocryphon in demonstration of the fact that, despite assertions to the contrary, בר אנש, in both its indefinite and definite forms, was used by the rabbis and (presumably) other Jews of the time of Jesus for the generic idea of man and as a deferential circumlocution for the first person pronoun 'I'. In addition, he points out that neither form of בר אנש was ever employed among the rabbis with messianic import or as a title of eschatological significance, even though Dan. 7.13 had been accepted in Judaism as a messianic text; and from this concludes that the expression itself was never employed by Jews as a messianic title – nor was it really suitable for such use.

Vermès' evidence is extremely important, and deserves to carry the day in demonstration of the facts that בר אנש was used by the rabbis (1) in the generic sense of 'a man' or 'any man', (2) as a circumlocution for 'I' when the speaker wanted 'to avoid undue or immodest emphasis on himself' or when he was 'prompted by fear or by a dislike of asserting openly something disagreeable in relation to himself',[102] and (3) without messianic

---

[101] G. Vermès, 'The Use of בר נשא/בר נש in Jewish Aramaic', Appendix E in M. Black, *An Aramaic Approach to the Gospels and Acts,* 3rd ed. (1967), pp. 310–28; see pp. 311–15 for a survey of work on the Aramaic expression.
[102] *Ibid.,* p. 320.

content or suggestion. What Vermès has failed to do, however, is to show that בר אנש was never employed in pre-Christian times, apart from the rabbis, as a title with messianic import, and that it was unsuitable for such a use within Palestine. This, of course, he assumes on the basis of his very thorough study of the rabbinic materials. But the presence of the term בר אנש in Dan. 7.13 has every appearance of just such a titular usage, meaning more than just that the figure looked human[103] – despite the rabbis' failure (and undoubtedly Judaism's failure generally) to pick it up. And the Gospels' portrayal of Jesus' employment indicates that at least on occasions he saw it as a suitable vehicle for the expression of a messianic consciousness. As Matthew Black has said, both earlier and in response to Vermès here: 'No term was more fitted both to conceal, yet at the same time to reveal to those who had ears to hear, the Son of Man's real identity.'[104]

In his work on Old Testament 'testimonia' portions employed in the New Testament, C. H. Dodd has shown that 'there are three passages in Scripture containing the term "Son of Man", and three only, which can be *proved* to have been employed for testimonies' and which can be used with any degree of confidence to elucidate the New Testament at this point: Pss. 8 and 80 and Dan. 7.[105] In Ps. 8.4–6, Son of Man, in parallelism with man, 'is simply man as such, man in his weakness and insignificance, yet "visited" by God, and by his merciful ordinance "crowned with glory and honour".'[106] In Ps. 80.17–19 it is the nation 'Israel, under the similitude of a human figure, humiliated into insignificance until visited by God and raised to glory'.[107] Though Pss. 8 and 80 are assuredly pre-Christian, it is only Dan. 7 which employs the term as a title and in a messianic sense, and which is therefore of significance here. Many have, of course, pointed to the recurrent son-of-man expression in the prophecy of Ezekiel as the basis for the use of the title in the Gospels.[108] But, again, C. H. Dodd has

---

[103] The wording 'one like a Son of Man' (כבר אנש) need not be damaging to a titular use in Dan. 7.13. The Greek equivalent is certainly understood as a title in Rev. 1.13 and 14.14, yet spoken of as ὅμοιον υἱὸν ἀνθρώπον. Cf. also the use of ὁμοίωμα in Phil. 2.7 and of ἀφομοιόω in Heb. 7.3.

[104] M. Black, *Aramaic Approach*, p. 329; see also pp. 328–30.

[105] C. H. Dodd, *According to the Scriptures*, p. 117.   [106] *Ibid.*   [107] *Ibid.*

[108] E.g., W. A. Curtis, *Jesus Christ, the Teacher* (1943), pp. 135–43; G. S. Duncan, *Jesus, Son of Man* (1947), pp. 145f.; A. Richardson, *An Introduction to the Theology of the New Testament* (1958), pp. 20f., 128ff.; E. M. Sidebottom, *The Christ of the Fourth Gospel* (1961), pp. 73–8.

shown that while 'Ezekiel may no doubt have been in the minds of early Christians, . . . proof that it was so is lacking in the New Testament. Ezekiel does not appear to have been a primary source of testimonies.'[109]

In laying sole dependence upon Daniel in understanding the titular use of Son of Man in pre-Christian Jewish thought, we cannot continue to interpret the seemingly enigmatic figure of Dan. 7 by the categories of I Enoch 37–71. Using the Enochian Similitudes to explicate Daniel's Son of Man, most scholars today assert that the one like a Son of Man in Dan. 7 is a transcendent and glorified redeemer figure who is exalted above all sufferings. To this, however, C. F. D. Moule has pertinently remarked:

But the fact remains that in Dan. 7.21, 25, the specially agressive 'horn' on the beast's head 'made war with the saints, and prevailed over them' and was destined to 'wear out the saints of the Most High'; and it is precisely with these saints of the Most High that the Son of Man is identified. It is irrelevant that this interpretation of the Son of Man vision is a secondary interpretation [as at times asserted]: all that concerns the present investigation is that it was in Dan. 7 as Jesus and his disciples knew it – and I know of no evidence to the contrary. But, if so, the Son of Man, in the only document known to have been available then, stands for a loyal, martyr-group who are brought to glory and vindicated *through suffering*.[110]

Whether we are to understand the title in Dan. 7 in a strictly individualistic sense or along the lines of corporate personality is not principally the point at issue here. What is the point is that while Dan. 7.13f. indeed speaks of the glorification of the Son of Man, it is in context a glorification and vindication through

---

[109] C. H. Dodd, *According to the Scriptures*, esp. p. 117n. The proposal of E. Schweizer that Ps. 22 and Wisd. Sol. 2–5 are the pivotal passages here ('The Son of Man', *JBL*, LXXIX [1960], p. 128) is refuted in my discussion which follows.

[110] C. F. D. Moule, in review of H. E. Tödt's *Son of Man in the Synoptic Tradition* in *Theology*, LXIX (1966), p. 174. On a suffering motif in Dan. 7 and Ps. 80, see also W. D. Davies, *Paul and Rabbinic Judaism*, p. 280; C. H. Dodd, *According to the Scriptures*, p. 117; E. Best, *Temptation and Passion*, pp. 163f. On the corporate nature of Daniel's 'Son of Man', see also T. W. Manson, 'The Son of Man in Daniel, Enoch and the Gospels', *BJRL*, XXXII (1950), pp. 171–93; M. D. Hooker, *Son of Man in Mark*, pp. 13f., *passim*. One need not see in the son-of-man image the sole source for a suffering christology in the New Testament, as Moule and Hooker tend to do, to appreciate the glorification through suffering motif of Dan. 7.

suffering. Both aspects of (1) humiliation and suffering, on the one hand, and (2) vindication and glory, on the other, are signalled by the expression Son of Man in the one passage in pre-Christian Jewish literature which employs the term as a title.[111] And this is of immense significance for its employment in the New Testament, even though late Judaism made nothing of the term itself in its eschatological expectations and could not reconcile the seeming paradox to which in its titular use it pointed.

As a Self-Designation of Jesus. Since Bultmann, it is commonly asserted that (1) Jesus never employed the expression Son of Man of himself, (2) Jesus only used the title in regard to a coming apocalyptic figure who would vindicate his own earthly ministry at some time in the future and with whom he would be associated in some manner, (3) it was the early church which first applied the title to Jesus, first in an apocalyptic manner identifying him with the coming Son of Man and then to Jesus himself in his earthly ministry and in his suffering, and (4) all evidence to the contrary must be discounted as being *vaticinia ex eventu.*[112] But though this line of argument is convincing on its own presuppositions, it runs roughshod over *prima facie* interpretations of the evidence and bases itself upon hypothetical reconstructions in favour of a more normal reading of the data. We must not deny that there were theological motives and tendencies at work in the composition of the Gospels, so that the reporting of the words of Jesus was conditioned in each case by the author's background, interests, purpose, and audience. But we handle the evidence much too loosely if we interpret the records as indicating the exact reverse of what they purport. 'The Gospels', as Borsch rightly insists, 'do not offer it [Son of Man] to us as one title among many; they clearly state that this is the designation of which Jesus spoke, and spoke consistently, as most revelatory of his work.'[113]

The term Son of Man occurs eighty-one times in the Gospels, sixty-nine of them in the Synoptic Gospels. And with just two

[111] Cf. G. H. Dalman, *The Words of Jesus* (ET 1909), pp. 264–6; E. Best, *Temptation and Passion,* p. 164.

[112] R. Bultmann, *Theology of the New Testament,* I, pp. 29–31, 49. For detailed expositions, see the treatments by Tödt, Higgins, Hahn, and Fuller cited above. For an extension of the position beyond the guidelines laid out by Bultmann, see Vielhauer (cited above) and H. M. Teeple, 'The Origin of the Son of Man Christology', *JBL,* LXXXIV (1965), pp. 213–50.

[113] F. H. Borsch, *Son of Man in Myth and History,* p. 16.

exceptions, Luke 24.7 (where the angel quotes Jesus' words) and John 12.34 (where the people ask Jesus regarding his use of the term) – neither of which are true exceptions since both reflect Jesus' own usage – all of the occurrences are attributed to Jesus himself. In no instance is the title recorded as given to Jesus by others, nor is it employed in any explanatory manner by the Evangelists themselves. Furthermore, it is found in all the strata of the tradition: in Mark, in the non-Marcan material common to Matthew and Luke (Q), in the material peculiar to Matthew (M), and in the material peculiar to Luke (L). Apart from the Gospels, it appears only in the quotation of Ps. 8.4–6 in Heb. 2.6–8, on the lips of the dying Stephen in Acts 7.56,[114] and in the parabolic description of the exalted Jesus in Rev. 1.13 and 14.14. It is only in the latter three cases (Acts 7.56; Rev. 1.13; 14.14), however, that it is employed as a christological title outside of the Gospels. On the face of it, therefore, it would seem that there is a widely based tradition that Jesus used the term of himself and little evidence that there was any extensive use of Son of Man as a christological title on the part of Christians during the first century.

The Bultmannian position which assigns the title exclusively to the eschatological hope is unconvincing. The devotees of this view may justly be asked: Why should the church have been so careful to insert the title Son of Man into the words of Jesus alone, when (as the Bultmannians assert) it really represented their christology and not his? And further: Why were Christians so circumspect as to preserve such a saying as that of Luke 12.8 (where Jesus supposedly distinguishes between himself and the coming Son of Man) when for them (as the Bultmannians acknowledge) there was no such distinction between Jesus and the Son of Man?[115]

The title, as Ernest Best points out, 'is varied very little by Matthew and Luke in their adoption of the passages in which it occurs in Mark', which suggests 'a particular reverence for it' and supports the conclusion that 'it was continued because it lay deep in the tradition'.[116] We cannot, therefore, speak of the Gospels'

---

[114] Though P[74] reads τοῦ θεοῦ for τοῦ ἀνθρώπου. G. D. Kilpatrick suggests that this stems from a date older than the scribe of P[74] and may therefore be more than a secondary reading ('Acts vii. 56: Son of Man?', *TZ*, XXI [1965], p. 209).

[115] Rephrasing slightly the question put by E. Schweizer, 'Son of Man Again', *NTS*, IX (1963), p. 257n.

[116] E. Best, *Temptation and Passion*, p. 162.

use of Son of Man as being simply editorial. It may have had meaning for the Evangelists, or it may have been almost as ambiguous to them as when Jesus first used it. But though it was not a current designation for Jesus in their circles at the time of writing, the Evangelists received it and preserved it – probably in large measure because they did not know to what other title they might change it.[117]

Son of Man as a title seems to have been enigmatic in meaning and ambiguously understood in Jesus' day. It is not found in the Qumran literature to date as a title, and only by association with the 'Servant of Yahweh' or the generic idea of 'Man', understood as a symbolic appellation of messianic import, can the concept be inferred to have had some currency within popular Judaism.[118] The question, 'Who is this Son of Man?' of John 12.34, indicates something of this ambiguity in the peoples' inability to apprehend Jesus' preference for this title rather than that of Messiah.

Perhaps, as Eduard Schweizer and Howard Marshall suggest, Jesus 'adopted the term Son of Man just because it was an ambiguous term, revealing as well as hiding'.[119] Though in view of his explicit reference to Daniel's 'abomination of desolation' in the Olivet Discourse (Matt. 24.15; Mark 13.14) and his allusions to the imagery of Dan. 7.13, first in that same discourse (Mark 13.26, par.) and later in his reply before the Sanhedrin (Mark 14.62, par.) – and both with explicit reference to the Son of Man – it can hardly be doubted that Dan. 7 was the source upon which Jesus based his own understanding and to which he pointed in his use of the term.[120] Evidently, as Gustaf Dalman insisted, what he meant to say in using this expression of himself was 'that He was

[117] Ibid., p. 163.

[118] On 'Servant of Jahweh', see M. Black, 'Servant of the Lord and Son of Man', SJT, VI (1953), pp. 1–11; F. F. Bruce, Biblical Exegesis in the Qumran Texts (1960), pp. 63–6, 87. On 'Man', see O. Cullmann, Christology of the New Testament, pp. 141f. (on 1QS 4.20–23); G. Vermès, Scripture and Tradition (1961), pp. 56–66 (on targumic treatments of Jer. 31.21 and Zech, 6.12, on 1QH 3.7–10 and 1QS 4.20–23, and on the LXX translations of II Sam. 23.1 and Num. 24.7, 17).

[119] E. Schweizer, 'Son of Man', JBL, LXXIX (1960), p. 128. Cf. also idem, 'Son of Man Again', NTS, IX (1963), p. 359; I. H. Marshall, 'The Divine Sonship of Jesus', Interp., XXI (1967), p. 93; idem, 'Synoptic Son of Man Sayings', NTS, XII (1966), pp. 350f.

[120] In this regard, I Enoch 37–71 and IV Ezra 13 are comparable: I Enoch 71 has clear references to Dan. 7; I Enoch 46 is virtually a midrash on Dan. 7.13; and IV Ezra 13.3 is dependent on Dan. 7.13 as well.

that one in whom this vision of Daniel was to proceed to its realisation'.[121] In so doing, he possessed a title which combined both the elements of suffering and of glory – thus signalling both aspects of his redemptive ministry. And in effect, by reaching back to the enigmatic figure of Dan. 7, he sought to explicate his person and redemptive ministry in terms of glorification and suffering in fulfilment of the prophet's vision. As Dalman has said: 'In using the title He purposely furnished them with a problem which stimulated reflection about His person, and gave such a tendency to this reflection that the solution of the problem fully revealed the mystery of the personality of Jesus.'[122]

In the Early Church. That Son of Man was not a common christological designation in the early church is indicated by its almost complete absence in Acts and the letters of the New Testament, notwithstanding a *Gemeindetheologie* understanding of the Gospels to the contrary. And this was probably so for at least two reasons.

First, the title could not be understood in the Greek world other than referring simply to the humanity of Jesus. While the Jewish Christian Gospel of the Hebrews, the Nag Hammadi materials, and the historian Hegesippus as he is quoted by Eusebius retain in varying degrees something of its earlier flavour,[123] the Gentile fathers from Ignatius and Justin 'with one consent, though in variously conceived modes, have seen in this title a reference to the human side in the descent of Jesus'.[124] And this is typical of its reception outside a Jewish milieu. Thus from the Apostolic Fathers to the present, the title, with but few exceptions, has come to be regarded in the dogmatic theology of the church as but the converse of the title Son of God, the one speaking of Jesus' humanity and the other of his divinity. But in the early church it was not so.[125]

[121] G. H. Dalman, *Words of Jesus*, p. 258.

[122] *Ibid.*, p. 259.

[123] See Jerome's report regarding the Gospel of the Hebrews (*NT Apoc.*, I, p. 165); Jesus' words as given in the Gospel of Thomas 86, 106, and the Gospel of Philip 54, 120; the statement of De Resurrectione (Epistle to Rheginus) 44.21–33 that the Son of God was also the Son of Man in order that as the Son of God he might vanquish death and that 'through the Son of Man the restoration into the Pleroma might take place'; and Hegesippus' report of James ascribing the title to Jesus in Eusebius, Eccl. Hist. II, 23.

[124] G. H. Dalman, *Words of Jesus*, p. 253. Cf. Ignatius, Ephesians 20.2; Irenaeus, Contra Heresies V. 21. 3; Barnabas 12.10; Justin, Apology, I. 51.9.

[125] Paul's 'Second Adam' doctrine (Rom. 5.12–21; I Cor. 15.21f., 45–49; Acts 17.31), which was probably introduced into the church in its explicit

Secondly, a son-of-man designation for Jesus in the period between his redemptive sufferings and his coming glory was not strictly appropriate. Just as the title Messiah was not considered entirely fitting until he had completed the work of the Messiah, and was declared to be such by the evident acceptance of his work by God in the resurrection from the dead,[126] so the title Son of Man was not the most suitable in the period between the completion of his redemptive work and the assumption of his full glory. It is only in those portions where suffering and glory are brought together on the part of his people, and Jesus is portrayed as standing with his afflicted saints (i.e., Acts 7.56; Rev. 1.13; 14.14), that he is spoken of in terms of the Son of Man. But these are exceptions in the literature of the early church, and seem to be considered in some sense extensions of Jesus' own sufferings in the experiences of his people and anticipations of his final glory in their vindication.[127]

How then did the church's conviction regarding the messiahship of Jesus give rise to further thought about him and lay the basis for the earliest christology? Well, in the first place, it negated the appropriateness of his own favourite designation of himself during his ministry, displacing a son-of-man ascription in favour of that of Messiah. For the early Christians, Jesus *was* the suffering Son of Man in line with Daniel's representation, and he *would be* the glorified Son of Man who would return to complete the prophetic picture. As C. F. D. Moule observes: 'Half its content was already a thing of the past, and half was – at any rate in the eyes of the early Church – yet in the future. . . . It was naturally assumed that the Church was in a *Zwischenzeit*, between the going and the return; and what relevance has the term Son of Man to that?'[128] The earliest Christians remembered that Jesus preferred to speak of himself as the Son of Man, and thus took

form by the apostle himself (the hymn of Phil. 2.6–11 may presuppose a similar imagery, but does not explicate it), may be a variation of the son-of-man motif. But if so, it only indicates to what extent the son-of-man concept required reconstruction if it were to be understood in a non-Jewish milieu (cf. Schweizer, 'Son of Man', *JBL*, LXXIX [1960], pp. 127–29; W. D. Davies, *Paul and Rabbinic Judaism*, pp. 41ff.).

[126] Cf. above, pp. 71–4.
[127] Cf. C. F. D. Moule, 'Influence of Circumstances on the Use of Christological Terms', *JTS*, X (1959), pp. 256f.
[128] *Ibid.*, p. 257.

pains to record it as on his lips alone. But they took the title Messiah to be the appropriate designation for him in this interim period of redemptive history, and thus refrained for the most part from speaking of him as the Son of Man themselves.

SON OF GOD

Conviction regarding Jesus as the Messiah also incorporated some rather important positive consequences in the formulation of early Christian thought and some rather immediate implications as to the attribution of other titles to him by the church. Of major importance was the ascription of 'Son of God' to Jesus.

In a number of passages, the titles 'Messiah' and 'Son of God' are brought together:

1. In Peter's confession, as given by Matthew and Sinaiticus Mark, the wording is: 'You are the Christ, the Son of (the living) God' (σὺ εἶ ὁ χριστὸς ὁ υἱὸς τοῦ θεοῦ [τοῦ ζῶντος]).[129]

2. Caiaphas' query, as recorded by Matthew and Mark, is: 'Are you the Christ, the Son of God?' (σὺ εἶ ὁ χριστὸς ὁ υἱὸς τοῦ θεου).[130]

3. The demonic recognition of Jesus as 'the Son of God' is said by Luke to have been based upon a knowledge that he was 'the Christ' (σὺ εἶ ὁ υἱὸς τοῦ θεοῦ . . . ὅτι ᾔδεισαν τὸν χριστὸν αὐτὸν εἶναι).[131]

4. Martha's affirmation, as reported by John, is: 'You are the Christ, the Son of God, the One coming into the world' (σὺ εἶ ὁ χριστὸς ὁ υἱὸς τοῦ θεοῦ ὁ εἰς τὸν κόσμον ἐρχόμενος).[132]

5. The Fourth Evangelist explicitly declares his purpose in writing to be that his readers might believe that 'Jesus is the Christ, the Son of God' ('Ιησοῦς ἐστιν ὁ χριστὸς ὁ υἱὸς τοῦ θεοῦ).[133]

6. Paul's preaching in the synagogues of Damascus is represented as focusing on Jesus as 'the Son of God' and Jesus as 'the Christ' (οὗτός ἐστιν ὁ υἱὸς τοῦ θεοῦ . . . οὗτός ἐστιν ὁ χριστός).[134]

There is no reason to assume in the above instances that Son

[129] Matt. 16.16; Mark 8.29. A. Richardson suggests that even 'the Son of the *living* God' may have been a current messianic title (*Introduction to the Theology of the New Testament*, p. 151); cf. W's reading of Mark 8.29.
[130] Matt. 26.63. The reading ὁ υἱὸς τοῦ εὐλογητοῦ of Mark 14.61 is a locution for God. The separation of the titles Christ and Son of God in Luke 22.67–71 is probably to be circumstantially explained.
[131] Luke 4.41.
[132] John 11.27.
[133] John 20.31.
[134] Acts 9.20–22.

of God is used either as a synonym for or to supersede the title Christ,[135] or that by this term the idea of a Messiah has been translated into vocabulary more familiar to the Gentile world.[136] Rather, where the two titles are brought together there is the indication that the writers were aware of their discrete connotations and considered Son of God the logical implication of Messiah – and that they expected these nuances and this relationship to be appreciated by the readers whom they addressed.

Since the flat denial of Dalman and Bousset on the point, the majority of scholars have asserted that Son of God had no messianic associations in pre-Christian Judaism.[137] And even those who have been hesitant to deny so roundly such messianic significance for the term in late Judaism have been able only to argue that possibly it was so used on certain occasions, though they have been at a loss to cite positive and unambiguous evidence to this effect.[138] The reference to 'I and my Son' in I Enoch 105.2 is probably a Christian interpolation.[139] And the significance of the identification of the Messiah as God's Son in IV Ezra 7.28f.; 13.32, 37, 52 and 14.9 has been disputed on the basis of lateness of date and greater affinity to a servant concept than the idea of sonship.[140]

[135] E.g., E. F. Scott, *The Fourth Gospel* (1906), pp. 182f.

[136] E.g., R. Bultmann, *Primitive Christianity in its Contemporary Setting* (ET 1956), pp. 176f. Note, however, W. C. van Unnik's significant counter to this approach in 'Purpose of St. John's Gospel', *Studia Evangelica,* I, pp. 389–91. Cf. also V. H. Neufeld, *Earliest Christian Confessions,* pp. 116f., on the close association of 'the Christ' and 'the Son of God', yet the derivative nature of the title 'the Son of God' in the Johannine *homologia* (though, admittedly, on pp. 70–4 Neufeld somewhat inadvertently tends to equate them, despite his thesis).

[137] G. H. Dalman, *Words of Jesus,* pp. 271f.; W. Bousset, *Kyrios Christos,* pp. 53f. See also E. Huntress, ' "Son of God" in Jewish Writings Prior to the Christian Era', *JBL,* LIV (1935), pp. 117ff.; W. Michaelis, *Engelchristologie im Urchristentum,* pp. 10ff.; V. Taylor, *Person of Christ in New Testament Teaching,* pp. 173f.; W. G. Kümmel, *Heilsgeschehen und Geschichte* (1965), pp. 215f.; J. Jeremias, *The Prayers of Jesus* (ET 1967), p. 37.

[138] Cf., e.g., P. Volz, *Eschatologie der jüdischen Gemeinde,* p. 174; R. Bultmann, *Theology of the New Testament,* I, p. 50; O. Cullmann, *Christology of the New Testament,* pp. 274, 278–82; C. H. Dodd, *Fourth Gospel,* p. 253.

[139] Chapters 105 and 108 are absent in the final section of the sixth-century 'Beatty-Michigan Papyrus', which is thought to be a Greek version quite close to the semitic original (cf. C. Bonner, *The Last Chapters of Enoch in Greek* [1937].)

[140] The thesis of B. Violet is widely accepted (*Die Apokalypsen des Esra und des Baruch in deutscher Gestalt* [1924], pp. 74f.). The concepts represented by παῖς and υἱός, however, are quite indistinguishable at times. Furthermore, these

In the recently discovered 4Q Florilegium, however, the words 'I will be to him a father, and he shall be to me a son' of II Sam. 7.14 are given explicit messianic import in the comment: 'The "he" in question is the Scion of David who shall function in Zion in the Last Days, alongside the Expounder of the Law.' Admittedly, the connection of 'Son' with a nationalistic idea of messiahship as represented in Qumran's understanding of the 'Scion of David' is a feature not paralleled in Christian usage. Nor is this quite a titular use of the term. None the less, it does seem fair to conclude with R. H. Fuller on the basis of this passage that 'son of God *was just coming into use* as a Messianic title in pre-Christian Judaism, and was ready to hand as a tool for the early Christians to use in interpreting Jesus of Nazareth'.[141]

We need not assert that 'Son of God' and 'the Son' find their places in the Gospel narratives only because first placed on the lips of Jesus by the church.[142] Even if we are not permitted an initial appeal to such passages as Matt. 11.27 (cf. Luke 10.22), the οὐδὲ ὁ υἱός clause of Mark 13.32, the parable of the vineyard of Mark 12.1–9 (and par.), the trinitarian formula of Matt. 28.19, or the frequent self-designations in the Fourth Gospel,[143] the evidence from his use of 'Father' for God indicates that divine sonship was the basic datum for Jesus in his ministry.[144] And if Jesus

---

portions must now be restudied in light of the pesher comment on II Sam. 7.14 in 4QFlor.

[141] R. H. Fuller, *Foundations of New Testament Christology*, p. 32.

[142] So F. Hahn (*Christologische Hoheitstitel*, pp. 280–350) and R. H. Fuller (*Foundations of New Testament Christology*, pp. 114f., 164–6, 187, 192–7, 231f.), who argue that the title 'Son of God' was first given to Jesus by the church in a *parousia* context, then applied to his earthly ministry, and finally understood ontologically. O. Cullmann (*Christology of the New Testament*, pp. 278–81) and E. G. Jay (*Son of Man, Son of God*, p. 46) also speak of the possibility that 'Son of God' was put into Jesus' mouth by the church since they can find no evidence for its pre-Christian messianic usage.

[143] On Matt. 11.27, see A. M. Hunter, 'Crux Criticorum – Matt. XI. 25–30 – a Re-appraisal', *NTS*, VIII (1962), pp. 241–9. Whether it be held that Mark 13.32 has been wholly fabricated or partially distorted, it seems scarcely imaginable that the church would have attributed words of ignorance to Jesus even under the most extreme pressure of eschatological disillusionment. That the reading was originally 'Son of Man' is wholly conjectural. In John's Gospel, see 5.19–26; 6.40; 8.35f.; 9.35–37; 10.36; 14.13; 17.1

[144] Cf. T. W. Manson, *The Teaching of Jesus* (1931), pp. 99–115; J. Jeremias, *The Central Message of the New Testament* (1965), pp. 9–30; idem, *The Prayers of Jesus*, pp. 11–65.

spoke of God and to God in such a manner as to indicate that he
was uniquely his Father – which seems beyond doubt from the
data[145] – it is difficult to see why he could not have spoken of
himself as 'the Son' and 'the Son of God' in the manner actually
preserved in the Gospels.[146]

But while 'the evidence strongly suggests that the fundamental
point in Jesus' self-understanding was his filial relationship to
God and that it was from this basic conviction that he undertook
the tasks variously assigned to the Messiah, Son of Man and
Servant of Yahweh, rather than that the basic datum was consciousness of being the Messiah',[147] the primary factor in the
application of the title Son of God to Jesus by the church was the
conviction regarding his status as the Messiah. In the narratives
regarding his youthful delay in the temple, his baptism, and the
temptation in the wilderness,[148] the Gospels make the point that
for Jesus the underlying presupposition of his teaching and
ministry was that of sonship; that is, that it was his realization of
God as his father and of the Father's acknowledgment of him as
Son which was the basic datum of his ministry – even the point of
departure for Satan in two of the three temptations. For Jesus,
then, awareness of his own character preceded and gave insight
into the nature of his mission. But these same Gospels also indicate
that for the disciples it was the conviction of Jesus as Messiah –
weak and fluctuating as it was, and only finally established by the
resurrection – which was the basic datum in their understanding of
Jesus. For them, apprehension of his mission preceded and gave
guidance into the nature of his person.

This diverse epistemic relationship seen in the Gospels is also
reflected in early portions of the Epistles. Paul introduces the
confessional bit incorporated in Rom. 1.3f. by a reference to the

---

[145] Though for an opposing view, see H. Montefiore, 'God as Father in
the Synoptic Gospels', *NTS*, III (1956), pp. 31–46.

[146] Cf. I. H. Marshall, 'Divine Sonship of Jesus', *Interp.*, XXI (1967),
pp. 87–103: where also the claim of Hahn and Vielhauer that 'the Son' and
'Son of God' are two distinct titles with separate provenances is pertinently
demolished (*ibid.*, pp. 87f.).

[147] *Ibid.*, p. 93; see also pp. 98f. Cf. V. Taylor, *Person of Christ in New
Testament Teaching*, p. 186; G. S. Duncan, *Jesus, Son of Man*, pp. 115–17;
and A. J. B. Higgins, *Jesus and the Son of Man*, p. 13, where, though differing
on the titles Messiah and Son of Man, there is agreement that Jesus' sense of
sonship was the basic factor in his own consciousness.

[148] Luke 2.41–50; Mark 1.9–11 and par.; Matt. 4.1–11; and Luke 4.1–13.

status of Jesus as God's Son, and then quotes the confession to the effect that this sonship was declared in the resurrection from the dead. This need not be assumed to be a correction of a traditional formula. The thought is similar in the hymnodic portion of Phil. 2.6–11, where pre-existent union with God and post-resurrection exaltation to lordship are joined. Throughout the New Testament there is no suggestion that the consciousness of the disciples in any way negated the correctness of Jesus' own self-awareness, or that the resurrection in any way altered his essential character. Rather, as in Rom. 1.3f., the resurrection confirmed and manifested an existing reality.[149] In that act, the earliest Christians saw both the culmination of Jesus' messianic function and the validation of his person. In that act, he was declared Messiah in fact. And as Messiah, other ascriptions associated with messiahship were seen to be appropriate as well – chiefly, that of Son of God.

In the literature of Israel, the nation itself and the Jewish people are spoken of in terms of sonship.[150] They were the sons of God in a manner not true of any other nation or people because of their election by God and the establishment of his covenant with them. In that relationship, God pledged himself to them and they were pledged to a response of loving obedience. Together with this corporate understanding of sonship, however, there also exists in the Old Testament the idea of the king, God's anointed representative, as God's Son.[151] Contemporary Old Testament scholarship lays emphasis upon the centrality of the king in the religion of Israel, maintaining that sonship was originally a royal epithet which only took on a corporate significance through a process of democratization. However that may be, in first-century Judaism the ideas of Israel as God's Son and the anointed king as God's Son existed side by side.[152] Furthermore, as we now know from 4Q Florilegium, the category of sonship was beginning to be extended to the Davidic Messiah in at least certain Jewish circles prior to Christianity.

[149] Cf. W. C. van Unnik, 'Jesus the Christ', *NTS*, VIII (1962), p. 108; I. H. Marshall, 'Divine Sonship of Jesus', *Interp.*, XXI (1967), p. 102; E. Schweizer, 'The Concept of the Davidic "Son of God" in Acts and its Old Testament Background', *Studies in Luke-Acts*, ed. L. E. Keck and J. L. Martyn (1966), pp. 186f.

[150] Ex. 4.22f.; Hos. 11.1; Isa. 1.2; 30.1; 63.16; Jer. 3.19–22; Sir. 4.10; Pss. Sol. 13.9; 17.27–30; 18.4; Jub. 1.24f. Cf. also Wisd. Sol. 2.13, 16, 18.

[151] II Sam. 7.14; Ps. 2.7; 89.26f.; 110.3 (LXX).

[152] Cf. B. Gerhardsson, *The Testing of God's Son* (ET 1966), pp. 22f.

It is in the light of this background that the title as used in the New Testament must be seen. 'Son of God' was no alien import, and certainly cannot be interpreted simply in terms of popular religious notions circulating in the hellenistic world. Contrary to the assumption of a hellenistic provenance, it is in the literature of the Jewish mission of the church that the ascriptions 'Son of God' and 'the Son' come most to expression, and not, it must be noted, in that representing the Gentile cycle of witness. It is Matthew among the Synoptists who gives increased prominence to the sonship of Jesus,[153] John who makes this theme the high point of his christology,[154] and Hebrews that devotes more than two chapters to its explication. In comparison, Paul's employment of 'Son of God' only three times and 'the Son' twelve seems rather surprising.[155] Mark and Luke unquestionably believe Jesus to be the Son of God; but with the possible exception of Mark 1.1, only repeat traditional wording. Their omission of the title in Peter's confession[156] and in the rulers' taunt,[157] together with Luke's treatment of the centurion's acclaim,[158] are more likely due to a tendency to downplay distinctive Jewish motifs in the Gentile mission than to an expansionist practice of Matthew.[159]

Undoubtedly the title received elaboration and extension of meaning in its use by Christians during the first century. Under the guidance of the Spirit, the church's understanding certainly grew. But while Son of God very soon came to signify divine nature, it was probably used in a more functional manner by the earliest Jewish believers to denote Jesus' unique relationship with

[153] W. Kümmel points out that a major interest of Matthew's Gospel is 'the proof that Jesus is "the Christ, the Son of the living God" (16.16)' (*Introduction to the New Testament* [ET 1965], p. 83).

[154] In addition to the explicit statement of John 20.31, see I John 4.15 and 5.5. Cf. also John 1.34, 49; 10.36; I John 2.23; 3.23; 5.11f., 13, 20.

[155] Son of God: Rom. 1.4; II Cor. 1.19; Gal. 2.20. The Son (or, his Son): Rom. 1.3, 9; 5.10; 8.3, 29, 32; I Cor. 1.9; 15.28; Gal. 1.16; 4.4, 6; I Thess. 1.10. W. Kramer observes: 'In comparison with the passages in which the titles *Christ Jesus* or *Lord* occur, this is an infinitesimally small figure' (*Christ, Lord, Son of God* [ET 1966], p. 183). Kramer further notes that 'Paul's use of the title *Son of God* depends primarily on external factors, in that it is prompted by what has gone before' (*ibid.*, p. 185).

[156] Mark 8.29 (non-Sinaiticus); Luke 9.20; cf. Matt. 16.16.

[157] Mark 15.30; Luke 23.35; cf. Matt. 27.40, 43.

[158] Luke 23.47; cf. Matt. 27.54; Mark 15.39.

[159] Contra G. Dalman (*Words of Jesus*, pp. 274f.), *et al.* Likewise, the separation of the titles 'Christ' and 'Son of God' in Luke 22.67–71 and Acts 9.20–22 may be similarly understood.

God the Father and his obedience to the Father's will. As Israel and her sons were understood to be uniquely God's own among the peoples of the earth and the anointed king God's Son – and in that relationship pledged to loving obedience – so Jesus as Israel's Messiah, who united in his person both the corporate ideal and descent from David and who exemplified an unparalleled obedience to the Father's will, was the Son of God *par excellence*. That a corporate understanding of sonship was understood to be fulfilled and heightened in Jesus is indicated by the retention in the tradition of the argument of John 10.34–36, where, by means of an *a minori ad maius* inferential approach, Jesus is presented as saying: 'Is it not written in your law, "I said: You are gods"? If those are called gods to whom the word of God came and the Scripture cannot be set aside, why are you charging me, whom the Father consecrated and sent into the world, with blasphemy because I said, "I am the Son of God"?'[160] That a fulfilment in terms of royal sonship was understood as well is signalled in the application of II Sam. 7.14 and Ps. 2.7 to Jesus.[161] In Jesus, therefore, the corporate and royal Son-of-God motifs were brought together, whether or not they were ever so united before.

Further significance was soon to be seen in the title Son of God – especially when joined with other attributions and as the church's reflection was providentially deepened through circumstances. But this more functional appreciation of Jesus' unique relationship with the Father and his complete obedience to the Father's will seems to have been the initial implication and the primal understanding of the earliest Jewish believers in explication of their conviction of Jesus as the Messiah.

GOD'S SALVATION

A significant aspect in Jewish messianology is indicated by the 'messianically charged variants' in the text of Isaiah found at Qumran. The passage in 1QIs^a 51.4f. reads:

---

[160] Cf. also the quotation of Hos. 11.1 in Matt. 2.15.

[161] Acts 13.33; Heb. 1.5; 5.5. Cf. E. Lövestam, *Son and Saviour: A Study of Acts 13.32–37* (ET 1961), who argues in the body of his work that 'the covenant promise to David of permanent dominion for his house and its fulfilment in Jesus the Messiah has a dominating place in Paul's sermon in Acts 13.16ff.' (p. 84), and in an appendix on ' "Son of God" in the Synoptic Gospels' that 'the royal aspect plays a very important role in the designation of Jesus as "God's Son" in the Synoptics' (p. 110).

Attend to me, my people;
 and give ear to me, my nation.
For a Torah from me goes forth,
 and my Judgment (ומשפטי) I will establish as a light for peoples.

Near is my Righteousness (צדקי).
My Salvation (ישעי) has gone forth,
 and *his* arm (וזרועו) will rule the peoples;
in *him* (אליו) the coastlands trust,
 and for *his* arm (זרועו) they wait.

The textual variations concern the three pronouns, where the third person masculine suffix replaces the first person suffix. And in such an alteration there is the suggestion that the covenanters of Qumran understood God's functions and attributes as messianic titles: in this passage, at least, understanding 'my Salvation' as a title for the Messiah, and possibly also viewing 'my Judgment' and 'my Righteousness' in like manner.[162]

'Salvation' (ישע, ישועה) appears as a messianic title in other portions of Jewish literature as well. Jubilees, in speaking of the expectations associated with the tribe of Judah, says: 'In thee shall be the Help of Jacob, and in thee be found the Salvation of Israel.'[163] The Hymns of the Qumran community tell of waiting 'for Salvation to bloom and for a Shoot to grow up to give shelter with might'.[164] The Damascus Document assures the faithful that a 'book of remembrance' is being written for them 'until Salvation and Righteousness be revealed',[165] and that they 'shall see his Salvation'.[166] In the comment on II Sam. 7.14 in 4Q Florilegium where the Davidic Messiah is identified as the 'son' in question, Amos 9.11 is quoted in substantiation and applied to 'him who will arise to bring salvation to Israel' – thus equating 'sonship', the 'Scion of David', and the One 'who will arise to bring salvation to Israel'. The rabbis, too, seem to have appreciated this equation, for in commenting on Gen. 49.11 and Zech. 9.9 – two

---

162 Cf. W. H. Brownlee, 'Messianic Motifs', *NTS*, III (1957), pp. 195–7; D. Barthélemy, 'Le grand rouleau d'Isaie trouvé près de la Mer Morte', *RB*, LVII (1950), p. 548n.; J. V. Chamberlain, 'Functions of God as Messianic Titles', *VT*, V (1955), pp. 366–72.
163 Jub. 31.19.
164 1QH 7. 18f.
165 CDC 20.20 (9.43).
166 CDC 20.34 (9.54).

passages considered by them to be messianically related – 'Salvation' and 'Messiah' are employed interchangeably in the tractate Berakoth.[167] This identification is continued in the Testaments of the Twelve Patriarchs. Testament of Dan 5.10 reads: 'And there shall arise unto you from the tribe of Judah and of Levi the Salvation of the Lord, and he shall make war against Beliar'; and the Test. Naph. 8.3; Test. Gad 8.1, and Test. Jos. 19.11 exhort the people to 'honour' and 'be united to' Levi and Judah, 'for from them shall arise the Salvation of Israel'.[168] In speaking of one Messiah from the two tribes of Levi and Judah, the Testaments of the Twelve Patriarchs evidences, on the one hand, its Essene background and, on the other, its distinction from Jubilees and the earlier Qumran writings. But whether judged strictly Jewish or more probably Jewish Christian in its fuller form, its testimony at this point is important in demonstrating the Jewishness of the ascription 'Salvation' to the Messiah.

From the passages cited above, it seems probable that 'God's Salvation' or simply 'Salvation' were Jewish epithets for the expected Davidic Messiah. It should be noted as well, however, that the ascription is brought into close proximity to the servant motif in the Dead Sea materials. Besides being set in the midst of the Servant Songs themselves, 1QIs^a 51.4–5 has verbal affinities to Isa. 42.1–4 and 49.6.[169] And the description in *Hodayot* 7.18f. recalls the language of Isa. 53.2, as well as that of Isa. 11.1–5.

All this throws considerable light on certain statements in regard to Jesus in the New Testament, particularly in the early chapters of Luke's Gospel, Peter's sermon before the Sanhedrin in Acts, the Fourth Gospel, and that of Matthew – portions reflecting in varying degrees early Jewish Christian expression. In Luke's Gospel, the aged Simeon is presented as saying:

[167] In a lengthy section on dreams, b. Ber. 56b reads: 'If one sees an ass in a dream, he may hope for salvation, as it says, "Behold thy king cometh unto thee; he is triumphant and victorious, lowly and riding upon an ass" (Zech. 9.9)'; b. Ber. 57a: 'If one sees a choice vine, he may look forward to seeing the Messiah, since it says, "Binding his foal unto the vine and his ass's colt unto the choice vine" (Gen. 49.11).' The union of Zech 9.9 and Gen. 49.11 in rabbinic messianic *testimonia* seems to have been traditional.

[168] A late Slavonic recension and two Greek versions, however, read 'one who saves Israel' for 'the Salvation of Israel' at Test. Jos. 19.11; which probably only indicates later inabilities to appreciate this as a title.

[169] Cf. C. H. Dodd, *According to the Scriptures,* p. 91; W. H. Brownlee, 'Messianic Motifs', *NTS,* III (1957), p. 196.

Now let your servant depart in peace, Lord,
   according to your word.
For my eyes have seen your Salvation (τὸ σωτήριόν σου),
   which you have prepared before the face of all people;
a light to lighten the nations,
   and the glory of your people Israel.[170]

Here is a piecing together of quotations from the second part of
Isaiah which not only identifies the Messiah Jesus as God's Salvation but also describes him in servant terminology. In Zechariah's
hymn of praise, the Messiah from the house of David is described
as a 'horn of salvation' (κέρας σωτηρίας) who would save his
people from their enemies.[171] Probably quoting John the Baptist,
Luke also includes a reference to the Messiah as 'God's Salvation'
(τὸ σωτήριον τοῦ θεοῦ).[172] Peter's proclamation that 'there is *the*
salvation (ἡ σωτηρία) in no one else, for there is no other name
under heaven given among men whereby we must be saved'
probably reflects an earlier titular use in Jewish Christian circles,
which in Luke's literary recasting has become somewhat ob-
scured.[173] And possibly Jesus' statement to the Samaritan woman
that '*the* Salvation (ἡ σωτηρία) is of the Jews' likewise stems from
such a titular idea;[174] if so, thereby viewing Jesus as saying only
that it is well-known that the Messiah is to come from Judah,
rather than necessarily imputing to him a nationalistic pride and
soteriological prejudice. Matthew rather cryptically indicates his
awareness of 'Salvation' as a messianic appellative in his quotation
in Matt. 21.5: 'Say to the daughter Zion, behold your king comes
to you.' The quotation is conflated from Isa. 62.11, which reads
'Say to the daughter Zion, Behold your salvation comes', and
Zech. 9.9, which has 'your king comes to you'. Certainly the
affinity between Jesus (ישוע) and Salvation (ישע or ישועה) was
present in his mind when composing his Gospel, as is clear from
the explicit correlation in Matt. 1.21.

   This is not to suggest that the understanding of Jesus as 'God's
Salvation' was reserved for only the Jewish Christian stratum of
early Christian faith. The concept of salvation in Christ was highly

[170] Luke 2.29–32.
[171] Luke 1.68–79.
[172] Luke 3.6.
[173] Acts 4.12.
[174] John 4.22.

important in Paul's preaching as well, as C. A. Anderson Scott
has so ably argued. And this is true, whether or not we go on with
Scott to insist that 'salvation' was the central theme in Paul's
theology.[175] What the evidence cited above does mean, however,
is that the early Jewish believers in Jesus appreciated the fact that
as the Messiah he was the one who both embodied and effected the
salvation promised of old, and that they expressed this consciousness by means of the title 'God's Salvation' in speaking of him.

The idea of the saviourship of the Messiah was not one which
could have arisen only on Gentile soil, being compatible only with a
hellenistic outlook.[176] There were, of course, revisions required
within the church regarding the nature and extent of this salvation
as the gospel went out into the Gentile world. But already expectations concerning the future messianic salvation in pre-Christian
Judaism were beginning to be joined to a servant theme as well as
to nationalistic conceptions, as the Dead Sea Scrolls indicate. What
the early Christians seem to have done, on the basis of their conviction regarding Jesus as the Messiah and their understanding as
derived from him of the nature of that messiahship, was to minimize the political associations in the idea of messianic salvation
and to highlight the spiritual – and thus to ascribe to him the
appellation 'God's Salvation'. Where the apostle Paul is quite
obviously reproducing traditional formulations, there is an emphasis upon the sacrificial obedience and vicarious action of Jesus in
the accomplishment of salvation. Philippians 2.6–11 speaks of his
adoration as based upon the facts of his humiliation and death.
I Corinthians 15.3 says that 'Christ died for ($\acute{v}\pi\acute{\epsilon}\rho$) our sins'; and
I Cor. 11.24 records Jesus' words as being 'this is my body which
is (broken) for you.'[177] Other credal formulations could be cited
as well.[178] But these are sufficient to demonstrate that a spiritual
understanding of messianic salvation in terms of vicarious expia-
tion was part of the warp and woof of primitive confession and
proclamation, and not a later theological development.

[175] C. A. A. Scott, *Christianity According to St. Paul* (1927). On this latter
point, Scott asserts: 'The concept of Salvation provides both a centre and a
framework for all the religious and ethical ideas which have real importance
in Christianity as St. Paul understood it.' Every chapter in Scott's work is
then concerned to explicate this theme in Pauline thought.

[176] See below on 'Saviour', pp. 141–4.

[177] Cf. R. H. Mounce, 'Continuity of the Primitive Tradition: Some Pre-
Pauline Elements in I Corinthians', *Interp.*, XIII (1959), pp. 417–24.

[178] E.g., Rom. 3.24f.; 4.25.

SUFFERING SERVANT

In addition to the explicit christological attributions cited above, conviction regarding Jesus as the Messiah gave rise to other appellations which, for one reason or another, appear in the literature of the Jewish mission of the church in varied measure somewhat muted;[179] that is, there are in the New Testament certain christological affirmations and titles which stem from the Jewish Christian cycle of witness and which are based upon the designation of Jesus as Messiah, but which for various reasons, both theological and circumstantial, do not come to such explicit expression as those previously mentioned. They are none the less important and should be noted. And one of the most significant of these is 'Suffering Servant'.

In the Old Testament and the writings of late Judaism, 'Servant of God' (עבד יהוה, παῖς θεοῦ) is employed in a religious sense as (1) a self-designation of the pious worshipper, (2) an ascription in the plural of pious persons, (3) a collective term for the elect nation Israel, (4) a title of honour for outstanding instruments of God, and (5) a denotation of the Messiah.[180] Jeremias has shown that not only are there passages where the Messiah is spoken of as God's Servant – though always 'only in the form "my servant" and only in the mouth of God', never as a title ascribed by others[181] – but also that Isa. 42.1ff.; 43.10; 49.1ff.; and 52.13ff. were understood messianically in at least certain sectors of Palestinian Judaism during the first centuries BC and AD.[182]

But while there is evidence that the concept of God's servant carried messianic connotations in certain contexts and in certain circles within late Judaism, the accompanying demonstration of a 'suffering servant' motif in these same circles rises no higher than that of tentative possibility. The Talmud, indeed, speaks of suffering sent by God as having atoning efficacy,[183] and there are many indications that 'humility and self-humiliation, or acceptance of

---

[179] I.e., muffled, though not entirely silent.

[180] Cf. W. Zimmerli and J. Jeremias, *The Servant of God* (ET 1957), pp. 13–50.

[181] *Ibid.*, pp. 49f., citing Ezek. 24.23f.; 37.24f.; Zech. 3.8; IV Ezra 7.28f.; 13.32, 37, 52; 14.9; II Bar. 70.9; and the Targums on Isa. 42.1; 43.10; 52.13; Zech. 3.8; Ezek. 34.23f.; 37.24f.

[182] *Ibid.*, pp. 52–78. M. D. Hooker's attempted counter to Jeremias at this point is very inadequate (cf. *Jesus and the Servant* [1959], pp. 53–61)

[183] Cf. W. D. Davies, *Paul and Rabbinic Judaism*, pp. 262–5.

humiliation from God's hand, were expected of a pious man and thought to be highly praiseworthy'.[184] But there is no explicit evidence that this general attitude towards suffering was ever consciously carried over to ideas regarding the Messiah, God's Servant *par excellence*. The Hymns of Thanksgiving from Qumran bring us close to this concept in their association of both suffering and the servant of God with ideas about the coming Messiah(s): (1) that the psalmist (the Teacher of Righteousness himself?) was conscious of being God's servant;[185] (2) that persecution and suffering were the lot of both the Teacher and the community in following what they believed to be the divine will;[186] and (3) that the group at times expressed itself in language taken over from the Servant Songs of Isaiah.[187] But that these ideas were ever connected at Qumran to form a suffering servant messianology is at best very uncertain. It may be that rabbinic Judaism purged a suffering servant interpretation of the Isaian Servant Songs from its own traditions because of the use made of them by Christians, as J. Jeremias suggests.[188] It seems, however, that the lack of clarity regarding such an identification at Qumran – from whence we might reasonably have expected greater precision on this point, had it existed in pre-Christian Judaism – points to the fact that while 'Servant of God' was thought of in some circles within late Judaism in a messianic fashion, a 'suffering servant' conception of the Messiah had not as yet been consciously formed. It may have been in the process of crystalization in some quarters; though it seems that a 'son of David' messianology in most cases negated it.

In the New Testament, Jesus is called God's Servant (ὁ παῖς αὐτοῦ or σου) in Acts 3.13, 26, and 4.27, 30, with both Isaian and Davidic nuances present. And in five passages quotations from the Servant Songs are applied to his person and to aspects of his ministry: (1) Matt. 8.17, quoting Isa. 53.4 regarding his healing ministry; (2) Matt. 12.18–21, quoting Isa. 42.1–4 regarding his avoidance of notoriety; (3) Luke 22.37, quoting Isa. 53.12 regarding his sufferings; (4) John 12.38, quoting Isa. 53.1 regarding the peoples' unbelief; and (5) Acts 8.32f., quoting Isa. 53.7f. regarding

---

[184] E. Schweizer, *Lordship and Discipleship*, p. 23; also pp. 23–31.
[185] 1QH 13.18f.; 14.25; 17.26.
[186] 1QH 8.26f.; cf. 5.15f.; 8.35f.
[187] E.g., 1QH 4.5f. is an expanded paraphrase of Isa. 42.6.
[188] J. Jeremias, *Servant of God,* pp. 75f.

Philip's preaching of the Gospel to the Eunuch.[189] Of these express designations in the New Testament, only Jesus' quotation of Luke 22.37, Philip's text in Acts 8.32f., and possibly Peter's statement in Acts 3.13 directly connect Jesus with a suffering servant concept as well as a servant motif. As has been frequently pointed out, however, in addition, the traditional formulations of I Cor. 15.3–5; 11.23–25; Phil. 2.6–11 and I Peter 2.21–25 – together with such confessional bits as found in Rom. 4.25; 8.32, 34; I Tim. 2.6 and I Peter 3.18 – evidence in varying degrees both a verbal and a conceptual affinity to Isa. 53.[190]

Surveying the passages where Jesus is explicitly identified as God's Servant, where the Isaian Songs are applied to him or to aspects of his ministry, and where the language of confession is based on Isa. 53, there is little doubt that early Christians thought in terms of a servant christology – even a suffering servant christology.[191] Whether or not this was as foundational as some have argued, it was at least an important element in their total conception of Jesus. And judging by the facts that such a conception exists in Paul's letters principally (if not exclusively) in confessional portions and in the writings of the Apostolic Fathers only in prayers and liturgical formulae,[192] it is reasonable to conclude that a suffering servant christology did not arise from a hellenistic milieu but stems from the earliest stratum of Christian conviction.[193]

The understanding of Jesus' messianic ministry in terms of the Suffering Servant seems, in the first place, to be attributable ulti-

[189] Also Paul quotes Isa. 52.15 in Rom. 15.21, though not christologically.
[190] On the 'pre-synoptic stock of traditional formulae' alluding to Isa. 53, see J. Jeremias, *Servant of God*, pp. 88–93, 97f.; *idem, Central Message of the New Testament*, pp. 45–50; A. M. Hunter, *Paul and his Predecessors*, pp. 31, 43f.; O. Cullmann, *Christology of the New Testament*, pp. 64–9.
[191] Miss Hooker's thesis to the contrary (*Jesus and the Servant*) must be faulted on three counts: (1) the atomistic exegesis in which she takes pride; (2) the refusal to see significance in either pre-Christian or Christian messianic uses of Isa. 53 unless they explicate the suffering element; and (3) the total neglect of any interaction with such circumstantial factors as I here propose in explanation of the admittedly almost complete lack of 'sustained interpretation' of Isa. 53 in the New Testament. These criticisms pertain as well to those treatments upon which she builds: W. Bousset, *Kyrios Christos*, pp. 69–72; F. J. Foakes Jackson and K. Lake, *Beginnings*, I, pp. 381–92; H. J. Cadbury, *Beginnings*, V, pp. 364–70; F. C. Burkitt, *Christian Beginnings*, pp. 38f.; and R. Bultmann, *Theology of the New Testament*, I, p. 31.
[192] I Clem. 59.2–4; Didache 9.2f.; 10.2f., 7; Mart. Pol. 14.1–3; 20.2.
[193] Cf. J. Jeremias, *Servant of God*, pp. 83–5, 93f.

mately to Jesus himself, and, in the second, to have been connected
with the church's consciousness of Jesus as the Messiah. Someone
within the Christian movement very early took the original step of
fusing the concepts of Messiah and Suffering Servant, for it does
not appear to have been done prior to the rise of Christianity and
it comes to expression in the earliest stratum of Christian literature. Luke 22.37 directly asserts that it was Jesus, and the Gospels
throughout point back to him. Probably, as Jeremias believes:

Jesus only allowed himself to be known as the servant in his esoteric
and not in his public preaching. Only to his disciples did he unveil the
mystery that he viewed the fulfilment of Isa. 53 as his God-appointed
task, and to them alone did he interpret his death as a vicarious dying
for the countless multitude.[194]

However that may be, it is only on the basis of a suffering servant
self-consciousness that the various elements in the Gospels' portrayal of the ministry of Jesus take on a coherent pattern and find
a sufficient rationale.[195] In addition, the juxtaposition of the
ascriptions 'God's Christ' ($\tau o\hat{v}$ $\chi \rho \iota \sigma \tau o\hat{v}$ $a\vec{v}\tau o\hat{v}$) and 'God's Servant' ($\tau o\hat{v}$ $\pi a\iota \delta \acute{o}s$ $\sigma o\upsilon$) in the prayer of the church in Acts 4.24–30
indicates that the earliest appreciation of Jesus as the Suffering
Servant was inextricably tied up with the conviction regarding
Jesus as the Messiah.[196] While, therefore, a suffering servant interpretation of Jesus' ministry ultimately stemmed from Jesus himself, it seems to have been only established in the church's consciousness on the basis of conviction regarding his messiahship.

Having said all this, we are confronted with the problem with
which every interpreter has wrestled: Why are not the suffering
servant theme and Isa. 53, the only clearly redemptive suffering
servant passage in the Old Testament, employed more explicitly
in the canonical Christian writings? If indeed such an understanding permeates the whole of the Gospels and the earlier New
Testament materials, we would expect the concept, together with
its main Old Testament proof-text, to come to explicit expression

---

[194] *Ibid.*, p. 104.
[195] Cf. H. W. Wolff, *Jesaja 53 im Urchristentum* (1942), esp. pp. 55–70;
W. Manson, *Jesus the Messiah* (1943), pp. 110–13; J. W. Bowman, *The Intention of Jesus* (1945), pp. 32ff.; H. E. W. Turner, *Jesus, Master and Lord* (1953),
pp. 149, 207–11; F. V. Filson, *The Gospel according to St. Matthew* (1960), p. 40.
[196] Note also the designation of Acts 4.27: $\tau \grave{o}\nu$ $\ddot{a}\gamma \iota o\nu$ $\pi a\hat{\iota}\delta \acute{a}$ $\sigma o\upsilon$ '$I\eta \sigma o\hat{v}\nu$, $\grave{o}\nu$
$\ddot{\epsilon}\chi \rho \iota \sigma a s$.

frequently in the Christian literature. Yet only in three passages, Luke 22.37; Acts 8.32f.; and I Peter 2.21–25, is this done directly. 'Here,' as C. F. D. Moule points out, 'is a phenomenon that still awaits explanation.'[197]

It will not do to equate this problem with issues faced in regard to a 'son of man' christology, and suggest that the early church ceased to employ a suffering servant theme for the same reasons.[198] The situations are not at all similar; for while Son of Man appears openly and extensively on the lips of Jesus and almost never as an acclamation or in a comment on the part of the church, suffering servant christology appears in almost equal measure in the thought of both Jesus and the church – though muted in much the same measure for both. Nor is it sufficient to argue that the very antiquity and dominance of servant christology in the early church 'explains the infrequency of express quotations',[199] as though the more prominent a concept the less it will be mentioned. If we are to offer any explanation for this phenomenon, it seems that that explanation must proceed more along circumstantial than theological lines.

In all probability, Paul is of aid here. In I Cor. 1.23 he says quite plainly that the proclamation of Christ as crucified was central to his message, but also acknowledges that this was 'a scandal to Jews' and 'foolishness to Gentiles'. In Gal. 5.11 he speaks of 'the scandal of the cross', which he considers to lie inherent in the Christian gospel. As one trained as a rabbi, Paul well knew the reaction of the Jew to the Christian proclamation of a suffering Messiah.[200] And as a citizen of the empire, he was aware of the seeming absurdity and indignity of such a redemptive figure in the eyes of Greeks. Probably, therefore, ideas current within both Judaism and Grecian religious philosophy regarding the nature of divine salvation must be credited in large measure for the muting of a suffering servant motif in the church. That this understanding of Jesus' messianic office was firmly rooted in the consciousness of early Jewish Christianity seems beyond doubt. But it had little to which it could appeal in contemporary religious thought, and much that stood against it. In view of the circumstances, in fact, it

---

[197] C. F. D. Moule, *Birth of the New Testament,* p. 83.
[198] See above, pp. 91–93.
[199] J. Jeremias, *Servant of God,* p. 98.
[200] Cf. also Rom. 9.33; I Peter 2.8; Luke 20.18.

may even be considered surprising that the church proclaimed a redemption based upon vicarious suffering at all. Its continuance, however, is some indication of the fixity of a suffering servant concept in the consciousness of early believers.

DAVIDIC KING

Firmly associated with messiahship in both Judaism and early Jewish Christianity was the concept of Davidic kingship. In Judaism, in fact, 'son-of-David' expectations tended to be dominant, with other themes subsumed under this motif; while among the early Christians Davidic kingship seems to have been a derivative of messiahship, and appears in the New Testament in a severely muted fashion and in a radically redefined form.

Davidic Origin. In all branches of Jewish opinion there was the settled conviction that the Messiah would be a descendent of David; even born in Bethlehem, the city of David.[201] The promise to David in II Sam. 7.16, 'thy house and thy kingdom shall be established for ever before thee, and thy throne shall be established for ever', underlies the messianic prophecies of Isaiah, Micah, Jeremiah, Ezekiel, and Zechariah; and is explicitly recalled in such diverse intertestamental portions as Sir. 47.11, 22; I Macc. 2.57; and Pss. Sol. 17.5. Even where the Davidic hope was subjugated under a priestly emphasis, it was considered too important to be negated.[202] And rather than displace the traditional belief of a Davidic deliverer, earlier priestly sectarianism developed a two-Messiah theory which could accommodate both their distinctive emphasis and a traditional expectation.[203]

That Jesus was of Davidic descent is a view firmly embedded in Christian tradition from an early date. Paul includes this as part of the common confession of the church in Rom. 1.3, 'descended from David according to the flesh' (τοῦ γεγομένου ἐκ σπέρματος Δαυὶδ κατὰ σάρκα). In Acts 13.23 he is represented as highlighting this as a vital element in his preaching at a synagogue in Antioch of

---

[201] Cf. L. Ginzberg, *The Legends of the Jews,* V (1955), p. 130. C. H. Dodd's doubt that a Bethlehemite birth was part of pre-Christian Jewish messianology and his suggestion that 'it was the fact that Jesus was actually born there that revived in Christian circles interest in a prophecy which played little part in contemporary Jewish thought' (*Fourth Gospel,* p. 91) cannot be maintained.

[202] Cf., e.g., Jub. 31.13–20.

[203] E.g., 1QS 9.11.

Pisidia, and II Tim. 2.8 presents it as a common theme in the apostle's proclamation of the Gospel. The rationale for the genealogies of Matthew and Luke is the conviction that Jesus' ancestry is demonstrably Davidic, as is expressly stated in the caption of Matt. 1.1. Revelation 3.7; 5.5; 22.16, portions which very well may be liturgically derived, refer to Davidic descent as a heavenly ascription and self-designation of the exalted Jesus. And it is taken for granted in Heb. 7.14. It is true, of course, that Mark 12.35–37 (and par.) presents Jesus as challenging the dominant son-of-David understanding of messiahship current in his day. But that is not to say that he repudiated the idea of Davidic descent either for himself or for the understanding of messiahship generally. Certainly the earliest Christians did not take it as such.[204]

It need not be supposed that the church's ascription of messiahship to Jesus made him a descendant of David in their eyes when in fact he was not. Neither the acclaim of Jesus as 'Son of David' on the part of the people nor the Evangelists' recording of that fact are plausible 'had it been believed that He did not satisfy the genealogical conditions implied by the name'.[205] And, as Dalman further pointed out:

As the scribes held to the opinion that the Messiah must be a descendant of David, it is certain that the opponents of Jesus would make the most of any knowledge they could procure, showing that Jesus certainly or probably did not fulfil this condition. And there can be no doubt that Paul, as a persecutor of the Christians, would be well instructed in regard to this point. As he, after mingling freely with members of the Holy Family in Jerusalem, shows that he entertained no sort of doubt on this point, it must be assumed that no objection to it was known to him. Nowhere in the New Testament do we find a single trace of conscious refutation of Jewish attacks, based on the idea that the derivation of Jesus from David was defective.[206]

What the affirmation of Jesus' messiahship did involve and, ultimately, what was effected by the resurrection was a focusing of attention on the lineage of Jesus. This may not seem important to us. And certainly it was not the factor which established commit-

[204] There may be a polemic against a son-of-David messianology in Acts 2.29ff., but that is not the same as a repudiation of Davidic descent. A non-Davidic understanding of Ps. 110.1 first appears in Christian tradition with Barn. 12.10.

[205] G. Dalman, *Words of Jesus*, pp. 319–21.

[206] *Ibid.*, pp. 320f.

ment to Jesus as the Messiah on the part of the earliest believers. But judging by the prominence given it in the confession of Rom. 1.3f., the genealogy of Matthew's Gospel,[207] and the quasi-formula of II Tim. 2.8, Davidic descent was a significant element in the *raison d'être* constructed in hindsight by first-century Jewish Christians and important in the proclamation of the gospel, especially in the Jewish mission. Perhaps a 'seed-of-David' ascription came to be considered to some extent the converse of 'Son of God', so that in union these two appellations represent a 'two-existence Christology'.[208] Probably, however, all that the earliest Jewish believers meant to signal by the inclusion of Davidic descent in their confession was the factor of continuity which exists between the messianology of the Old Covenant and Jesus as the embodiment of the New.

Spiritual Kingship. The Gospels report that Jesus was frequently hailed or spoken of as king: (1) by the Magi in their query to Herod;[209] (2) by Nathanael in his initial response to Jesus;[210] (3) by various persons acclaiming Jesus to be the 'Son of David', where it is evident that the expected Messiah of royal status is connoted;[211] (4) by the festival pilgrims on the occasion of Jesus' entry into Jerusalem;[212] (5) in Pilate's questioning of Jesus;[213] (6) in the mocking taunt of the soldiers; [214] and (7) in the title placed over the cross.[215] The retention of this designation in the records has some significance of itself, even though not credited to any early Christian except Nathanael (whose acclaim, it need be noted, is promptly minimized by Jesus' reply).[216] And the relatively greater emphasis laid upon the concept of the kingship of

---

[207] Luke's relegation of the genealogy to ch. 3 and his tracing of the lineage back to 'Adam, the son of God' evidences and is a result of the tension which exists in relating traditions stemming from one ideological milieu for a mentality saturated in another. So also the reversal of elements in II Tim. 2.8.

[208] Though a three clause construction of Rom. 1.3f. is proposed by H. Windisch, 'Zur Christologie der Pastoralbriefe', *ZNW*, XXXIV (1935), pp. 213–38; A. M. Hunter, *Paul and his Predecessors*, pp. 27f.

[209] Matt. 2.2.

[210] John 1.49.

[211] Matt. 9.27; 12.23; 15.22; 20.30f. (par. in Mark 10.47f.; Luke 18.38f.).

[212] Matt. 21.9; Mark 11.9f. speak in terms of Davidic relationship; Luke 19.38; John 12.13 in terms of kingship. Both, however, in context, come to the same end.

[213] Matt. 27.11; Mark 15.2; Luke 23.3; John 18.33.

[214] Matt. 27.29; Mark 15.18.

[215] Matt. 27.37; Mark 15.26; Luke 23.38; John 19.19.

[216] John 1.50f.

Jesus in the First and Fourth Gospels supports to some extent our thesis of characteristic christological motifs in the Jewish Christian sector of the early church.[217]

Even more significant here, however, are instances (admittedly few) where the idea of Jesus as king exists as one element underlying early Christian preaching and where it comes to expression in the New Testament on the part of the authors themselves. The Jewish claim before the magistrates of Thessalonica was that Paul and Silas were presenting Jesus as a king, thereby threatening Caesar's exclusive prerogatives.[218] As stated, the narrative of Acts indicates that this assertion was patently false. Yet the maxim *ex nihilo nihil fit* seems applicable here; for while the Christian mission was assuredly no political threat to the empire, as the Jewish opponents tried to make out, there was undoubtedly something in the apostles' message to which they could appeal in support of their assertion – whether something expressly said or something implied in the proclamation of Jesus as the Messiah. Only Matthew and John among the Evangelists apply Zech. 9.9 to Jesus' entry into Jerusalem;[219] evidently, because it was only to their audiences that the combination of kingship, fulfilment, and humility was meaningful. In so doing, of course, they present on their own part a kingly motif, among others, for Jesus. The Letter to the Hebrews speaks of the kingship of Jesus in a spiritual sense, connecting it with the Melchizedekian priesthood.[220] And the Apocalypse includes three or four references to Jesus as king in a blended religious and cosmic manner.[221]

But though there are such veiled allusions and indirect evidences in support of Davidic kingship as an early christological ascription among Jewish Christians, there is also the absence of explicit attribution of kingship to Jesus in the New Testament. At first

[217] See W. A. Meeks, *The Prophet-King* (1967), pp. 61–80, on the centrality of the kingship of Jesus and the prominence of βασιλεύς in the passion narrative of the Fourth Gospel.

[218] Acts 17.7.

[219] Matt. 21.5; John 12.15.

[220] Heb. 7.1f.

[221] Rev. 15.3f.; 17.14; 19.16. 'The bright morning star' of Rev. 22.16 is probably an allusion to Balaam's oracle of the Star of Jacob (Num. 24.15–19), which was understood at Qumran as a royal conqueror (cf. 4QTes. 9–13 and 1QM 11.6–7; though see also CDC 7.19–20 [9.8], and contrast Test. Jud. 24.1–6; Test. Levi 18.3). Note also I Tim. 1.17 and 6.15, which, if christological, are pertinent as well. Cf. J. Daniélou, 'L'étoile de Jacob et la mission chrétienne à Damas', *VC*, XI (1957), pp. 121–38.

glance, this is quite surprising. Along with the transference from the Psalter of the titles 'Lord' and even 'God' to Jesus, we would have expected at some point in the development of Christian thought that of 'King' as well – especially when God is spoken of so often in Israel's devotional literature as King. What was it that caused the Christians to ignore the clause 'I have set my king upon my holy hill of Zion' in Ps. 2.6, when Ps. 2 was widely acknowledged as having messianic import in contemporary Judaism and they employed Ps. 2.7 as a proof-text for the sonship of Jesus? And how is it that Ps. 24.7–10, with its fivefold mention of 'the King of glory' (ὁ βασιλεὺς τῆς δόξης), was never applied to Jesus? Even though it would have been exceedingly appropriate both to the thought and to the context, I Cor. 2.8, for instance, reads 'the Lord of glory' (ὁ κύριος τῆς δόξης) for the expected septuagintal term.

Undoubtedly, such a reluctance to affirm explicitly the Davidic kingship of Jesus was due to both theological and situational factors. Remembering Jesus' own attitude towards political messiahship and his endeavours to redefine his kingship in spiritual terms,[222] and recognizing that such an appellation would foster grave misconceptions in both Palestine and the Roman empire, the Christians seem to have steered clear of an explicit affirmation of Jesus' Davidic kingship. That they considered him of royal status and the nation's rightful ruler is clear in the First and Fourth Gospels. And that they expressed their faith at times in terms of his spiritual kingship is seen in the Letter to the Hebrews. Further, as evidenced in the Apocalypse, as the church's thought developed and matured, Jesus' kingship was also cast into cosmic categories. Conviction regarding messiahship logically entailed the attribution of Davidic kingship. But Davidic King as a christological title, while allusively present in their consciousness, was severely muted in the expression of early Jewish Christianity, and that for both theological and circumstantial reasons.

HIGH PRIEST

It is commonly maintained that the doctrine of the priesthood of Jesus in the Letter to the Hebrews represents a new and individual feature of that author, and not a remoulding of current ideas or an

---

[222] See the dialogue with Pilate in John 18.33–38a and the discussion with the Pharisees in Mark 12.35–37 (and par.). Cf. also the words ὑμεῖς ἐκ τῶν κάτω ἐστέ, ἐγὼ ἐκ τῶν ἄνω εἰμί of John 8.23.

appeal to any existing messianic expectation.[223] Such an opinion, however, stands in need of considerable revision in view of recent evidence.

The Dead Sea Scrolls have brought to the fore the realization that there existed within sectarian Judaism prior to and contemporary with early Christianity a messianic hope that included priestly features. Roughly speaking, messianic thought within what can be called an Essene cycle of expectation seems to have worked itself out according to something approximating the following pattern of development: (1) from an emphasis upon the supremacy of the tribe of Levi over the tribe of Judah, as in the 'proto-Essene' Jubilees;[224] (2) to a doctrine of two Messiahs, a priestly and a Davidic, as in the Manual of Discipline;[225] (3) to a concept of one Messiah who would fulfil both priestly and royal functions, as in the Damascus Document.[226] In addition, though warrior characteristics are so stressed as to leave us with no certain references to the priesthood, 11Q Melchizedek indicates that the figure of Melchizedek had messianic associations in certain sectors of late Judaism.[227]

The New Testament reflects at times a priestly understanding of the person and work of Jesus. In addition to the many references to Jesus as the High Priest of the New Covenant in the Letter to the Hebrews,[228] the Fourth Gospel strikes a similar note in its presentation of Jesus as assuming the place of centrality in the nation's religious festivals[229] and as praying after the manner of a priestly mediator.[230] And in the Pauline letters, the exalted Christ

[223] Cf., e.g., G. Friedrich, 'Beobachtungen zur messianischen Hohepriestererwartung in den synoptikern', *ZTK*, LIII (1956), pp. 265–311; J. Gnilka, 'Die Erwartung des messianischen Hohepriesters in den Schriften von Qumran und in Neuen Testament', *RQ*, II (1960), pp. 395–426; F. Hahn, *Christologische Hoheitstitel*, p. 240; H. Montefiore, *The Epistle to the Hebrews* (1964), pp. 96, 117f.; R. H. Fuller, *Foundations of New Testament Christology*, p. 33; A. J. B. Higgins, 'The Priestly Messiah', *NTS*, XIII (1967), esp. pp. 233f.

[224] Jub. 31.13–20.

[225] 1QS 9.10f.

[226] CDC 19.11 (9.10); 20.1 (9.29); 12.23–13.1 (15.4); 14.19 (18.8); cf. Test. Levi 8.11–15; 18.1–14, though the question of provenance is accute here.

[227] Cf. M. de Jonge and A. S. van der Woude, '11QMelch. and the New Testament', *NTS*, XII (1966), pp. 301–26.

[228] Heb. 2.17; 3.1; 4.14–46; 5.1–10; 6.20, 7.24–27; 8.1ff.; and 9.11ff.

[229] Esp. John 7–8.

[230] John 17.

is spoken of as making intercession for his own[231] and as being the mediator between God and man.[232] Other portions may yield further inferential support here,[233] but these instances at least are fairly direct.

Likewise, we are probably correct in viewing some of the passages which speak of Jesus' death as a sacrifice as echoing the 'binding of Isaac' (the *'Akedath Isaac*) motif, which seems to have been employed quite widely in first-century Judaism.[234] Testament of Levi 18.6f. draws the comparison between the heavenly voice at the baptism and Abraham's call to Isaac, in these words:

The heavens shall be opened, and from the temple of glory shall come upon him sanctification, with the Father's voice as from Abraham to Isaac. And the glory of the Most High shall be uttered over him, and the spirit of understanding and sanctification shall rest upon him in the water.

Now whether the Testaments are to be considered a Jewish composition with Christian interpolations or a Christian writing throughout, the passage in question suggests that in certain circles of Christian speculation the proposed sacrifice of Isaac and the completed sacrifice of Jesus were paralleled. Just as in talmudic Judaism Isaac's 'willingness to lay down life at God's bidding is reckoned by God as though the sacrifice had been accomplished, and was pleaded by his descendants as a ground for the remission of their sins',[235] so it is likely that the early Jewish Christians viewed the redemptive work of Jesus as the antitype of the Old Testament Isaac narrative. Possibly the *'Akedath Isaac* stands behind the designation of Jesus in the Fourth Gospel as the 'Lamb of God', that is, the One foretold in Abraham's promise of a lamb

[231] Rom. 8.34.
[232] I Tim. 2.5.
[233] Cf. L. Mowry, 'The Dead Sea Scrolls and the Background for the Gospel of John', *BA*, XVII (1954), pp. 86–9; F. M. Braun, 'L'arrièrefond judaique due quatrième evangile et la Communauté de l'Alliance', *RB*, LXII (1955), pp. 29–31; W. H. Brownlee, 'Messianic Motifs', *NTS* III (1957), p. 206. Note also the language of Rom. 12.1; I Peter 2.5, 9; and Rev. 1.6; 5.10.
[234] Cf. G. F. Moore, *Judaism*, I, pp. 539–41, 549; H. J. Schoeps, *Paul* (ET 1961), pp. 141–9; G. Vermès, *Scripture and Tradition*, pp. 194–225; E. Best, *Temptation and Passion*, pp. 169–73. C. K. Barrett, *From First Adam to Last* (1962), pp. 26–30, however, is more sceptical regarding the prevalence of this idea in New Testament times.
[235] G. F. Moore, *Judaism*, I, p. 549.

to be provided by God himself and typified in the offered ram.[236] And possibly, as well, it underlies the repeated emphasis in the Letter to the Hebrews that as High Priest, of whom it is required that something be in hand to be offered, Jesus 'offered up himself'.[237]

It is no longer necessary to assume a hellenistic provenance for the portrayal of Jesus as High Priest in the New Testament. All of the elements brought together in such a conception – messianic priesthood, the association of Melchizedek with the Messianic Age, redemptive sacrifice, and heavenly intercession[238] – were part of Christianity's Jewish heritage; though, assuredly, not in the same proportions or already brought together in the same manner. Knowing the character of his person and experiencing reconciliation with God through his sacrifice, believers within at least certain sectors of the early church seem to have found the categories of high priest and priestly ministry to be appropriate to some extent of Jesus as well. And, on analogy with Qumran and in conformity with what we have found regarding other hebraic christological ascriptions, it seems proper to say that they came to such an appreciation on the basis of their conviction of Jesus as the Messiah.

Having said all this, however, it yet remains true that a high priest christology in the New Testament is definitely muted. There are undoubtedly reasons for this which will continue to elude us. But two, at least, immediately suggest themselves.

In the first place, the widespread antipathy among the Jewish populace towards the Sadducean ideal of a priest-king sovereignty must be noted. From the Assumption of Moses, the historian Josephus, and the Talmud – and less directly from other sources as well – we learn that the Hasmonean rulers adopted the title

[236] John 1.29, 36. Note also the twenty-eight times the exalted Jesus is designated the 'Lamb' in the Apocalypse, though this probably is in line more with the apocalyptic imagery of the bull and the lamb (e.g., I Enoch 90.37f.). See above, pp. 49f.

[237] Heb. 7.27ff.

[238] On heavenly intercession, see I Enoch 12–16 (esp. 15.2); 104.1; 4QAng.Lit.; and b. Ḥag. 12b (also I Enoch 47.2 and Test. Levi 3.5f., though here methodologically ruled out). As J. Strugnell points out: 'The statement in b. Ḥag. 12b that Michael only exercised his function of heavenly high priest after the destruction of the Jerusalem Temple perhaps refers to a shift in religious interests after that time' ('Angelic Liturgy at Qumran', *VTS*, VII [1960], p. 335).

'(High) Priest of the Most High God'.[239] In so doing, of course, they applied to themselves the title used of Melchizedek in Gen. 14.18 – undoubtedly attempting thereby to legitimize their reign by declaring themselves priest-kings 'forever after the order of Melchizedek', as is said in Ps. 110.4.[240] At the height of their power during the reigns of Simon (142–134 BC) and John Hyrcanus (134–104 BC), it may very well have seemed to many that they deserved the ascription; though it is hardly likely that the Hasidim and other pietistic quietists would have accorded them the honour. But such illusions were completely dispelled by the conduct of Alexander Jannaeus (103–76 BC) and his sons. And soon intense antagonism towards such a Hasmonean claim arose, as is indicated by the tone of Assump. Mos. 6.1 and probably by the lacuna in Jub. 13.25 as well.[241] The Genesis Apocryphon[242] and 11Q Melchizedek indicate that the Qumran convenanters continued to respect the priesthood of the biblical Melchizedek and to expect that he would be associated in some significant manner with the Messianic Age, even while they denied the legitimacy of the

---

[239] Assump. Mos. 6.1: 'Then there shall be raised up unto them kings bearing rule, and they shall call themselves priests of the Most High God. They shall assuredly work iniquity in the holy of holies.'

Antiq. XVI. 6.2 (163): Caesar Augustus decreed that 'the Jews may follow their own customs in accordance with the law of their fathers, just as they followed them in the time of Hyrcanus, high priest of the Most High God'.

B. Rosh. Hash. 18b: 'The Grecian [Syrian] Government had forbidden the mention of God's name by the Israelites, and when the Government of the Hasmoneans became strong and defeated them, they ordained that they should mention the name of God even on bonds, and they used to write thus: "In the year so-and-so of Johanan, High Priest of the Most High God".'

Cf. Jub. 32.1: 'And he [Jacob] abode that night at Bethel, and Levi dreamed that they had ordained and made him the priest of the Most High God and his sons for ever.' Also note Tos. Sot. 13.5; b. Sot. 33a; b. Suk. 52b; Test. Levi 8.14.

[240] Cf. R. Leszynsky, *Die Sadduzäer* (1912), p. 94; R. H. Charles, *Ap. & Ps.*, II, 9, 61; G. F. Moore, *Judaism*, II, pp. 327f. Also note A. D. Nock, 'The Guild of Zeus Hypsistos', *HTR*, XXIX (1936), pp. 65–7. One need not take the older view that Ps. 110 is Maccabean on this basis. The Hasmoneans could just as plausibly have attempted to validate their sovereignty by its employment as by its invention.

[241] Note the 'they shall assuredly work iniquity in the holy of holies' of Assump. Mos. 6.1. On the lacuna of Abraham's meeting with Melchizedek in Jub. 13.25, which has every appearance of an intentional deletion, see R. H. Charles, *Ap. & Ps.*, II, 9, 33. Contrariwise, note K. Kohler, 'Melchizedek', *JE*, VIII, p. 450.

[242] 1QApoc. 22.14–17 retells the biblical story without embellishment at this point, including the title 'Priest of God Most High'.

Hasmonean-Sadducean assertion. But the rabbinic materials reveal that the rabbis, and presumably the earlier Pharisaic teachers as well, stood in such essential opposition to these priestly claims that they even denied the supremacy of the biblical Melchizedek in the Genesis narrative and tended to disparage his inclusion in the messianic hope.[243] The fact that the priesthood and the sacrificial system are minimized in talmudic literature[244] should probably be credited as much to this antagonism as to the destruction of the Temple and the rabbis' own Torah-centricity. Conversely, it may also be credited in part for preparing Judaism for the shock which might otherwise have been disastrous in the loss of the cultus in AD 70. But whatever advantages or disadvantages it may have had in other areas, the factor of widespread antipathy to such Hasmonean-Sadducean claims must be taken into account in evaluating the position of the early Jewish Christians in speaking of the priesthood of Jesus.

In such a situation, it is not surprising that a priestly christology should be severely muted in the New Testament. Further, it need not be considered strange that where it does come to explicit expression it is in an epistle dealing with impending apostasy back into Judaism and written to converts whose background would have enabled them to appreciate the point.[245] In all probability, therefore, both the reticence of the author of Hebrews to use the argument from Melchizedek in ch. 5 and then his full-blown development of Jesus as a 'priest forever after the order of Melchizedek' in chs. 7 through 10 are to be accounted for in large measure by the ambivalence existing within the Jewish world of (1) general antipathy towards a Melchizedekian priesthood and Melchizedekian claims because of Sadducean assertions, yet (2) a retention in certain circles (Essene?) of Melchizedek himself as a messianic figure.[246]

But this, of course, is at best only a partial explanation. The

---

[243] Note Lev. R. 25.6 and b. Ned. 32b, where the priesthood is said to have been taken from Melchizedek and given to Abraham because 'he blessed Abraham before blessing the Omnipresent'. In Song of Songs R. II. 13. 4 and b. Suk. 52b, Melchizedek is included among the 'four craftsmen' (the eschatological חרשים); though in b. Suk. 52b, Rabbi Shesheth is recorded as strenuously objecting.

[244] Cf. W. D. Davies, *Paul and Rabbinic Judaism*, pp. 253–9.

[245] Cf. M. de Jonge and A. S. van der Woude, '11QMelch. and the New Testament', *NTS*, XII (1966), esp. pp. 318f.

[246] For a contrary opinion, see H. Montefiore, *Hebrews*, p. 118.

earliest Christians were also guided by their remembrance of Jesus' attitude towards the priesthood, the cultus, and his own ministry in relation to them. While there is no indication that they recalled any opposition on his part to the temple *per se* – it was his Father's house, and even his cleansing of it could not be viewed so as to dispute that – the general impression gained from the portrayal of Jesus in the Gospels is that of passivity to the priesthood and to the cultus. In addition, he did not expressly speak of himself in terms of a priest. And taking their cue from him, neither did they.

Stemming from their conviction regarding the messiahship of Jesus, therefore, at least some within early Jewish Christianity seem to have conceptualized the ministry and exalted status of Jesus in terms of the High Priest *par excellence*. Yet the explicit expression of this christological motif is quite definitely muted in the New Testament, and that for both theological and circumstantial reasons.

IV

LORDSHIP AND ATTENDANT FEATURES

THE SERMON OF Peter at Pentecost concludes with the assertion: 'Therefore let all the house of Israel know assuredly that God has made him both Lord and Christ, this Jesus whom you crucified.'[1] In the Acts of the Apostles, the two major titles used of Jesus are 'Christ' and 'Lord'. And in the New Testament, the two major confessions are 'Jesus is the Christ (Messiah)' and 'Jesus is Lord'.[2] While κύριος at times appears first in the combination of titles, particularly in Peter's sermon cited above and Paul's references to the 'Lord Jesus Christ',[3] it is the ascription χριστός which is more prominent in the Jewish Christian materials of the New Testament – though not, it must be insisted, to the exclusion of the title κύριος. The previous chapter has considered the confession 'Jesus is the Christ' and its immediate implications. We must now deal with the affirmation 'Jesus is Lord' and its attendant features.

LORD

The Title as an Early Acclamation. There is little question today regarding the pre-Pauline character of κύριος as a designation for Jesus. It is generally agreed that the title was employed in regard to Jesus both as a term of respectful address and as a worshipful acclamation prior to the ministry of Paul.[4] The contemporary issues have to do with (1) the ideological milieu in which the ascription took the character of an acclamation (whether hebraic Jewish Christianity or a pre-Pauline hellenistic form of Christi-

[1] Acts 2.36.

[2] As V. H. Neufeld points out in *Earliest Christian Confessions*, particularly chs. IV–V, pp. 42–107.

[3] For a suggested explanation for this order in Acts 2.36, see below, pp. 149f. Paul's usage is understandable in light of his Gentile mission, as explicated in what follows.

[4] To mention only a varied and representative few, G. Dalman, *Words of Jesus*, pp. 324–31; R. Bultmann, *Theology of the New Testament*, I, p. 125; O. Cullmann, *Christology of the New Testament*, pp. 203–22; W. Kramer, *Christ, Lord, Son of God*, pp. 65–7.

anity), (2) the criteria upon which distinctions of this sort may be based, and (3) the meaning of the title in an early Palestinian Christian context.

A. Marana tha *of I Corinthians 16.22*

Discussion regarding the use of 'Lord' in the early church invariably centres on the doxology of I Cor. 16.22–24:

If any one does not love the Lord, let him be accursed (ἀνάθεμα). Μαράνα θά! The grace of the Lord Jesus be with you. My love be with you all in Christ Jesus. Amen.

The crucial phrase is the transliterated Aramaic expression μαράνα θά, and the important word is the term for Lord which it expresses, מר or מרא, which usually appears in Aramaic in the possessive as מרי or מראי (first person singular) and מרן, מרנא, or מראנא (first person plural).

The transliterated expression in I Cor. 16.22 is notoriously difficult philologically. In the first place, it is not clear where the division should appear. And even when the division has been made, there is the possibility of the second word being interpreted in more than one way. Thus, it may be read as follows:

1. Μαράνα θά: 'Our Lord, Come!' (present imperative), understood as a prayer set in either a eucharistic or an eschatological context, or, perhaps, both.

2. Μαρὰν ἀθά: 'Our Lord comes!' (future indicative), or 'Our Lord is here!' (perfect indicative), understood as a confession.

While it is possible linguistically to view the formula as indicative, its correspondence with 'Come, Lord Jesus' of Rev. 22.20, where ἔρχου κύριε Ἰησοῦ appears to be a translation of the transliterated μαράνα θά, makes it probable that the expression should be understood primarily as a prayer rather than as a confession – though, of course, every request is also indirectly a declaration.

Bousset argued that μαράνα θά was an expression coined from the Greek in bilingual Antioch for the sake of Aramaic-speaking believers of Syria and Cilicia, and therefore that it arose within a hellenistic Christian community and cannot be viewed as an expression of early Palestinian Christianity.[5] Bultmann believes that

---

[5] W. Bousset, *Kyrios Christos* (1913), pp. 98f. Later Bousset altered his position, advocating that it was a Jewish oath which Palestinian Christians employed with reference to God and which hellenistic believers later applied

the phrase was probably first employed by Palestinian Christians
as an oath sworn before God and with reference to God alone,
and at a later time was taken over in hellenistic Christian circles to
refer to Jesus.[6] But both of these positions have failed to carry
conviction in the light of more cogent interpretations, and are
widely seen today as desperate attempts to fabricate a plausible
setting in justification of a theory. Currently it is generally accepted
that 'since *maranatha* was preserved as an Aramaic formula even in
Greek-speaking churches we must assume that it originated [as a
christological ascription] in the early Aramaic-speaking church',[7]
for it would hardly have been retained untranslated in a Greek
text had it originated as the translation of a more primary Greek
term. 'The only explanation for the reverent preservation of the
Aramaic form is that there must have been a memory that its
source was the original Church in Jerusalem.'[8]

But while the provenance of the phrase μαράνα θά seems to be
fairly well established on the basis of its Aramaic form, and there
exists little reason to deny its reference to Jesus, the question of
its meaning within the Palestinian church is frequently debated.
Representative of a sizeable sector within contemporary New
Testament scholarship is W. Kramer's claim that '*Mara* was a
relatively harmless title, without heavy religious overtones', and
that it must be distinguished from the uses of κύριος which arose
in the worship of hellenistic believers.[9] In elaboration of this
thesis, Kramer proposes that we should think of two types of
κύριος affirmations in regard to Jesus: (1) a '*Mare-Kyrios*' ascription
which was employed in the Aramaic-speaking church in a purely
honorific fashion without any metaphysical connotations, and (2)

---

to Jesus (*Jesus der Herr* [1916], pp. 22f.); though in the second edition of
Kyrios Christos (1921), p. 84, he abandoned his 1916 suggestion and restated
his earlier position.

[6] R. Bultmann, *Theology of the New Testament*, I, pp. 51f., resurrecting
Bousset's 1916 thesis, though without crediting Bousset or mentioning his
abandonment of it in 1921.

[7] W. Kramer, *Christ, Lord, Son of God*, p. 100; cf. also J. C. O'Neill, *The
Theology of Acts in its Historical Setting* (1961), p. 129, and R. H. Fuller,
Foundations of New Testament Christology, p. 157.

[8] O. Cullmann, *Christology of the New Testament*, p. 214. Cullmann goes on
to point out: 'It was respected for that reason, just as the Aramaic form of the
words "*Abba*", "*Talitha cumi*", and "*Eli, Eli, lama sabachthani*" was respected because one knew that Jesus himself had spoken them in this way.'

[9] W. Kramer, *Christ, Lord, Son of God*, p. 101.

the 'acclamation-*Kyrios*' title which came about as a result of the pervading influence of hellenism in Gentile centres of Christianity.[10] Thus, Kramer insists, it is an error to believe that the identification of μαράνα θά as a formula stemming from the earliest community of believers at Jerusalem and as having reference to Jesus is the 'Achilles' heel' of Bousset's hellenistic theory (even though Bousset was in error in working out some of the details of his theory), for 'the same title was used by two different churches in connection with two different complexes of ideas and in this double usage entered the stream of tradition. No genetic connection between the two can be discovered.'[11]

It is, of course, extremely difficult to say with any degree of finality precisely what the early Jewish Christians really thought when they uttered the word מרן or μαράνα ('our Lord') with respect to Jesus. After all, the transliteration of the Aramaic appears only once in the New Testament (though its Greek counterpart appears in Rev. 22.20); and מר, like κύριος, is 'a term of deferential homage, the scope of which can vary widely, according to the position of the person addressed'.[12] But it is no good to assert the impossibility of the designation being used in the early church at Jerusalem in an acclamation manner on the grounds that (1) such would be 'unthinkable' for Jewish Christians who shared in Israel's monotheistic faith;[13] or that (2) the parallels between the acclamation usages of κύριος in the New Testament and usages of κύριος in the Greek world prove that an acclamation sense is hellenistic *per se* and therefore not hebraic.[14] The first objection determines the issue by the presuppositions of the investigator rather than by the data at hand. And the second works from the *a priori* of a dichotomous cleavage between hebraic and hellenistic thought – which may be neat and tidy, but is much too simplistic – and ignores the effect of the intermingling of cultures and the factor of basically similar responses to common phenomena in men of even differing cultural orientations.

What could be legitimately argued against an acclamation use

---

[10] *Ibid.*, esp. pp. 104–7.   [11] *Ibid.*, p. 104.

[12] G. Dalman, *Words of Jesus*, p. 326; cf. also pp. 324–6.

[13] As, e.g., R. Bultmann, *Theology of the New Testament*, I, p. 51; W. Kramer, *Christ, Lord, Son of God*, pp. 101f.

[14] As, e.g., Kramer, *Christ, Lord, Son of God*, p. 103: 'On account of the many similarities with the idea of *Kyrios* in the Hellenistic *Kyrios*-cults we took it that the title must have come from Hellenism.'

of מר by the earliest Jewish Christians is that because of their entirely futuristic eschatology they did not entertain thoughts about the exaltation of Jesus; that is, that Jesus was regarded by them as being inactive from his resurrection to his *parousia*, and that only with the waning of hope regarding the latter did thoughts arise about the present lordship of Jesus.[15] If this could be demonstrated, one would have an effective counter to any claims for an early acclamation of Jesus in the Jerusalem community. Our investigation of the ἀρχή and πρωτότοκος complex of expressions and of the κατάβασις–ἀνάβασις theme, however, has suggested that as a matter of fact early Jewish Christians did think of Jesus as exalted.[16] And, as Oscar Cullmann points out, 'nothing indicates better . . . how vital was the present lordship of Christ in early Christian thought' than the repeated citation of Ps. 110.1 in the canonical Jewish Christian materials.[17] Almost no other Old Testament passage is quoted or alluded to as often.[18] And none, once having been interpreted messianically, expresses the ideas of exaltation and present lordship more clearly.

As a prayer, μαράνα θά is set in the context of worship. It may have been first employed in a eucharistic liturgy invoking the presence of Jesus in the feast, whether devoid of eschatological connotations or in anticipation of a future presence.[19] Or it may have originated as part of the *anathema* ban-formula, requesting that the Lord come soon in judgment to redress wrong and establish right.[20] But whatever its original purpose, its note of worshipful acclamation in respect to Jesus seems not to be able to be set aside. Undoubtedly the concepts of exaltation, lordship, and Lord received development and further explication as time went on and within the Gentile mission. But there is no evidence that מר and κύριος as titles applied to Jesus in the New Testament must be distinguished as separate and distinct entities.

---

[15] E.g., F. Hahn, *Christologische Hoheitstitel*, pp. 126–32.

[16] Cf. above, pp. 53–62.

[17] O. Cullmann, *Christology of the New Testament*, p. 223.

[18] Acts 2.34f.; 5.31; 7.55; Heb. 1.3; 8.1; 10.12f.; I Peter 3.22; Rev. 3.21. In the Gospels, see Mark 12.36 (and par.); 14.62 (and par.); 16.19. In Paul's letters, Rom. 8.34; I Cor. 15.25; Col. 3.1; Eph. 1.20.

[19] Analogous to the use of μαράναθα in Didache 10.6. Cf. H. Lietzmann, *Messe und Herrenmahl* (1926), pp. 236–8; O. Cullmann, *Christology of the New Testament*, pp. 210–13.

[20] Cf. C. F. D. Moule, 'A Reconsideration of the Context of *Maranatha*', *NTS*, VI (1960), pp. 307–10.

B. *The Confession of Philippians 2.11*

In the Pauline corpus there are three instances where literary form and manner of citation indicate that the apostle is employing an earlier formula-confession (*homologia*) in saying 'Jesus is Lord' (Κύριος Ἰησοῦς): Rom. 10.9; I Cor. 12.3; Phil. 2.11. In two of the passages the quasi-technical term 'to confess' (ὁμολογεῖν) is used.[21] But though all three are widely accepted as containing a pre-Pauline confessional formula, little more than this can be said regarding the provenance for Rom. 10.9 and I Cor. 12.3. Discussion therefore must centre upon the confession 'Jesus is Lord' of Phil. 2.11.

On the basis of its semitic features, it may plausibly be argued that the hymn of Phil. 2.6–11 took form originally in a Palestinian milieu and reflects to a considerable degree the convictions and piety of Jerusalem Christianity.[22] Various objections, of course, have been raised against such a view. Only two, however, seem to be critically based and pertinent here.

Reginald Fuller builds his case against an early provenance for the hymn among Aramaic-speaking believers at Jerusalem on the thesis that 'the exaltation Christology of the second strophe was probably quite foreign to Aramaic Christianity', and therefore 'its *Sitz im Leben* must be sought in Hellenistic Jewish Christianity'.[23] Again, however, as I said above in discussing the expression μαράνα θά, I do not believe that the evidence sustains such an elimination. It is the methodology of Bultmann, Käsemann, Fuller, Hahn, and company, which is at fault. Assuredly motifs in the christology of the New Testament can be paralleled by those in the hellenistic world, and some quite legitimately so. But many also find a basis in Palestinian Judaism, whether of an orthodox or a sectarian type. If our procedure is to declare everything hellenistic which finds similarity with Grecian religious philosophy, we will, of course, have precious little to identify as hebraic. But if, on the other hand, we recognize the intermingling of hebraic and

---

[21] Rom. 10.9 (ὁμολογήσῃς) and Phil. 2.11 (ἐξομολογήσηται). Cullmann understands the primary theme of I Cor. 12.3 to be not *glossolalia* but the confession of the lordship (and thus kingship) of Jesus in face of current emperor worship and state persecution (*Christology of the New Testament*, pp. 218–22), though this is difficult to validate.

[22] See above, pp. 58f.

[23] R. H. Fuller, *Foundations of New Testament Christology*, p. 205.

hellenistic orientations in Palestine and are prepared to emphasize
those analogies which exist between early Christianity and those
Jewish antecedents of which it claims to be the fulfilment – without
however, ignoring comparisons with features found in the non-
Jewish world – a different state of affairs results. It is this latter
procedure which I consider more historiographically valid and
which recent discoveries have pressed upon us. And therefore, I
fail to be impressed by the thesis of Fuller and others at this point,
based as it is upon a methodology which I consider to be faulty.

Werner Kramer observes that the wording of the confession in
Phil. 2.11 is not just 'Jesus is Lord' but 'Jesus Christ is Lord'
(Κύριος 'Ιησοῦς Χριστός), and points out that 'since the *homologia*
consists of the title Lord and a name, we may regard the combination *Jesus Christ* as being essentially a name'.[24] His conclusion is
that since χριστός is here used as a second name for Jesus, 'it
follows that the hymn must have originated in a Hellenistic setting,
for only there was *Jesus Christ* regarded as a double name'.[25] The
point is well taken, for, as I have noted earlier, χριστός seems to
have been taken primarily as an appellative and not usually as a
name among early Jewish believers.[26] But before relegating the
hymn of Philippians to a non-Aramaic provenance on this basis
alone (as Kramer does), certain other matters should be noted:

1. First, while it is true that the early Jewish believers seem to
have usually used χριστός ascriptively rather than as a proper
name, the assertion that they never employed it as a name is difficult to maintain. James, for example, is reported as referring to
Judas and Silas as 'men who have risked their lives for the sake of
the name of our Lord Jesus Christ (τοῦ ὀνόματος τοῦ κυρίου ἡμῶν
'Ιησοῦ Χριστοῦ);[27] and the Fourth Gospel, despite its heavy emphasis
on χριστός as an appellative, twice employs 'Ιησοῦς Χριστός as a
double name.[28]

2. Secondly, there is the possibility that Χριστός did not appear
in the original wording of the hymn at all (it is omitted in quotations by the third-century Origen, the fourth-century writers

---

[24] W. Kramer, *Christ, Lord, Son of God,* pp. 67f.
[25] *Ibid.,* p. 68.
[26] See above, pp. 74–77.
[27] Acts 15.26. While this may be attributed to the literary styling of Luke,
it is set in what is probably a quasi-liturgical composition which may be
expected to reflect early expression.
[28] John 1.17; 17.3.

Eusebius, Hilarius, and Ambrosiaster, and in the ninth-century manuscript G), and that Paul simply assimilated the wording at this point for the benefit of his audience to include the fuller name familiar at Philippi. After all, the apostle was not above the occasional interjection in quoting traditional material, as probably the inserted θανάτου δὲ σταυροῦ of v. 8 in this same hymn indicates.

3. Thirdly, there is the possibility that originally the hymn not only included χριστός but also the article, bringing together in effect the dual confessions of messiahship and lordship, and that in employing the hymn in his Gentile mission Paul omitted the article because of the inability to speak meaningfully regarding messiahship in a Gentile milieu. In so doing, he would have neither wrecked the form of the stanza nor perpetuated an expression incomprehensible to a non-Jewish audience.

Any of the three suggestions may possibly have been the case. We have, however, no means by which to pursue the matter further.[29] Kramer's observation, therefore, is pertinent; but his conclusion is somewhat premature.

While acknowledging the difficulty of the use of χριστός as a name in Phil. 2.11 (though also insisting upon the possibility of a solution), it yet remains probable that the confession of Jesus as Lord (κύριος) is rooted in the thought of the earliest Christian community at Jerusalem. And what is true here is also likely in the cases of Rom. 10.9 and I Cor. 12.3. These passages indicate that Paul was not the creator of the conviction regarding the lordship of Jesus, but that the confession 'Jesus is Lord' stems from the earliest stratum of Christian conviction. Undoubtedly Paul extended the concept, for in the hymn of Phil. 2.6–11, while worshippers 'in heaven and on earth and under the earth' are referred to, the lordship mentioned appears to be entirely within a religious context and not extended to cosmic concerns. What the apostle's quotations do specifically evidence, however, is that he believed his proclamation of Jesus as Lord was in direct continuity with the proclamation of the earliest church. And there seems little reason to deny it.

C. *The Name and the Lord*

Of significance as well are the instances in the Jewish Christian

---

[29] Interaction with the confession as it appears in Rom. 10.9 and I Cor. 12.3 aids us little here, for relationships may be variously evaluated and with less to go on in these cases.

materials of the New Testament where the name (τὸ ὄνομα) interpreted christologically and the title Lord are brought into close
association.[30] It is true, of course, that there are passages where
'the name' is associated with 'the Son'[31] and with 'Christ' or 'Jesus
Christ'.[32] But there are also portions where it is correlated with the
ascription Lord. Foundational in this association are Peter's quotations of Joel 2.32 in Acts 2.21 and Ps. 110.1 in Acts 2.34f., both
being included in his Pentecost sermon. And this collation is continued in Acts 8.16; 9.10–17; 15.26; and 22.13–16. It appears most
clearly, however, in Phil. 2.9–11: 'God has highly exalted him and
given him the name which is above every name, that at the name of
Jesus every knee should bow, in heaven and on earth and under
the earth, and every tongue confess that Jesus Christ is Lord
(κύριος), to the glory of God the Father.' What name is this that is
above every name? Undoubtedly, it is the name by which God
himself has been known; that is, in Greek, κύριος. Or perhaps it
would be truer to early Jewish Christian thought to say that since
Jesus is the name of God, evidencing the presence and power
of God, it is appropriate that the Old Testament title for God be his
as well.[33]

Paul also joins at times τὸ ὄνομα and ὁ κύριος, and speaks of
calling on 'the name of the Lord Jesus (Christ)'.[34] Interestingly,
however, his letters indicate that his rationale in such a procedure
was strictly traditional: (1) because 'whoever shall call upon the
name of the Lord shall be saved', as he says in Rom. 10.13 quoting
Joel 2.32; and (2) because God 'raised him from the dead and made
him sit at his right hand in the heavenly realms, far above all rule
and authority and power and dominion – and above every name
that is named, not only in this age but also in that which is to
come – and has put all things under his feet', as he says in Eph.
1.20–22 freely paraphrasing the church's hymn quoted in Phil.
2.6–11 and alluding to Ps. 110.1 as christologically understood.

Lordship and Lord. Twentieth-century scholarship has been
sharply divided as to the basis for the application of the title Lord
in an acclamation sense to Jesus. Four positions have been ad-

[30] See above, pp. 41–46, on 'the Name' as a christological title.
[31] E.g., John 3.18; Heb. 1.4f.; I John 5.13.
[32] E.g., I Peter 4.14; Acts 2.38; 3.6; 4.10; 8.12; 10.48.
[33] Note the consciousness expressed in John's presentation of Jesus as
having come in the Father's name (John 5.43; 10.25; 12.13).
[34] II Thess. 1.12; 3.6; I Cor. 1.2, 10; 5.4; 6.11; Eph. 5.20; Col. 3.17.

vanced: (1) that the LXX supplied both the term and the theology for the original ascription;[35] (2) that belief in Jesus as Lord stemmed directly from the expression and thought of Hellenism;[36] (3) that belief in Jesus as Lord must be credited in the first instance to the recognition of Jesus' authoritative teaching and supernatural activity during his ministry;[37] and (4) that the conviction rests primarily upon the resurrection and exaltation of Jesus.[38]

Undoubtedly many factors played a part in the establishing of this title in the consciousness of the early church, as most commentators – even while identifying one element as primary – acknowledge. The Jewish Christian materials of the New Testament indicate, however, that 'Lord' (1) was a post-resurrection title, and (2) found its point of departure and initial rationale in the resurrection and exaltation of Jesus. In Phil. 2.9–11, the bestowal of 'the name' and the confession 'Jesus Christ is Lord' are predicated upon the fact that 'God has highly exalted him' (δ $\theta\epsilon\delta\varsigma$ $a\upsilon\tau\delta\nu$ $\upsilon\pi\epsilon\rho\upsilon\psi\omega\sigma\epsilon\nu$). In Acts 2.36, the declaration of Jesus as Lord is based upon the facts that God raised him from the dead and exalted him to his right hand. Therefore Peter can assert: 'God has made him both Lord and Christ' ($\kappa a\iota$ $\kappa\upsilon\rho\iota\upsilon\nu$ $a\upsilon\tau\delta\nu$ $\kappa a\iota$ $\chi\rho\iota\sigma\tau\delta\nu$ $\epsilon\pi\upsilon\iota\eta\sigma\epsilon\nu$ δ $\theta\epsilon\delta\varsigma$). And in John 20.28, a verse which along with John 20.31 brings to a climax the argument of the Fourth Gospel, Thomas proclaims Jesus as his Lord only after assurance of the reality of the resurrection.

The Gospels offer little support for an acclamation use of 'Lord' in regard to Jesus during his ministry. Matthew and Luke speak of him being addressed many times by the title $\kappa\upsilon\rho\iota\epsilon$, both by disciples and by others. But in that the vocative $\kappa\upsilon\rho\iota\epsilon$ ranges in meaning from simple respect to reverential worship (with God alone knowing for sure what is meant in most cases), such instances afford little aid in determining attitudes. Interestingly, Mark has this form of address only in 7.28. And at times, other ascriptions

---

[35] B. B. Warfield, *The Lord of Glory* (1907), pp. 43f., 217; W. W. Graf von Baudissin, *Kyrios als Gottesname im Judentum*, 4 vols. (1929), esp. III, pp. 709f.
[36] W. Bousset, *Kyrios Christos*, pp. 95–9 (1913 ed.) and pp. 78–84 (1921 ed.); R. Bultmann, *Theology of the New Testament*, I, pp. 51f.
[37] G. Vos, *The Self-Disclosure of Jesus* (1954), pp. 118–40; E. von Dobschütz, '$KYPIO\Sigma$ $IH\Sigma OY\Sigma$', *ZNW*, XXX (1931), esp. p. 119. The position does not, however, deny later developments.
[38] V. Taylor, *Names of Jesus*, pp. 49–51; O. Cullmann, *Earliest Christian Confessions*, p. 58.

are employed for that of κύριε in parallel Synoptic passages: (1) κύριε in Matt. 8.25, but διδάσκαλε in Mark 4.38 and ἐπιστάτα in Luke 8.24; (2) κύριε in Matt. 17.4, but ῥαββί in Mark 9.5 and ἐπιστάτα in Luke 9.33; (3) κύριε in Matt. 17.15, but διδάσκαλε in Mark 9.17 and Luke 9.38; and (4) κύριε in Matt. 20.31, 33 and Luke 18.41, but ῥαββουνί in Mark 10.51. It seems fair to say that, especially for Mark, but also for the other Synoptists, the vocative κύριε had no special significance during Jesus' ministry beyond that of respectful address – often of profound respect, indeed, but not necessarily worshipful acclamation. John's Gospel indicates essentially the same. Only the response 'Lord, I believe' (πιστεύω κύριε) of the blind man cured by Jesus in John 9.38 can be definitely said to include the note of worship; though even here, as the narrative makes plain, the understanding expressed in the ascription was minimal.

In regard to 'the Lord' (ὁ κύριος) with reference to Jesus in the Gospels, the situation is similar. It is not found in the non-Marcan sayings common to Matthew and Luke (Q). And only once does it appear in Matthew and Mark: in Jesus' instruction to his disciples to say that 'the Lord has need of him' when questioned about taking the donkey.[39] In a similar set of directions regarding preparing for the Passover, however, Jesus is represented as referring to himself as 'the Teacher' (ὁ διδάσκαλος), thereby indicating, perhaps, that he employed the terms of himself rather interchangeably.[40] That Jesus thought of himself as ὁ κύριος is implied in his discussion of Ps. 110.1,[41] and the frequent citation of this verse indicates that his point was remembered. But there is no evidence in either Matthew or Mark that he was ever called Lord during his ministry on the basis of Ps. 110.1, even though after his exaltation the verse became very important in Christian thought. Luke's

[39] Matt. 21.3; Mark 11.3 (also Luke 19.31); perhaps to be understood as 'its Lord', or possibly even as a sort of prearranged password. The use of 'the Lord' in Mark 5.19 is of uncertain bearing; for though the restored demoniac proclaimed what the Lord had done for him by telling what Jesus had done for him, this is not decisive in determining the intent of either Jesus or the Evangelist in the use of the title. Luke, at any rate, understood 'the Lord' in Jesus' words to refer to God (Luke 8.39). The appearance of the title in Matt. 28.6 lacks adequate textual support, and there is less evidence for Mark 16.9.

[40] Matt. 26.18; Mark 14.14; Luke 22.11. Cf. also John 13.13f., where Jesus refers to himself as 'the Teacher and the Lord' and then as 'the Lord and the Teacher'; perhaps thereby again indicating in the alteration of terms the roughly synonymous character of the titles as Jesus was then using them.

[41] Matt. 22.45; Mark 12.37; Luke 20.44.

Gospel uses 'the Lord' frequently in regard to Jesus. Usually it employs the title in the narrative, which probably must be seen as reflecting the author's own terminology and that of his Gentile audience. Once it appears on the lips of others as a christological ascription – but then, significantly, it is expressed by the disciples *after* the resurrection in the declaration 'the Lord is risen indeed'.[42] John's Gospel uses the title infrequently of Jesus. In the first nineteen chapters, it appears at most only three times: 4.1; 6.23; 11.2; though recent critical texts class the first two as of 'dubious textual validity',[43] and John 11.2 may possibly be questioned as well.[44] At best, however, all three verses in which the title occurs in the first nineteen chapters of the Fourth Gospel are of the nature of parenthetical remarks on the part of the Evangelist himself, into which it may be assumed a later usage contemporary with the time of the writer is more likely to manifest itself.[45] In chs. 20 and 21, the title is used nine times in the resurrection narrative and post-resurrection sayings.[46] 'It is clear,' as Vincent Taylor observes, 'that the Evangelist feels it appropriate to speak of "the Lord" in these contexts, but does not feel at liberty to use the title in connexion with the earlier ministry.'[47]

From the above data, certain conclusions seem inevitable. In the first place, the christological title Lord seems to have stemmed from the early Christians' consciousness of the lordship of Jesus, which itself rested upon their assurance regarding his resurrection and present exaltation. This is directly signalled in Phil. 2.9–11; Acts 2.36; and John 20.28. And it is implied as well in Paul's words of Rom. 14.8f.: 'Whether we live or die, we are the Lord's. For this purpose Christ died and lived [again], in order that he might be Lord [κυριεύσῃ: establish his lordship] over both dead and living.' Christ's lordship, as Paul understands it, was established by means of his death and resurrection. And by the almost inci-dental manner in which he alludes to this relationship, he gives evidence of reproducing a traditional rationale. This understanding also underlies the commission of Matt. 28.18–20, for it is the Risen One who says 'All authority in heaven and on earth has been given

[42] Luke 24.34.
[43] Cf. the 1966 Bible Society's Greek New Testament.
[44] Cf. V. Taylor, *Names of Jesus*, p. 43.
[45] Cf. G. Vos, *Self-Disclosure of Jesus*, p. 120.
[46] John 20.2, 13, 18, 20, 25, 28; 21.7a, 7b, 12.
[47] V. Taylor, *Names of Jesus*, p. 43.

to me' – and now as the Lord exercising his lordship is able to command his disciples to 'go therefore and make disciples'.

The data cited above also indicate, secondly, that while conviction regarding the lordship of Jesus and the acclamation use of the title Lord for Jesus were grounded in the Easter faith, they were buttressed theologically and biblically from the very inception of the Christian movement. Though the early Christians did not come to these views first of all on the basis of the Old Testament or even the teachings of Jesus, they nevertheless, having witnessed recent events and experienced his exalted lordship, were able to look back upon the Old Testament and the ministry of Jesus in a new light and find valuable support there. Jesus himself was probably the one who furnished the key for this re-examination of Holy Writ and who by his Spirit gave guidance into the significances of past occurrences; and though they failed to grasp his meaning then, they now saw that in his treatment of Ps. 110.1 Jesus had pointed out biblical validation for their present conviction[48] and in his use of κύριος had indicated an awareness regarding his own person which was in basic continuity with their present affirmation.[49] Though these factors had not been foundational in their own experience, they were none the less vitally necessary for a mature faith and a full appreciation.

Thirdly, such correspondences as exist between early Christian thought and hellenistic religious philosophy in the use of the title Lord and in the understanding of lordship must be classed as essentially incidental and secondary. The earliest Christian ascription was born in the matrix of religious rather than cosmological concerns. And while parallels with Grecian concepts came to the the fore as Christian thought developed, the relationship of such analogous features should probably be understood more in the sense of a catalyst than a base. Terms, however, were in the air. And certainly the use of κύριος for two centuries or so in the LXX had some effect on Palestinian usage.

---

[48] Bultmann's observation regarding the secondary character of the LXX in the ascription of Lord to Jesus is sound (*Theology of the New Testament*, I, p. 124), though his implications and conclusions are faulty.

[49] While Jesus' references to himself as 'Lord of the Sabbath' (Mark. 2.28, par.), 'your Lord' (Matt. 24.42, though cf. Mark 13.35), and possibly 'the Lord' (Mark 11.3, par., though cf. Mark 14.14, par.) are not necessarily acclamation usages, they are in continuity with later ascriptions and when viewed from the post-exaltation perspective they fit in.

Fourthly, the evidence drawn from the Jewish Christian materials and from the letters of Paul indicates that the title Lord with reference to Jesus, while definitely an early christological acclamation, was not employed in the Jewish Christian cycle of witness as frequently as it was in the Gentile mission. While both 'Jesus is the Christ' and 'Jesus is Lord' were central confessions in the Christian community at Jerusalem, it is the former which was more prominent in early Jewish Christianity and the latter which came to expression most frequently among those ministering to Gentiles.

Extensions in Appreciation. The fact that early Jewish Christians thought of Jesus as Lord in an acclamation sense is not, however, the whole story, for there were also developments and extensions in the apprehension of that lordship and there are differences between early Jewish believers and Paul on his Gentile mission which must not be overlooked.

The conviction regarding Jesus' lordship and the attribution of the title Lord to him seem to have been largely explicated in the earliest stratum of Christian thought within contexts of religious and historical concerns. This is not to say that cosmological and speculative considerations were not implicit in such affirmations. But it is to point out that the passages cited in support of an early acclamation use of the title give little reason to believe that the earliest Jewish believers were thinking at the time in cosmic or philosophic categories, and furnish some support for the view that they were speaking in terms primarily religious and historical.

The μαράνα θά of I Cor. 16.22, together with its Greek parallel in Rev. 22.20, reflect interests dominantly religious and historical: the Jesus to whom prayer is properly addressed and who is rightly the object of his people's love is requested to come soon in eschatological judgment or to anticipate his future coming by a manifestation of his immediate presence. The imperative 'Come!' (θά) suggests an awareness of Jesus as living and transcendent. But no necessary inference is able to be drawn regarding his relationship to the structure of the universe, nor is the nature of transcendence consciously explicated. Philippians 2.9–11 speaks of Jesus being 'highly exalted' and receiving worship from creatures 'in heaven and on earth and under the earth'. But though the hymn begins by asserting that 'the divine nature was his from the first' (NEB), there is no necessary indication in the words regarding his exaltation that anything more than sovereignty in the religious sense was originally entertained. And it is of some significance to note that it is not Jesus himself but the worshippers who are related to cosmic localities. The parenthetical comment of Acts 10.36, 'he is Lord of all ($\pi\acute{\alpha}\nu\tau\omega\nu$)', probably has reference to 'Lord of all men' (the immediate context concerns righteous ones of every nation who are accepted by God), and thus connotes first of all supremacy and sovereignty of a religious nature. Even Paul's statement in Rom. 14.8f. regarding the purpose of Jesus' death and resurrection being 'that he might be Lord over both dead and living', and Jesus' words of Matt. 28.18–20 regarding 'all authority in heaven and on earth' having been given him, need not of themselves be interpreted to connote more than religious lordship; though, of course, in union with other passages they may be seen as signifying more.

There is, admittedly, little evidence upon which to build here. While only a few instances may be sufficient to establish the fact that Jesus was worshipfully acclaimed as Lord within the earliest Christian community, many passages would be required to substantiate and to explicate a thesis regarding development in apprehension. Yet it is a possible view that lordship and Lord with respect to Jesus were first conceptualized within the matrix of dominantly religious and historical concerns, and that it was only *via* the pressures of alien ideologies and the need to speak meaningfully to the concerns of the day that cosmological and philosophical factors inherent in these early commitments were later explicated as well.

Such a thesis receives *a priori* support from the general tendency of semitic thought to follow more functional than speculative lines; and, while not able to be fully substantiated by the evidence at hand, at least is not refuted in the few passages from the earliest stratum of Christian expression which speak of Jesus as the Lord. Furthermore, it has the pragmatic value of enabling us to understand better the historical circumstances involved in the ascription of the titles 'God' and 'Saviour' to Jesus in the New Testament (as discussed in the sections that follow). Oscar Cullmann has insisted: 'The lordship of Christ must extend over every area of creation. If there were a single area excluded from his lordship, that lordship would not be complete and Christ would no longer be the

Kyrios.'[50] But while that is true for the understanding of the title in Paul and the later canonical writings of Jewish Christianity, it is doubtful that this maturity of thought can be identified in the earliest stratum of Christian conviction, though it may be assumed to have been latent there.

In comparing the use of 'Lord' as a christological title among the early Jewish Christians and on the part of Paul, certain distinctives, therefore, appear. In the first place, whereas the confession of lordship among the early Jewish believers consisted of the one article 'Jesus is Lord',[51] Paul, when not citing traditional formulations, employs the bipartite form of 'One God the Father' and 'One Lord Jesus Christ'.[52] There may, of course, be conceptual differences involved here; though probably this variation should be understood circumstantially. For the earliest Jerusalem believers the implications of deity contained in the ascription as yet lay in the substratum of thought. The title seemed to pose no overt threat to Jewish monotheism, and thus required no delineation in respect to that doctrine. In the Gentile mission, however, another lordship could easily be mistaken as a support for polytheism. And thus Paul, as in I Cor. 8.5f., spoke of 'One God' in conjunction with his proclamation of 'One Lord Jesus Christ'.

Secondly, while the statements stemming from the earliest stratum of Christian faith speak of a risen, exalted, and coming Lord, the apostle Paul's emphasis, without negating these convictions, was on the nearness of the Lord in the experience of the Christian – in fact, by means of the ministration of the Spirit, being 'in the Lord' (ἐν κυρίῳ).[53] This may have been included in the thought of the earliest Christians. But it is Paul who gave it expression in the New Testament.

And thirdly, while the earliest believers thought of Jesus as Lord in dominantly religious and historical contexts, Paul seems to have been the one who enlarged, expanded, and enriched the

---

[50] O. Cullmann, *Christology of the New Testament,* p. 228.

[51] See Phil. 2.11; Rom. 10.9; I Cor. 12.3.

[52] I Cor. 8.5f.; cf. also Eph. 4.5; I Tim. 2.5; Gal. 3.20. Tripartite liturgical portions and doxologies are found in both Jewish Christian and Pauline materials (e.g., Matt. 28.19 and II Cor. 13.14). On their relation to the original confessions, see O. Cullmann, *Earliest Christian Confessions,* pp. 41–51.

[53] E.g., I Thess. 3.8; II Thess. 3.4; I Cor. 7.22, 39; II Cor. 10.17; Phil. 3.1; 4.2, 4; Eph. 5.8. Note the close association of 'the Lord' and 'the Spirit' in II Cor. 3.17: ὁ δὲ κύριος τὸ πνεῦμά ἐστιν. Cf. also his ἐν χριστῷ formula.

church's understanding of what lordship entailed. Even in Paul, however, it should be noted that a concept of cosmic lordship comes to expression most clearly only where the supremacy of Christ was challenged on speculative and metaphysical grounds, as in Colossians.[54] Perhaps a cosmic understanding of Jesus' lordship was only brought to its fulness in his own mind in debate with such an alien philosophic orientation. But however a maturity of concept was formed and a fulness of expression attained, an appreciation of Jesus' lordship in cosmic and metaphysical terms seems to have been very soon acknowledged within Jewish Christian circles as well to be a legitimate extension of early conviction – as the Prologue to the Fourth Gospel and the Apocalypse indicate.

GOD

Though the attribution of the title 'God' to Jesus undoubtedly was based upon several strands of conviction in the early church, the terminological bridge from the title's unambiguous meaning in Judaism to its occasional use in the New Testament as a christological ascription seems to have been the designation of Jesus as Lord. This is directly suggested in the association of titles in John 20.28, where Thomas is recorded as exclaiming: 'My Lord and my God'. And as soon as Ps. 110.1 came to be recognized as a christological *testimonium*, which the book of Acts reports occurred on the Day of Pentecost, such a collation of titles for Jesus would have been inevitable – though perhaps, at least for most, not immediate. The titles κύριος and θεός commonly appear together in the LXX as well as in pagan religious literature, and as C. K. Barrett points out, 'When this confession ['Jesus is Lord'] was interpreted in terms of the Old Testament, where κύριος = θεός, the fuller formula was close at hand.'[55] Indeed, as Raymond Brown asserts:

If Jesus could be given this title [κύριος], why could he not be called *theos*, which the Septuagint often used to translate *'elohim*? The two Hebrew terms had become relatively interchangeable, and indeed YHWH was the more sacred term.[56]

---

[54] A cosmic understanding may be anticipated to some extent in I Cor. 8.6, though its explication is left for Col. 1.15ff.

[55] C. K. Barrett, *The Gospel according to St. John* (1955), p. 476.

[56] R. E. Brown, *Jesus, God and Man* (1967), p. 29.

The New Testament passages which speak of Jesus as God, however, are comparatively few.[57] John 20.28, of course, unequivocally calls the resurrected Jesus both 'Lord' and 'God' (ὁ κύριός μου καὶ ὁ θεός μου); and though the Evangelist usually focused on messiahship and sonship in his portrayal of Jesus, this spontaneous and devotional cry but illustrates a further aspect of his christology. The Prologue to the Fourth Gospel begins by speaking of the Logos as not only existing 'in the beginning', but also as being 'with God' (πρὸς τὸν θεόν) and 'divine' (θεὸς ἦν ὁ λόγος). The reading 'the unique God' (μονογενὴς θεός) of John 1.18 is better attested textually than 'the unique Son' (μονογενὴς υἱός), though it is often set aside on theological grounds.[58] And the phrase 'this is the true God' (οὗτός ἐστιν ὁ ἀληθινὸς θεός) of I John 5.20 probably refers to Jesus as well, who is both its antecedent and the centre of focus in the argument of the immediate context.[59]

Hebrews 1.8f. quotes Ps. 45.6f. as having reference to Jesus, with the result that 'God' (ὁ θεός understood as a vocative) becomes a title for Jesus. While it is true, of course, that the author of the Letter to the Hebrews was employing the language of the Psalm to establish his point, it cannot from that be argued that therefore no significance can be attached to the address of the Son as God.[60] As R. E. Brown points out, 'we cannot presume that the author did not notice that his citation had this effect'; and this being so, 'we can say, at least, that the author saw nothing wrong in this address'.[61] By his employment of Ps. 102.25–27 in the following verses with reference to Jesus, there is little doubt that the writer to the Hebrews had every intention of attributing not only the title but also the creative activity of God to the Son. And in II Peter 1.1 the phrase 'the righteousness of our God and Saviour Jesus Christ' (τοῦ θεοῦ ἡμῶν καὶ σωτῆρος Ἰησοῦ Χριστοῦ) is very likely

---

[57] For varied and representative treatments of the passages in question, see R. Bultmann, 'The Christological Confession of the World Council of Churches', *Essays Philosophical and Theological* (ET 1955), pp. 273–90; O. Cullmann, *Christology of the New Testament*, pp. 306–14; V. Taylor, 'Does the New Testament call Jesus God?', *ExpT*, LXIII (1962), pp. 116–18; and R. E. Brown, 'Does the New Testament call Jesus God?', *TS*, XXVI (1965), pp. 545–73 (reprinted in *Jesus, God and Man*, pp. 1–38).

[58] This same consciousness underlies John 5.18 and 10.33.

[59] Cf. R. Schnackenburg, *Die Johannesbriefe* (1963), pp. 290f.

[60] Cf. V. Taylor, 'Does the New Testament call Jesus God?', *ExpT*, LXXIII (1962), p. 117.

[61] R. E. Brown, *Jesus, God and Man,*, p. 25.

a similar ascription, the use of the article evidently signalling the idea that the two titles are to be understood as referring to the one person, Jesus Christ.[62]

In the Pauline letters, somewhat surprisingly, the use of 'God' as a christological title is rarer still. And even where it is possible to understand it in this manner, there are real syntactical problems in interpretation. At the close of a recitation of the privileges of the Jews, Paul says in Rom. 9.5: 'Of whom is the Christ according to the flesh, who is over all, God blessed for ever (ὁ ὢν ἐπὶ πάντων θεὸς εὐλογητὸς εἰς τοὺς αἰῶνας.) Amen.' Scholarly opinion has been long and almost equally divided on the question as to whether 'God blessed for ever' should be understood as an ascription of Jesus, a description of the Father, or a doxology directed to God.[63] On the strength of the immediately preceding 'who is over all', which I believe clearly has reference to the contextual antecedent ὁ Χριστός, the balance of probability seems to fall on the side of Jesus as the object of the acclamation. II Thessalonians 1.12 and Titus 2.13 follow the pattern observed in II Peter 1.1 in the use of the article, and probably are to be understood as expressing christological titles as well: 'our God and Lord Jesus Christ' (τοῦ θεοῦ ἡμῶν καὶ κυρίου 'Ιησοῦ Χριστοῦ) in the first, and 'the great God and our Saviour Christ Jesus' (τοῦ μεγάλου θεοῦ καὶ σωτῆρος ἡμῶν Χριστοῦ 'Ιησοῦ) in the second. The major problem in interpreting II Thess. 1.12 in this fashion is that its immediate context is bipartite, speaking of both 'our God' and also of 'our Lord Jesus Christ', which has led many to conclude that the phrase under consideration must also be viewed as bipartite.[64] While this may very well be the case, 'the grace of the Lord Jesus Christ' is a

[62] Though often disputed it is none the less a generally reliable rule that 'when the copulative καί connects two nouns of the same case, if the article ὁ or any of its cases precedes the first of the said nouns or participles, and is not repeated before the second noun or participle, the latter always relates to the same person that is expressed or described by the first noun or participle; i.e., it denotes a further description of the first-named person' (usually attributed to Granville Sharp).

[63] The almost classical excursus on the question is by W. Sanday and A. C. Headlam, *The Epistle to the Romans* (1895), pp. 233–8, who view it on balance as ascribed to Jesus. Also O. Cullmann, *Christology of the New Testament*, pp. 312f., and A. Nygren, *Commentary on Romans* (ET 1952), pp. 358f. Taking the opposite position, see C. H. Dodd, *The Epistle of Paul to the Romans* (1932), pp. 152f., and C. K. Barrett, *The Epistle to the Romans* (1957), pp. 178f.

[64] Cf. O. Cullmann, *Christology of the New Testament*, p. 313; L. Morris, *The First and Second Epistles to the Thessalonians* (1959), p. 212.

typically Pauline expression[65] and allows the possibility that 'the grace of our God and Lord Jesus Christ' was but a variant and extension of thought on the part of the apostle. Other than these three possible instances, however, passages in Paul where $\theta\epsilon\acute{o}s$ is employed of Christ are lacking. The appeal to I Tim. 3.16 is undoubtedly illegitimate, for the reading 'who ($\acute{o}s$) was manifested in the flesh' has much stronger textual support than 'God ($\theta\epsilon\acute{o}s$) was manifested in the flesh'.

Certain observations immediately present themselves in surveying the New Testament evidence for the use of 'God' as a christological ascription. In the first place, it is obvious that the title appears quite infrequently (only eight or nine times, at best) and is reserved principally for the later canonical writings (John 1.1, 18; 20.28; I John 5.20; Heb. 1.8f.; and II Peter 1.1 in the literature from the Jewish Christian cycle of witness; Rom. 9.5; Titus 2.13; and possibly II Thess. 1.12 in Paul). Secondly, it need be noted that the appellative as applied to Jesus usually appears in association with cosmic categories (John 1.1; Heb. 1.8f.), the title 'Lord' (John 20.28; II Thess. 1.12), or the title 'Saviour' (II Peter 1.1; Titus 2.13). And thirdly, it is interesting to observe that six of its occurrences are to be found in the writings representative of the Jewish Christian cycle of witness (John's Gospel, I John, Hebrews and II Peter), whereas only two or three instances can be identified in the Pauline letters.

The generally late appearance of the title with reference to Jesus has been widely recognized to require some explanation, though a convincing rationale for this phenomenon seems yet to be forthcoming. Many earlier treatments of the passages in question have either denied the christological relevance of the title or ignored the fact that it appears principally in the later writings of the New Testament, and thus (for quite different reasons) have concluded that there is really no problem here at all. Where the title has been seen to have christological significance and where the phenomenon of its occurrence in the later canonical materials has been noted, the explanation has often centred on its association with Christian liturgy, suggesting that it came to be on the lips of Christians as a title for Christ only with the fuller development of liturgy in the latter part of the first century.[66]

---

[65] II Cor. 13.14; though see also II Cor. 1.2.
[66] Cf., e.g., R. E. Brown, *Jesus, God and Man,* pp. 30–38.

Probably a final explanation for the late employment of the title God for Jesus in the New Testament will continue to elude us, for the data with which to work is very scanty. Theologically, however, it appears that only as the understanding of the lordship of Jesus developed in the early church from a dominantly religious concept to include cosmic and philosophic categories as well that the title God, which carried an unambiguous definition as compared with the range of meaning inherent in Lord, came to be also ascribed to Jesus. Paul seems to have appreciated the metaphysical implications of Jesus' lordship earlier, and expressed them sooner, than most of his Jewish Christian colleagues for whom background, present situation, and missionary outreach tended to hold to basically functional and religious categories of thought and expression. Inevitably, however, implications inherent to their commitments were bound to come to the fore, which is evidently what we are witnessing in regard to the title θεός in the Johannine writings, Hebrews and II Peter. In addition, such an explication of their convictions may very well have been encouraged and stimulated by the circumstance of growing acknowledgment of the Imperial Cult. While official assertion of divinity was not made until Domitian's blasphemous claim to deification in the mid-nineties of the first century (apart from the insanity of Caligula and the veiled pretenses of Nero), the eastern provinces of the empire often rendered such homage none the less much earlier. It may therefore be that the express usage of θεός for Jesus in the later New Testament writings was in part a reaction to such assertions; especially so in the case of the Johannine materials, where the title may very well have been employed not only as a confession of faith but also as a counter-blast to the Imperial Cult which Christianity denied.

The problem as to why Paul so seldom ascribed the title to Jesus is a real one, which also calls for some explanation. Yet it seems that little can be offered along theological lines, for certainly Paul, if anyone, possessed a developed and high christology. He certainly thought of Jesus as divine, and it was he who seems to have employed the associated title Lord most frequently. While without sufficient evidence to be certain, it may well be that he did not usually attribute the title to Jesus due to the confusion it would cause among many in the Gentile world. To employ the title with respect to Jesus in a Jewish setting would have generated one of two reactions: (1) a rethinking of traditional monotheism in an attempt to include the idea of plurality within a basic unity, or (2) the charge of blasphemy. It would hardly have caused Jews to think along polytheistic lines. Everything in Israel's history and consciousness militated against that. But to employ the title with respect to Jesus in a Gentile milieu without in some way indicating its relationship to monotheism would have invariably resulted in the proclamation of Jesus as one god among many, and undermined the basic structure of Paul's message. In order to proclaim both the absolute lordship of Jesus and yet to preserve the proclamation of Jesus from being accepted as another polytheistic presentation, Paul employed the bipartite confession 'God the Father' and the 'Lord Jesus Christ' – using the title God to signal the note of monotheism and the title Lord to designate absolute supremacy, though for him they were roughly equivalent. But as occasionally the unitary confession of the early church that 'Jesus is Lord' appears in his writings, so his consciousness of the nature of his Lord occasionally expressed itself in the direct assertion that Christ is 'God blessed for ever' and in joining the titles God and Lord in respect to Jesus.

We might have expected that the designation of Jesus as God would have taken place more easily – and, as the argument often runs, therefore exclusively – in a hellenistic milieu. But, as a matter of fact, there is good reason to believe that it should be understood as (1) associated with the christological designation Lord, though the attitude expressed in the ascription was undoubtedly supported by several other strands of supplementary conviction as well; (2) coming to explicit expression as a result of the extension of Christian thought into cosmic and philosophic spheres, which extension was both inevitable and externally stimulated; and (3) more prominent in Jewish Christian circles than in the church's Gentile mission, though not frequent in either, for both theological and circumstantial reasons.

SAVIOUR

The title σωτήρ, as has been frequently pointed out, was widely current in the hellenistic world;[67] though, as has also been often

---

[67] See P. Wendland, 'ΣΩΤΗΡ', *ZNW*, V (1904), pp. 335–53; A. Deissmann, *Light from the Ancient East* (1927), pp. 363–5; W. Bousset, *Kyrios Christos*, pp. 293–301.

noted, it is present in the LXX as a title for God, and thus was part of the biblical heritage of Jewish Christianity as well.[68] But while the early Christians undoubtedly were aware of its use in Greek religious and quasi-religious materials, and certainly conscious of its employment in the Greek version of their own Scriptures, the designation of Jesus as 'Saviour' seems not to have been derived directly from either, though the term itself was part of the common coinage of the realm. The earliest christological use of the title appears rather to have stemmed from and been associated with the church's consciousness of the lordship of Jesus in general, and the extension of lordship into cosmic and metaphysical considerations in particular.

This is indicated by the contexts in which the title appears in the canonical Jewish Christian materials. Peter is reported in Acts 5.31 to have said: 'God exalted him [Jesus] at his right hand as Leader (ἀρχηγόν) and Saviour (σωτῆρα), to give repentance to Israel and forgiveness of sins.' The interests of the passage are admittedly more religious than speculative. Yet it is of significance to note that the appropriateness of the title for Jesus is based upon the fact of his exaltation and to observe that the title is associated with ἀρχηγός, a term readily lending itself to cosmic interpretation.[69] Consistently in II Peter the title appears in the double ascription 'our Lord and Saviour'.[70] And assuming a traditional basis of some type, though acknowledging a degree of assimilation for the sake of a Gentile audience, it is also of some importance that Luke 2.11 connects the title Saviour with that of Lord in the angelic announcement of 'a Saviour, who is Christ the Lord'. Jesus is referred to in John 4.42 and I John 4.14 as not only a Saviour, but more significantly here as 'the Saviour of the world' (ὁ σωτὴρ τοῦ κόσμου), thereby exhibiting both religious and cosmic interests.

Paul also employs Saviour with reference to Jesus, though relatively less frequently and with less specification as to the collation of titles. In Phil. 3.20, he says that 'we await a Saviour, the Lord

---

[68] Isa. 43.3, 11; 45.15, 21; 49.26; 60.16; 63.8; Jer. 14.8; Hos. 13.4; Pss. 24.5 (LXX); 26.9 (LXX); Micah 7.7 (LXX). Cf. Luke 1.47; I Tim. 1.1; 2.3; 4.10; Titus 1.3; 2.10; 3.4; Jude 25. On God as Saviour in talmudic literature, see *Str.-Bil.*, I, pp. 67–70.

[69] On the use of ἀρχηγός and its cognates in first religious contexts and then speculative discussions, see above, pp. 54–58.

[70] II Peter 1.11; 2.20; 3.2, 18.

Jesus Christ' (σωτῆρα ἀπεκδεχόμεθα κύριον 'Ιησοῦν Χριστόν), which suggests some association of titles. And in Eph. 5.23 Christ is spoken of as 'the head of the church' and 'the Saviour of the body' (κεφαλὴ τῆς ἐκκλησίας . . . σωτὴρ τοῦ σώματος), language which refers to spiritual lordship. Acts 13.23 and the Pastoral Epistles,[71] however, present Paul as designating Jesus simply as 'a Saviour' or 'our Saviour'.[72] Many, of course, are willing to accept the evidence of only Phil. 3.20 as being truly Paul. But even attributing these latter statements in the Acts, Ephesians, and the Pastorals to the apostle in one way or another, the use of σωτήρ as a christological title in Paul must be judged to be relatively infrequent and somewhat innocuous in its association of ideas.

It appears necessary, therefore, to conclude from the data above (1) that though Saviour was a common title in the religious and quasi-religious vocabularly of the Greek world, it was also part of first-century Judaism's heritage as a title for God, and thus also a part of the biblical heritage of early Jewish Christians; (2) that as a christological designation the term Saviour had some currency in early Jewish Christian circles along with the more common ascription 'God's Salvation'[73] and in conjunction with other appellations which were later to receive more specific definition;[74] (3) that whereas Jesus as God's Salvation was based upon the concept of messiahship, as demonstrated previously,[75] Jesus as Saviour stemmed originally from the strand of ideas having to do with lordship and received extension of meaning as the understanding of Jesus' lordship increased; and (4) that the title Saviour with reference to Jesus appears mainly, and as almost a *terminus technicus* only, in the later writings of the Jewish Christian cycle of witness and the Gentile mission of the church,[76] for it was only as it became extended into speculative spheres that it took on a rather fixed meaning and was able to displace the earlier ascription God's Salvation.

The explanation for the meagre use of Saviour as a christological

---

[71] II Tim. 1.10; Titus 1.4; 2.13; 3.6.

[72] Or 'Salvation' (σωτηρία) in Acts 13.23, as per P[74], the so-called *Koine* group of manuscripts, the Vulgate, and the major Syrian tradition.

[73] On 'God's Salvation' as a christological title, see above, pp. 99–103.

[74] Particularly, of course, κύριος and ἀρχηγός.

[75] See above, pp. 99–103.

[76] As a *terminus technicus,* see also Ignatius, Eph. 1.1; Mag. (Intro.), Phila. 9.2; Smy. 7.1.

title in the early New Testament materials along the lines that 'the use of the name in Greek religion, and above all in Caesar worship, restricted and delayed its currency in the primitive tradition'[77] fails to be convincing. After all, the title Lord was also used extensively in such contexts yet it suffers no similar limitation, at least in the Pauline letters. More likely the rationale behind the phenomena of its infrequent appearance and generally late use in the New Testament is to be explained by (1) the title's association with a cosmic understanding of lordship within the church, and (2) the already common employment of the expression God's Salvation to signal the religious and historical aspects in the salvation Jesus brought. And in this, its terminological history as a christological ascription in the New Testament is somewhat similar to that of the attribution of the title God to Jesus.[78]

THE WORD

The relation of the Johannine λόγος to the other christological titles of the New Testament is extremely difficult to determine, principally because it appears explicitly only in the Johannine writings and because it has so many parallels in the speech and literature of the day. John 1.1-5 refers to Jesus in terms of the λόγος who is pre-existent with God, essentially divine, the Creator of all that exists, and the source of life and light. John 1.14-18 continues this imagery, speaking of him as the incarnate glory of God the Father who is the promised bringer of grace and the revealer of God's person. I John 1.1 describes Jesus as the incarnate 'Word of Life' (τοῦ λόγου τῆς ζωῆς), and Rev. 19.13 as 'the Word of God' (ὁ λόγος τοῦ θεοῦ). The description of the Son in Heb. 1.3f. as 'the effulgence of [God's] glory and the express representation of his person' (ἀπαύγασμα τῆς δόξης καὶ χαρακτὴρ τῆς ὑποστάσεως αὐτοῦ), although using ῥῆμα rather than λόγος and although ascribing it to his activity rather than to his person (τῷ ῥήματι τῆς δυνάμεως αὐτοῦ) expresses a Logos christology in all but the name. And Paul's

---

[77] V. Taylor, *Names of Jesus*, p. 109.

[78] Understanding the titles God and Saviour to have been based principally on a cosmic understanding of Jesus' lordship, and thus to have been the product of a similar development of thought in the early church, goes a long way towards appreciating their union in the difficult passages of II Peter 1.2 and Titus 2.13 (also the union of God and Lord in II Thess. 1.12); and, in turn, tends to support our earlier treatment of the syntactical problems involved in these verses.

depiction of Christ in the Letter to the Colossians is very similar, even ascribing to Jesus such kindred designations as σοφία, ἀρχή, and πρωτότοκος, though in a slightly different context.[79]

Affinities to the Johannine Logos are present in the religious writings of ancient Greece and Iran, as has been frequently pointed out.[80] Many, however, have begun to be convinced that such parallels have been considerably overdrawn and that the connections between the New Testament and these bodies of literature are slight.[81] Probably more to the point in positing a terminological background for the Johannine usage are the statements regarding the Word, Wisdom, and Torah in early Jewish writings, both orthodox and sectarian. Judaism understood God's Word (דבר) to have almost autonomous powers and substance once it was spoken;[82] to be, in fact, 'a concrete reality, a veritable cause'.[83] Thus Sir. 42.15 says that 'by the Word of God are his works', and Wisd. Sol. 9.1–3 speaks of God as the One 'who made all things by thy Word, and with thy Wisdom formed man'; expressions built upon the reference to the creative word of God in Ps. 33.6 and the characterization of the near-personified word in Isa. 55.10f. More graphic still, Wisd. Sol. 18.15 reads: 'Thine all-powerful Word leaped from heaven down from the royal throne, a stern warrior.'

In the Targums, the term מימר occurs. Usually it means simply a word or message which is spoken or conveyed in some manner, without any hypostatization and with no ontological nuances involved. At times, however, מימר serves as a sort of buffer-word for God, as in Ex. 14.31: 'Israel believed in the Name of the Word (מימר) of the Lord'; and occasionally as a substitute for 'the Spirit of the Lord', as in Isa. 63.14. Thus, as Cullmann rightly observes, 'the fact that *memra* can be used instead of the divine name presupposes a special reflection about the "word of God" as such, independent of context'.[84]

---

[79] Cf. above, pp. 55–58.

[80] For an extensive bibliography, see *TWNT*, IV, pp. 69–71 (ET, pp. 69–71).

[81] See, e.g., E. M. Sidebottom's survey of opinion in *The Christ of the Fourth Gospel*, pp. 26ff.

[82] Cf. C. H. Dodd, *Fourth Gospel*, p. 264.

[83] G. F. Moore, *Judaism*, I, p. 414.

[84] O. Cullmann, *Christology of the New Testament*, p. 256. For a survey of discussion on the Targumic *Memra* and the Johannine *Logos*, see T. W. Manson, *On Paul and John* (1963), pp. 147–9, who believes it 'very improbable that the

Just when the concepts of Wisdom and Torah became joined with that of the Word is impossible to say. Probably they grew up together until they coalesced, so that at some time prior to the first century what was said about the one could be also said of the other. In Prov. 8.22–26, the hypostatized Wisdom speaks as follows:

The Lord created me at the beginning of his way,
  the first of his acts of old.
Ages ago I was set up, at the first,
  before the beginning of the earth.
When there were no depths I was brought forth,
  when there were no springs abounding with water.
Before the mountains had been shaped, before the hills,
  I was brought forth;
before he had made the earth with its fields,
  or the first of the dust of the world.

This conception of Wisdom as a pre-existent and personal entity is repeated elsewhere in Jewish Wisdom literature, probably coming to loftiest expression in the claim that Wisdom is 'the image of his [God's] eternal light' in Wisd. Sol. 7.26. For the rabbis, the Wisdom of God was the Torah, which they describe as pre-existent, first-born, the agent of creation, life, light, and truth.[85] In Test. Levi 14.4, the Torah is identified as 'the light to lighten every man', and in the Manual of Discipline 11.11 the 'divine thought' is the origin of all.

We need not espouse the thesis that the Prologue to the Fourth Gospel stems directly from an earlier hymn to Wisdom[86] to be impressed by the fact that the parallels between John's Logos christology and Jewish Wisdom and Torah motifs are striking. Nor can we deny that Logos concepts were widely employed in the religious and philosophic speculations of Hellenism. Undoubtedly both the Jewish and the Grecian uses of λόγος played their part in the explication of the Johannine Logos doctrine, for the religious language of Jewish Christians in Asia Minor during

---

Memra of the Targums has anything to do fundamentally with John's Logos doctrine' yet suggests that 'the linguistic usage of the Targum may have influenced the language of the Prologue'.

[85] See *Str.-Bil.*, II, pp. 353ff.; III, p. 131.

[86] Cf. J. R. Harris, *The Origin of the Prologue to St. John's Gospel* (1917); *idem*, 'Athena, Sophia, and the Logos', *BJRL*, VII (1922–23), pp. 56ff.

the latter part of the first century was certainly influenced by both
(1) the Wisdom literature and the rabbinic codifications of Torah,
on the Jewish side, and (2) current expressions employed in the
popular blend of Stoic and Platonic philosophy, on the Greek.
Probably, in fact, this overlapping of expression between Jewish
and pagan modes of conceptualization was the very reason why
John expressed his christology in this manner, employing a terminological bridge which had already been constructed.

But while the terminological bridge may well have drawn its
materials from the worlds of both Judaism and Hellenism, the
conviction upon which the New Testament Logos christology was
built and the consciousness which impelled it to expression seems
to have been that of the lordship of Jesus, understood in both
cosmic and religious terms. All of the passages in which a Logos
christology can be identified, whether expressly or more inferen-
tially so, are set in a context of both cosmic and religious concern.
And all appear in the later canonical writings. While Paul based his
understanding of Jesus to a large extent upon that of his Christian
predecessors, in the apprehension of Jesus in specifically cosmic
and metaphysical terms he seems to have led the way. The un-
equivocal christological use of λόγος in the Johannine writings,
therefore, is probably to be understood as based upon the conviction of Jesus' cosmic lordship and expressed by means of a
circumstantial adaptation to the appreciation of a particular audience for whom the expression was especially meaningful.[87]

---

[87] Cf. the emphasis of C. F. D. Moule, 'The Influence of Circumstances on
the Use of Christological Terms', *JTS*, X (1959), pp. 263.

V

THE CRYSTALLIZATION OF THOUGHT

THE PREVIOUS THREE chapters have dealt with separate titles and major strands of conviction in early christological thought. It is not enough, however, to stop there. Some attention must be given as well to issues regarding relationships between the individual titles, the rationale underlying developments, and the interaction of functional and speculative modes of conceptualization. It is with such questions that the present chapter is concerned in discussing the crystallization of christological thought in early Jewish Christianity.

THE POINT OF DEPARTURE

It has become fashionable of late to account for the origin of New Testament christology and the various stages of its early development by the theory of an original futuristic orientation and a series of gradual adjustments necessitated by the delay of the expected *parousia*. Taking the cue from Johannes Weiss and Albert Schweitzer, though with considerable refinement of methodology and variation of detail, Rudolf Bultmann and those owing their inspiration to him have largely carried the day on this point in Germany and in many quarters within New Testament scholarship generally.

The evidence cited in the previous two chapters, however, is to the effect that it was not the anticipated *parousia* and its delay which were foundational in early christology, but the resurrection of Jesus which served to trigger Christian thought in such a fashion as to establish solid convictions about Jesus. While Jesus made a decided personal impact upon his disciples during the course of his earthly ministry, it was the fact of his resurrection from the dead, as interpreted first by Jesus himself and then by the Spirit, which was the historical point of departure in their christological understanding. From the perspective of the resurrection, the earliest believers were able not only to surmount the scandal of the cross but also to appreciate that event as the climax of a ministry which was throughout the fulfilment and apex of redemptive history. And on this basis they came to understand the true character of their Master and the real nature of their mission. The older theological debates regarding the centrality of either Jesus' teaching or his death in Christian faith, important as they were, have tended to obscure the point that in the earliest days of the apostolic period it was the resurrection of Jesus which was central. Both the teaching and the death were interpreted in light of the resurrection, and both had significance for the early Christians only because Jesus had actually been raised from the dead.

Stemming from this historical point of departure was the conviction regarding the messiahship of Jesus, which, in turn, itself became the basis for the major christological titles in the Jewish mission of the church and the focal point in all further thought about Jesus in early Christianity. Contrary to a generally held opinion that the original motif was the confession of Jesus as Lord,[1] or the current post-Bultmannian insistence of son-of-man christology as foundational in the early church,[2] or Eduard Schweizer's suggestion that christological thought arose from the Jewish conception of the humiliation and exaltation of the pious man,[3] the evidence from the Jewish Christian materials of the New Testament indicates that the earliest consciousness of believers in Jerusalem in the post-resurrection period was that 'Jesus is the Christ', and that from this acknowledgment the major developments within early Jewish Christianity flowed.

The relation between the confessions 'Jesus is the Christ' and 'Jesus is Lord' is intricate. Both were employed in the Christian community at Jerusalem – Luke even represents Peter as placing

---

[1] O. Cullmann, e.g., notes the dual confession of Jesus as 'Lord' and as 'Christ' in the early church, but considers 'Lord' to be the common factor and fundamental element in all early Christian confession (*Earliest Christian Confessions*, esp. pp. 27–30, 57–62; *Christology of the New Testament*, p. 216); though he also argues for the title 'Messiah' as having 'a special place among all the other christological titles' (*Christology of the New Testament*, p. 111).

[2] F. Hahn begins his study of the christological titles on this premise (*Christologische Hoheitstitel*, p. 13). Cf. also H. E. Tödt, *Son of Man in the Synoptic Tradition, passim*. Bultmann argued for messiahship as the basic datum in the church's formulation (*Theology of the New Testament*, I, pp. 42f.), but in such a manner as to lay the foundations for the post-Bultmannian insistence on the *parousia* as determinative and Son of Man as the basic title in early thought.

[3] E. Schweizer, *Lordship and Discipleship*, esp. pp. 36, 41.

'Lord' first in the announcement that 'God has made this Jesus whom you crucified both Lord and Christ' in Acts 2.36 – and each seems to have influenced the other in their respective developments. As we have sought to demonstrate in what has gone before, the titles 'Christ' and 'Lord' stand as foundational motifs in two distinguishable strands of thought. But in that (1) the one is based upon the conviction regarding Jesus' resurrection from the dead and the other upon the consciousness of his present exaltation,[4] and (2) the proclamation of Jesus as the Christ was more prominent in the Jewish Christian cycle of early Christianity whereas that of Jesus as Lord was used in the Gentile mission almost exclusively, the conclusion seems inevitable that 'historically and logically the question of Jesus' messiahship preceded the question of his lordship or his sonship'.[5] Paul's treatment of the confession in Phil. 2.9–11 may reflect some assimilation for his Gentile audience,[6] as may very well be the case in Rom. 10.9 and I Cor. 12.3 as well. Likewise Luke's handling of Peter's words recorded in Acts 2.36 may evidence something of the same, at least in its order of titles.

While our study has been primarily concerned with early Jewish Christianity, it is possible to relate our findings here regarding the point of departure in christological thought to the other strata of understanding in the New Testament, as follows:

1. For Jesus, the evidence strongly suggests that the fundamental datum was that of sonship, and that it was from this basic conviction that he undertook the tasks assigned to the Messiah – understood, at least from his baptism, in terms of the Danielic Son of Man and the Isaian Suffering Servant. In explication of the nature of his mission, he spoke of himself as the Son of Man, thereby employing a term which was free from political connotations and which he could use to signal the idea of vindication through suffering. Only rarely was he willing to acknowledge the

---

[4] Understanding the resurrection and the exaltation of Jesus, while intimately connected, to be distinguishable; and suggesting that Paul's tendency to speak of these as almost one stems from his emphasis upon lordship, which was based upon both resurrection and exaltation, rather than messiahship, which was founded in the first instance upon resurrection.

[5] V. H. Neufeld, *Earliest Christian Confessions*, p. 142. Werner Kramer objects to such an understanding on the basis of his theory of separate and dichotomous provenances for these three titles (*Christ, Lord, Son of God*, cop. pp. 7₂f.).

[6] See above, pp. 126f.

ascription of Messiah, for that title was not really a fitting self-designation until after the fulfilment of the messianic office as he understood it and had become bound by nationalistic strictures.

2. For early Jewish Christians, the basic datum was that of messiahship as established on the basis of the resurrection of Jesus from the dead. In addition, on the basis of their consciousness of his exaltation into the presence of the Father and of his continuing ministry in their midst through the Spirit, they also confessed Jesus as Lord. But it was primarily Jesus as the Christ, the Son of God, and titles associated with this complex of ideas which were meaningful in a Jewish milieu, that received prominence in their thought and proclamation. Son of Man, though it had been the title Jesus used by way of self-designation, seems to have had little, if any, meaning for them in the interim period between his sufferings and final glory.

3. In the preaching of Paul and for Gentile Christians generally, the basic datum seems to have been that of lordship. Christological titles appropriate in the Jewish Christian cycle of witness appear to have lacked meaning for Gentile believers. Thus Christ, while too firmly wedded to the person of Jesus to be set aside, became primarily a proper name; Seed of David and Son of God appear mainly in traditional portions; Suffering Servant comes to expression only by way of allusion; God's Salvation is translated into Saviour; and priestly and kingly motifs disappear almost entirely. Likewise a son-of-man ascription is not employed by Paul for both theological and circumstantial reasons, though elements of it may appear in revised form in the apostle's Second Adam figure.

THE FUSING OF THE STRANDS AND MOTIFS

Three major groupings of christological titles are distinguishable in the materials of early Jewish Christianity: (1) motifs which were distinctive to Jewish Christian expression; (2) affirmations felt to be involved in the conviction of messiahship; and (3) appellations associated with the consciousness of lordship. It has not been too difficult to determine the point of departure in the theological enterprise of the early church, for the New Testament itself points to the resurrection as the basic factor in early Christian conviction and suggests that on the basis of this it was the Church's acknowledgment of Jesus as the Messiah which was the original theological foundation for its early christology. Scholarship's task here has been to test these claims as to plausibility with regard to first-century expectations, inherent consistency, and competing interpretations. While objections have been often voiced, the evidence and conclusions presented in this study have been in the direction of supporting this New Testament understanding.

But we are faced with a much more difficult problem in explicating how these strands and motifs became fused into a christology more or less structured. Here there are no explicit pointers as to the process. And the diversity of motifs, each with its own particular background and many able to reflect varied nuances of meaning, makes the task extremely complex. No hope is to be entertained for the explication of precise relationships. Yet some observations can be made regarding the fusing of the early christological strands generally, and of some of the individual titles in particular.

In the union of titles that took place during the apostolic period, two phenomena, at least, can be observed. In the first place, certain appellations appear to have had little direct impact upon the formulation of christological thought. Evidently, this was because (1) in a situation somewhat removed from the original context these terms failed to carry the meaning they had conveyed before, or (2) the meaning they conveyed before was felt to be expressed more adequately in other ascriptions more recently applied. As we have seen, there was a variety of christological titles employed in early Jewish Christianity. Undoubtedly, also, this variety of expression reflected to some degree differing foci of interests and differing conceptions of Jesus within Palestinian Christianity. But in the crystalization of thought which inevitably results in any movement (whether it be judged legitimate or not in any given situation), certain terms were found to be no longer as meaningful as originally considered, and the meaning of some was felt to be better expressed in other ways. This seems to have occurred very early in the case of angelomorphic christology. And from the fact that they tend to appear in the later Jewish Christian materials as more or less archaized titles, it seems to have been in the process of occurring for such ascriptions as the eschatological Mosaic Prophet, the Name, the Righteous One, the Copestone and God's Salvation. In effect, then, some of these more distinctive hebraic ascriptions did not find their place in the continuing mainstream of New Testament thought. That is not to say that they had no influence upon later christological formulation, for in many cases the positive features which each title signalled were incorporated into Christian thinking by the use of other titles or different groupings of ideas.

In the general christological consensus being formed in the apostolic period, there was also a basis for the rise of sectarian attitudes. We are able only to conjecture, yet it seems reasonable to suggest that as long as there existed a state of unexamined fluidity in the thinking of the earliest Christians there was little reason to distinguish between mainstream perspectives and those of a sectarian nature. But as christological thought became both crystalized, on the one hand, and expansive in scope, on the other, there would be those who for either traditional or doctrinal reasons would set themselves in opposition to such developments. In reaction to the direction that the crystalization of thought in mainstream Christianity was taking, some undoubtedly latched onto earlier titles which they felt were being ignored and certain perspectives which they considered illegitimately relegated to an inferior position in the structure of Christian thought. And though subdued in the New Testament which represents that mainstream development, these motifs found expression again in the Jewish Christian materials of the second century and following, as we have seen.

Secondly, it should be noted that in the fusing of titles in early Christian thought, new insights were gained and implications inherent in the believers' basic convictions were expressed. Thus, for example, the intimacy of relationship indicated in the title Son of God, ideas of divine presence and power signalled by the appellative the Name, and concepts regarding transcendence and sovereignty included in the ascription Lord, when collated, led to a heightened appreciation of the person of Jesus. This was undoubtedly the case as well in the association of the κατάβασις—ἀνάβασις theme, the copestone ascription, and the complex of designations that clustered about the terms ἀρχή and πρωτότοκος, with a cosmic understanding of the lordship of Jesus. While such details are not spelled out in the New Testament, this fusion of titles and the intertwining of their connotations was probably the terminological basis for the expression of such convictions as preexistence, divine status, and virgin birth. Likewise, the collation of loving obedience implied in the designation Son or Son of God, the suffering element contained in the concept of Servant as re-interpreted by Jesus, and the ascription of Saviour undoubtedly gave insight into the nature of their Messiah's mission.

FUNCTIONAL AND ONTOLOGICAL CATEGORIES

At many points in our discussion of early christology, a discernible pattern in the thought of the earliest Christians has emerged: the initial appreciation of Jesus in terms of his redemptive activity and the subsequent understanding of him in terms of his character or essential nature – or, to put it into the technical parlance more common today, a decided tendency to think first in functional and then in ontological categories.[7] The dogmatic treatments of christology have invariably followed the logical order of con-sidering first the person of Christ and then his work, as is im-mediately obvious in leafing through the volumes on systematic theology which have been written since the apostolic period. And there is evidence to suggest that for Jesus himself a filial conscious-ness preceded and was the basis for his messianic consciousness, so that for him an awareness of character preceded that of mission. But for the Jerusalem Christians the functional had epistemic priority, even though ontological categories may be logically prior and were inherent in the substratum of their thought. For them, Jesus was first understood and proclaimed principally in terms of his redemptive activity on behalf of man, and only through their own reflections and circumstances arising as catalytic challenges to thought (both, I believe, providentially directed) were the implications of those earliest commitments explicated in regard to his person.

Such a phenomenon, of course, is true in any commitment or in the rise of any movement. The bluntness of human perception, the failure to see immediately inherent relationships, and the necessity for all men to work from the concrete to the abstract in concep-tualization, all combine to make ontological affirmations in large

---

[7] For representative treatments on the relationship between functional and ontological categories of thought in the early church, see O. Cullmann, *Christology of the New Testament,* esp. pp. 325f.; V. Taylor, *Person of Christ in New Testament Teaching,* pp. 209–16; R. P. Meye, 'The Reply of Professor Cullmann to Roman Catholic Critics' (translating Cullmann's letter), *SJT,* XV (1962), pp. 36–43; R. H. Fuller, *Foundations of New Testament Christology,* esp. pp. 104–6; G. A. F. Knight, 'Building Theological Bridges', *Jews and Christians* (1965), pp. 108–36.

measure dependent upon the apprehension of the functional and derivative from it. And even when an awareness of reality and of its significances is born, it is an axiom of human experience that the underlying conviction precedes any adequate or precise expression.

And this was especially true in the case of the early Jewish believers in Jesus. By temperament, the Hebrew mind is more interested in acting than being, in the dynamic than the static, and in the historical than the speculative. As suggested earlier, such an outlook is probably best illustrated in Israel's messianic hope, where the greater emphasis in both canonical and noncanonical writings is laid upon the Messianic Age and the activity of God in that Age than upon the person of the Messiah who would bring it about.[8] And as to circumstances, the earliest Christians of Jerusalem were placed in a situation which both encouraged reflection along certain lines and stifled the full expression of their faith along others.

It has become popular of late to argue for the discontinuity of christological conviction between Jesus, the Aramiac church in Palestine, and hellenistic Christianity (whether Jewish, Gentile, or even Pauline). But our study has shown that while the christology of the earliest Jewish believers was primarily functional, it presupposed and carried in substratum ontological commitments; that while it received extensive development even within the Jewish Christian cycle of witness, that development was of the nature of explication and not deviation; that while it spoke mainly in terms understandable within a Jewish milieu, the proclamation of Christ in the Gentile mission in terms understandable in that context was in essentials not unfaithful to the earlier preaching; and that there is more than merely an implicit continuity existing between the self-consciousness of Jesus, the convictions of the earliest Jewish Christians regarding Jesus, and the affirmations of Paul in the Gentile mission.

It must therefore be concluded that the christology of early Jewish Christianity (1) found its initial point of departure in the resurrection and exaltation of Jesus; (2) gained support from the remembrance of Jesus' own teaching and consciousness, though neither were properly understood until after the resurrection; (3) derived substantiation from the Old Testament Scriptures, as those

---

[8] See above, pp. 63f.

biblical portions to which it looked were christocentrically understood; (4) received development through the guidance of the Spirit employing circumstances to deepen reflection; and (5) faced a situation in the Jewish mission of the church which caused it to develop and express itself along certain lines and tended to retard it along others. Although a breadth of conviction existed from the very first, undoubtedly containing within it also some diversity of opinion, a christological consensus forming the mainstream of Christian thought seems to have been formed very early. Under pressure, especially during the fifties and sixties of the first century, this consensus may at times have been for many more formal than real. But before the silencing of the Jerusalem church's effective ministry in the events of the sixties, the Gentile ministry of the church had taken root and was flourishing. And although the terminology was necessarily transposed to meet the concerns of another audience, it was the christology of Paul, the apostle to the Gentiles, which continued the main convictions of that earlier mainstream faith.

A SELECTED BIBLIOGRAPHY

I. JEWISH CHRISTIANITY

Bauer, W. *Rechtgläubigkeit und Ketzerei im ältesten Christentum* (Tübingen: Mohr, 1934).

Black, M. *The Scrolls and Christian Origins: Studies in the Jewish Background of the New Testament* (London: Nelson, 1961).

Brandon, S. G. F. *The Fall of Jerusalem and the Christian Church* (London: SPCK, 1951).

Bultmann, R. *Primitive Christianity in its Contemporary Setting,* trans. R. H. Fuller (London: Thames & Hudson, 1956).

Burkitt, F. C. *Christian Beginnings* (London: University of London, 1924).

Carrington, P. *The Early Christian Church,* 2 vols. (Cambridge: University Press, 1957).

Chadwick, H. *The Circle and the Ellipse* (Oxford: Clarendon, 1959).

Daniélou, J. *The Theology of Jewish Christianity,* trans. J. A. Baker (Chicago: Regnery, 1964).

— *The Dead Sea Scrolls and Primitive Christianity,* trans. S. Attanasio (Baltimore: Helicon Press, 1958).

Dix, G. *Jew and Greek* (London: Dacre Press, 1953).

Elliott-Binns, L. E. *Galilean Christianity* (London: SCM Press, 1956).

Filson, F. V. *Three Crucial Decades* (London: Epworth Press, 1963).

Fitzmyer, J. A. 'Jewish Christianity in Acts in Light of the Qumran Scrolls', *Studies in Luke-Acts,* ed. L. E. Keck and J. L. Martyn (Nashville: Abingdon, 1966), pp. 233–57.

Flusser, D. 'The Dead Sea Sect and Pre-Pauline Christianity', *Aspects of the Dead Sea Scrolls* (Scripta Hierosolymitana IV), ed. C. Rabin and Y. Yadin (Jerusalem: Hebrew University, 1958), pp. 215–66.

Goppelt, L. *Christentum und Judentum in erstem und zweiten Jahrhundert* (Gütersloh: Bertelsmann, 1955).

Haenchen, E. 'The Book of Acts as Source Material for the History of Early Christianity', *Studies in Luke-Acts,* ed. L. E. Keck and J. L. Martyn (Nashville: Abingdon, 1966), pp. 258–78.

Hare, D. R. A. *The Theme of Jewish Persecution of Christians in the Gospel according to St. Matthew* (Cambridge: University Press, 1967).

Harnack, A. *The Mission and Expansion of Christianity,* trans. J. Moffatt (London: Williams & Norgate, 1908).

Hort, F. J. A. *Judaistic Christianity* (London: Macmillan, 1894).

Knox, W. L. *St. Paul and the Church of Jerusalem* (Cambridge: University Press, 1925).

Koester, H., 'GNŌMAI DIAPHOROI: The Origin and Nature of Diversification in the History of Early Christianity', *HTR,* LVIII (1965), pp. 279–318.

Lampe, G. W. H. *St. Luke and the Church of Jerusalem* (London: Athlone Press, 1969).

Lietzmann, H. *The Beginnings of the Christian Church* (Vol. I of *A History of the Early Church*), trans. B. L. Woolf (London: Nicholson & Watson, 1937).

Lohmeyer, E. *Galiläa und Jerusalem* (Göttingen: Vandendoeck & Ruprecht, 1936).

Longenecker, R. N. 'Christianity in Jerusalem', Appendix in *Paul, Apostle of Liberty* (New York: Harper & Row, 1964), pp. 271–88.

Mowry, L. *The Dead Sea Scrolls and the Early Church* (Chicago: University of Chicago Press, 1962).

Munck, J. 'Jewish Christianity according to the Acts of the Apostles', *Paul and the Salvation of Mankind,* trans. F. Clarke (London: SCM Press, 1959), pp. 210–46.

— 'Jewish Christianity in Post-Apostolic Times', *NTS,* VI (1960), pp. 103–16.

Peake, A. S. *Paul and the Jewish Christians* (Manchester: University Press, 1929).

Pfleiderer, O. *Das Urchristentum,* 2 vols. (Berlin: Reimer, 1887).

Pines, S. 'The Jewish Christians of the Early Centuries of Christianity according to a New Source', *Proceedings of the Israel Academy of Science and Humanities* (in Hebrew), II (13, 1966), pp. 1–73.

Reicke, B. *Diakonie, Festfreude und Zelos* (Uppsala: Lundequistska, 1951).

— 'Der geschichtliche Hintergrund des Apostelkonzils und der Antioch-Episode', *Studia Paulina,* ed. W. C. van Unnik and G. Sevenster (Haarlem: Bohn, 1953), pp. 172–87.

— *Glaube und Leben der Urgemeinde* (Zürich: Zwingli, 1957).

Schlatter, A. *The Church in the New Testament Period,* trans. P. P. Levertoff (London: SPCK, 1955).

Schmithals, W. *Paul and James,* trans. D. M. Barton (London: SCM Press, 1965).

Schoeps, H. J. *Theologie und Geschichte des Judenchristentums* (Tübingen: Mohr, 1949).

— *Aus frühchristlicher Zeit* (Tübingen: Mohr, 1950).

— *Urgemeinde, Judenchristentum, Gnosis* (Tübingen: Mohr, 1956).

Scott, E. F. *The Beginnings of the Church* (New York: Scribner's, 1914).

— *The First Age of Christianity* (London: Allen & Unwin, 1926).

Simon, M. *St. Stephen and the Hellenists* (New York: Longmans, Green, 1958).

Spiro, A. 'Stephen's Samaritan Background', Appendix V in J. Munck's *The Acts of the Apostles* (New York: Doubleday, 1967), pp. 285–300.

Strecker, G. *Das Judenchristentum in den Pseudoklementinen* (Berlin: Akademie, 1958).

Streeter, B. H. *The Primitive Church* (London: Macmillan, 1929).

Turner, H. E. W. *The Pattern of Christian Truth: A Study of the Relations between Orthodoxy and Heresy in the Early Church* (London: Mowbray, 1954).

II. EARLY CHRISTOLOGY

Baudissin, W. W. graf von. *Kyrios als Gottesname im Judentum,* 4 vols. (Giessen: Töpelmann, 1929).

Borsch, F. H. *The Son of Man in Myth and History* (London: SCM Press, 1967).

Bousset, W. *Kyrios Christos* (Göttingen: Vandenhoeck & Ruprecht, 1913, 1921).

— *Jesus der Herr* (Göttingen: Vandenhoeck & Ruprecht, 1916).

Brown, R. E. *Jesus, God and Man* (Milwaukee: Bruce, 1967).

Black, M. 'Servant of the Lord and Son of Man', *SJT,* VI (1953), pp. 1–11.

— 'The Son of Man Problem in Recent Research and Debate', *BJRL*, XLV (1963), pp. 305–18.

Brownlee, W. H. 'Messianic Motifs of Qumran and the New Testament', *NTS*, III (1956), pp. 12–30, and III (1957), pp. 195–210.

Bultmann, R. *Theology of the New Testament,* vol. I, trans. K. Grobel (London: SCM Press, 1952).

— 'The Christological Confession of the World Council of Churches', *Essays Philosophical and Theological,* trans. J. C. Greig (London: SCM Press, 1955), pp. 273–90.

Burney, C. F. 'Christ as the APXH of Creation', *JTS*, XXVII (1926), pp. 160–77.

Caird, G. B. 'The Descent of Christ in Ephesians 4, 7–11', *Studia Evangelica,* II, ed. F. L. Cross (Berlin: Akademie-Verlag, 1964).

Campbell, J. Y. 'The Origin and Meaning of the Term Son of Man', *JTS*, XLVIII (1947), pp. 145–55.

Chamberlain, J. V. 'The Functions of God as Messianic Titles in the Complete Qumran Isaiah Scroll', *VT*, V (1955), pp. 366–72.

Cullmann, O. *The Earliest Christian Confessions,* trans. J. K. S. Reid (London: Lutterworth, 1949).

— *Christ and Time,* trans. F. V. Filson (London: SCM Press, 1951).

— *Peter: Disciple, Apostle, Martyr,* trans. F. V. Filson (London: SCM Press, 1953).

— *The Christology of the New Testament,* trans. S. C. Guthrie and C. A. M. Hall (London: SCM Press, 1959, 1963).

Dalman, G. H. *The Words of Jesus,* trans. D. M. Kay (Edinburgh: T. & T. Clark, 1909).

Daniélou, J. 'Trinité et Angelologie dans la Theolgie judéo-chrétienne', *RSR*, XLV (1957), pp. 5–41.

— *The Theology of Jewish Christianity,* trans. J. A. Baker (Chicago: Regnery, 1964).

Davies, W. D. *Torah in the Messianic Age and/or the Age to Come* (Philadelphia: Society of Biblical Literature, 1952).

— *The Setting of the Sermon on the Mount* (Cambridge: University Press, 1964).

Dobschütz, E. von. 'Kurios Iēsous', *ZNW*, XXX (1931), pp. 97–123.

Dodd, C. H. 'Jesus as Teacher and Prophet', *Mysterium Christi*, ed. G. K. A. Bell and A. Deissmann (New York: Longmans, Green, 1930), pp. 53–66.

Duncan, G. S. *Jesus, Son of Man* (London: Nisbet, 1947).

Friedrich, G. 'Beobachtungen zur messianischen Hohepriestererwartung in den synoptikern', *ZTK*, LIII (1956), pp. 265–311.

Flusser, D. 'Two Notes on the Midrash on 2 Sam. vii', *IEJ*, IX (1959), pp. 99–109.

Fuller, R. H. *The Foundations of New Testament Christology* (New York: Scribner's, 1965).

Glasson, T. F. *Moses in the Fourth Gospel* (London: SCM Press, 1963).

Gnilka, J. 'Die Erwartung des messianischen Hohepriesters in den Schriften von Qumran und im Neuen Testament', *RQ*, II (1960), pp. 395–426.

Hahn, F. *Christologische Hoheitstitel* (Göttingen: Vandenhoeck & Ruprecht, 1963).

Higgins, A. J. B. *Jesus and the Son of Man* (London: Lutterworth, 1964).

— 'The Priestly Messiah', *NTS*, XIII (1967), pp. 211–39.

— 'Is the Son of Man Problem Insoluble?', *Neotestamentica et Semitica*, ed. E. E. Ellis and M. Wilcox (Edinburgh: T. & T. Clark, 1969), pp. 70–87.

Holtz, T. *Die Christologie der Apokalypse des Johannes* (Berlin: Akademie, 1962).

Hooker, M. D. *Jesus and the Servant* (London: SPCK, 1959).

— *The Son of Man in Mark* (London: SPCK, 1967).

Iersel, B. M. F. *'Der Sohn' in den synoptischen Jesusworten* (Leiden: Brill, 1961).

Jay, E. G. *Son of Man, Son of God* (London: SPCK, 1965).

Jeremias, J. 'κεφαλὴ γωνίας—'Ακρογωνιαῖος', *ZNW*, XXIX (1930), pp. 264–80.

— 'Eckstein – Schlussstein', *ZNW*, XXXVI (1937), pp. 154–7.

— 'γωνία, ἀκρογωνιαῖος, κεφαλη γωνίας', *TWNT*, I, pp. 792f. (ET, pp. 791–3).

— 'λίθος', *TWNT*, IV, pp. 275–83 (ET, pp. 271–80).

— 'Μωυσῆς', *TWNT*, IV, pp. 852–78 (ET, pp. 848–73).

— *The Central Message of the New Testament* (London: SCM Press, 1965).

The Prayers of Jesus, trans. J. S. Bowden (London: SCM Press, 1967).

Jeremias, J. and Zimmerli, W., *The Servant of God,* trans. H. Knight *et al.* from *TWNT*, V, pp. 653–713 (London: SCM Press, 1957).

Jonge, M. de, 'The Use of the Word "Anointed" in the Time of Jesus', *NovT*, VIII (1966), pp. 132–48.

Jonge, M. de and Woude, A. S. van der, '11Q Melchizedek and the New Testament', *NTS*, XII (1966), pp. 301–26.

Kelly, J. N. D. *Early Christian Creeds* (London: Longman, 1950).

Klausner, J. *The Messianic Idea in Israel,* trans. W. F. Stinespring (London: Allen & Unwin, 1956).

Kramer, W. *Christ, Lord, Son of God,* trans. B. Hardy (London: SCM Press, 1966).

Leivestad, R. 'Der Apokalyptische Menschensohn ein Theologisches Phantom', *Annual of the Swedish Theological Institute,* VI (1968), pp. 49–105.

Lohmeyer, E. 'Kyrios Jesus. Eine Untersuchung zu Phil. 2, 5–11', *Sitzungsberichte der Heidelberger Akademie der Wissenschaften,* XVIII (1927–28), 89 pp.

Lövestam, E. *Son and Saviour: A Study of Acts* 13.32–37, trans. M. J. Petry (Lund: Gleerup; Copenhagen: Munksgaard, 1961).

McKelvey, R. J. 'Christ the Cornerstone', *NTS*, VIII (1962), pp. 352–9.

— *The New Temple: The Church in the New Testament* (London: Oxford University Press, 1969).

Manson, W. *Jesus the Messiah* (London: Hodder & Stoughton, 1943).

Manson, T. W. 'The Son of Man in Daniel, Enoch and the Gospels', *BJRL*, XXXII (1950), pp. 171–93.

Marshall, I. H. 'The Synoptic Son of Man Sayings in Recent Discussion', *NTS*, XII (1966), pp. 327–51.

— 'The Divine Sonship of Jesus', *Interp.*, XXI (1967), pp. 87–103.

Michaelis, W. *Zur Engelchristologie im Urchristentum* (Basel: Majer, 1942).

Moule, C. F. D. 'The Influence of Circumstances on the Use of Christological Terms', *JTS*, X (1959), pp. 247–63.

— 'A Reconsideration of the Context of *Maranatha*', *NTS*, VI (1960), pp. 307–10.

— 'The Christology of Acts', *Studies in Luke-Acts,* ed. L. E. Keck and J. L. Martyn (Nashville: Abingdon, 1966), pp. 159–85.
— *The Phenomenon of the New Testament* (London: SCM Press, 1967).
Neufeld, V. H. *The Earliest Christian Confessions* (Leiden, Brill, 1963).
Richardson, A. *An Introduction to the Theology of the New Testament* (London: SCM Press, 1958).
Robinson, J. A. T. *Twelve New Testament Studies* (London: SCM Press, 1962).
Sahlin, H. 'The New Exodus of Salvation', *The Root of the Vine,* A. Fridrichsen *et al.* (London: Dacre Press, 1953), pp. 81–95.
Schweizer, E. 'Der Menschensohn', *ZNW,* L (1959), pp. 185–210.
— 'The Son of Man', *JBL,* LXXIX (1960), pp. 119–29.
— *Lordship and Discipleship* (London: SCM Press, 1960).
— 'The Son of Man Again', *NTS,* IX (1963), pp. 256–61.
— 'The Concept of the Davidic "Son of God" in Acts and its Old Testament Background', *Studies in Luke-Acts,* ed. L. E. Keck and J. L. Martyn (Nashville: Abingdon, 1966), pp. 186–93.
Sidebottom, E. M. *The Christ of the Fourth Gospel* (London: SPCK, 1961).
Smalley, S. S. 'The Christology of Acts', *ExpT,* LXXVIII (1962), pp. 358–62.
— 'The Johannine Son of Man Sayings', *NTS,* XV (1969), pp. 278–301.
Stauffer, E. *New Testament Theology,* trans. J. Marsh (London: SCM Press, 1955).
Strugnell, J. 'The Angelic Liturgy at Qumran—4Q Serek Sirot 'Olat Hassabbat', *VTS,* VII (1960), pp. 318–45.
Takahashi, M. 'An Oriental's Approach to the Problems of Angelology', *ZAW,* LXXVIII (1966), pp. 343–50.
Taylor, V. *The Names of Jesus* (London: Macmillan, 1953).
— *The Person of Christ in New Testament Teaching* (London: Macmillan, 1958).
— 'Does the New Testament Call Jesus God?', *ExpT,* LXXIII (1962), pp. 116–18.
Teeple, H. M. *The Mosaic Eschatological Prophet* (Philadelphia: Society of Biblical Literature, 1957).
— 'The Origin of the Son of Man Christology', *JBL,* LXXXIV (1965), pp. 213–50.

Tödt, H. E. *The Son of Man in the Synoptic Tradition,* trans. D. M. Barton (London: SCM Press, 1965).

Turner, H. E. W. *Jesus, Master and Lord* (London: Mowbray, 1953).

Unnik, W. C. van. 'Jesus the Christ', *NTS*, VIII (1962), pp. 101–16.

Vermès, G. *Scripture and Tradition in Judaism* (Leiden: Brill, 1961).

— 'The Use of בר נשא/בר נש in Jewish Aramaic', Appendix E in M. Black's *An Aramaic Approach to the Gospels and Acts* (Oxford: Clarendon, 1967³), pp. 310–28.

Vielhauer, P. 'Gottesreich und Menschensohn', *Festschrift für Günther Dehn,* ed. W. Schneemelcher (Neukirchen: Moers, 1957), pp. 51–79.

— 'Jesus und der Menschensohn', *ZTK*, LX (1963), pp. 133–77.

— 'Ein Weg der neutestamentlichen Theologie. Prüfung der Thesen Ferdinand Hahns', *EvangT*, XXV (1965), pp. 24–72.

Vos, G. *The Self-Disclosure of Jesus* (Grand Rapids: Eerdmans, 1954).

Warfield, B. B. *The Lord of Glory* (London: Hodder & Stoughton, 1907).

Wendland, P. 'Sōtēr', *ZNW*, V (1904), pp. 335–53.

Wieder, N. 'The "Law-Interpreter" of the Sect of the Dead Sea Scrolls: The Second Moses', *JJS*, IV (1953), pp. 158–75.

— 'The Idea of a Second Coming of Moses', *JQR*, LXVI (1956), pp. 356–66.

Wolff, H. W. *Jesaja 53 im Urchristentum* (Berlin: Evangelische Verlag, 1942).

Wrede, W. *Das Messiasgeheimnis in den Evangelien* (Göttingen: Vandenhoeck & Ruprecht, 1901).

Zimmerli, W. *see* Jeremias, J.

INDEX OF AUTHORS

INDEX OF REFERENCES

I. Old Testament

II. *Jewish Apocrypha and Pseudepigrapha*

III. Dead Sea Scrolls

IV. Rabbinic Literature

V. Josephus and Philo

VI. New Testament

VII. *Jewish Christian Apocrypha*

VIII. Nag Hammadi Texts

IX. Church Fathers